T0193493

#NO FEAR

*A Guide to Overcome Fear
in Our Daily Lives*

SULY RIEMAN

WESTBOW
PRESS®
A DIVISION OF THOMAS NELSON
& ZONDERVAN

This book is a work of non-fiction. Unless otherwise noted, the author
and the publisher make no explicit guarantees as to the accuracy of
the information contained in this book and in some cases, names of
people and places have been altered to protect their privacy.

WestBow Press books may be ordered through booksellers or by contacting:

WestBow Press
A Division of Thomas Nelson & Zondervan
1663 Liberty Drive
Bloomington, IN 47403
www.westbowpress.com
844-714-3454

Because of the dynamic nature of the Internet, any web addresses or
links contained in this book may have changed since publication and
may no longer be valid. The views expressed in this work are solely those
of the author and do not necessarily reflect the views of the publisher,
and the publisher hereby disclaims any responsibility for them.

Any people depicted in stock imagery provided by Getty Images are
models, and such images are being used for illustrative purposes only.
Certain stock imagery © Getty Images.

Cover photograph by Suly Rieman.

Scripture quotations are from the Holy Bible, King James Version
(Authorized Version). First published in 1611. Quoted from the KJV Classic
Reference Bible, Copyright © 1983 by The Zondervan Corporation.

ISBN: 978-1-6642-9464-6 (sc)
ISBN: 978-1-6642-9463-9 (hc)
ISBN: 978-1-6642-9465-3 (e)

Library of Congress Control Number: 2023904483

Print information available on the last page.

WestBow Press rev. date: 03/20/2023

Suly Rieman

Go Forth and Get a Job! A Job Search Guide for College Grads
Surviving Grief, The Little Guide to Cope with Loss
Resume Writing Guide for College Students

This book is dedicated to my son, Jeremy E. Rieman
Your presence blessed me richly.
Your absence taught me to depend more and
more on the Lord Jesus Christ.
I love you, I miss you, and I will see you in Heaven.

CONTENTS

FOREWORD

It was one of those beautiful summer days that make you glad to be alive. The sun was shining, birds singing, and my boys and I were standing atop a ledge awaiting their first "cliff jumping" experience. We had been on a family hike making our way down a canyon when we spotted one of those perfect swimming holes – a sandy beach leading to cold, deep water along the wall of a small cliff. It was my 11-year-old son who first came up with the idea, "Dad, lets jump off that rock".

After working our way up the rock formation, prior to approaching the edge, I explained to my sons that the elevation would appear much higher from our current vantage point. My advice to them was to walk to the edge, make sure no one or nothing was underneath, take several steps back, and JUMP.

"If you think about it," I said, "you will talk yourself out of jumping. You have to JUMP FIRST, FEAR LATER."

I watched as my 11-year-old approached the edge and peered into the depths. Meanwhile, an evil smile appeared on the face of his younger brother. Before I could rebuke this wicked, albeit funny, idea, my youngest had taken the two steps toward his elder brother, extended his arms, and gave him the help needed to plunge into the depths below.

Similarly, in our personal journeys we often find ourselves on the edge of a precipice with a plethora of unknowns lying beyond our next decision. Unanswered questions, past failures, and an indefinite future make the leap increasingly difficult. As we stand teetering on the edge, attempting to peer over the ledge into the mysterious, we hear the voice of God whispering, "Trust me – JUMP". Yet, unlike my youngest child, God seldom, if ever, pushes us. He simply stands with us whispering, "Trust me and JUMP".

Every life holds these moments that forever change the trajectory of our days on this planet. Opportunities to sink or swim, trust or fear, jump or remain the same. It is these decisions, these instances in our lives, which move us from who we were to who we will be.

These moments of facing our fears are sometimes hard to see, but dangerous to miss. They are the moments that can change the trajectory of our life. They can link you to a life-long friend, help you recognize your destiny, or refresh the dreams you once held. These moments move us from the predictable and give us permission to trust God; to move from the ordinary to the extraordinary.

Regrettably, we too often allow our shame, regrets, and apprehensions of the unknown to "FEAR FIRST, JUMP LATER" rather than "JUMP FIRST, FEAR LATER." This truth begs the questions:

"How?"

"How do we avoid a life paralyzed by fears and anxiety?"

"How do we trade this regrettable life of would've, could've, should've for a life of courage, trust, and peace?

Suly, in her book "No Fear", does a masterful job of illuminating the fears we face, what those fears do to our bodies, and, most importantly, steps we can take to overcome these fears. If you're looking for a magic pill that will suddenly rid your life of fear, anxiety, and depression you will not find it in this book. Overcoming our irrational fears is certainly a journey and, in light of this truth, I implore you to slip into your proverbial shoes, grab your day pack and water, and allow Suly to take you on an excursion of life-changing discovery. The personal breakthroughs and understanding this book unpacks will have a profound impact on how you view and interact with yourself and others; it will indeed lead you to "JUMP FIRST – FEAR LATER."

Patrick McCalla
Executive Director, Operation JOY Foundation
President, Four Thirteen Productions
www.youtube.com/user/runnerdude55

For I am not ashamed of the gospel of Christ:
for it is the *power of* God *unto salvation to every one that believeth…*
Romans 1:16

INTRODUCTION

We never know what a day can bring, and somedays our lives are filled with fear. We may not want to admit that at times we are paralyzed by fear, so we socialize our situation with terms like concern, worry, anxiety, or we hide behind it with depression.

Our circumstances may drive us to experience fear in some way, be it rational or irrational. A visit to the doctor, and an unexpected diagnosis can send us into a complete fearful spiral for ourselves or the ones we love. The startling phone call in the middle of the night with tragic news. A job, or lack of one, attempting to find one, or losing one can fill our minds with all sorts of fear and unwelcomed thoughts. The challenges in life may drive us into a fearful mess: family circumstances, dysfunctional relationships, mental health issues, toxic co-workers, financial problems, divorce, domestic violence, acts of crimes, substance abuse, prison, and death. Add to that the daily issues we all face: work, unemployment, environmental issues, the rise and fall of the stock market, inflation, political unrest, bad neighbors, wars, and pandemics; it's a wonder any of us are able to get out of bed every morning.

As a Bible-believing Christian, a follower of Jesus Christ, I know that regardless of my circumstances, I am able to find strength and courage daily in the Lord and in His Word, the Bible. Each time I allow my mind to wander into the land-mine field of fearful thoughts, I search the scriptures for rock-solid truths on which I can depend and trust to guide me through the difficult, fearful days.

Several speakers on the topic of fear, refer to the Bible containing 366 verses on fear, one for every day of the year including leap year. Recently, I set out to find this long list of over 300 verses hoping to find an all-inclusive list, only to find partial lists. None of the searches produced a list of 366 verses. So I decided to keep track of such verses during my daily Bible reading. I made note of each verse which mentions fear, afraid, dismayed and similar words related to the topic. I set out to do this as a resource, a reference for myself, and then, I decided to share it with others. I figured since this information was helpful to me, it may be helpful to others. However, I realized that by the time I found every verse on fear, in every chapter of every book of the Bible, that endeavor would be very time consuming and would require lots of organization, and I was afraid that I may not find all of them!

Then one day, I remembered that when seminary students and pastors seek information on Bible verses, they reach for a Biblical concordance. A concordance is a wonderful reference index filled with details and information about the Bible. In my quest to find sound resources, I found two Bible reference classics in one volume published by Thomas Nelson: *The New Strong's Concise Concordance & Vine's Concise Dictionary of the Bible*. Over a century ago, Dr. James Strong, did some incredible research and cataloged every word in the Bible and he created an index of the location of each word. I cannot even imagine what his study or office looked like, with a plethora of paperwork, where he took notes on every Bible verse, or how he organized his findings, and then created an exhaustive list of every reference where each word is found! This very wise man created one of the most used Biblical resources known to us! This concordance is used by seminary students, teachers, pastors, and anyone, like average people like me, looking for details on the location of specific Bible verses. During my personal Bible reading, I kept track of the verses which contain the word fear and it was wonderful to compare my list to the listing found in the concordance.

As I did some research on fear and wrote a few chapters for this book, I sold my house, and got ready to move; one day my phone rang. It was the wife of my dear friend and editor, Steve. She let me know that Steve had passed away several days prior to her phone call. This news was not easy to hear, and I remember feeling like I was in fog. It was one of those moments in life, where I realized that my last conversation with him, was the last time I would ever speak with him again. I paused the research and writing; it took about two years for me to return to work on my writing projects. I met Steve long ago in Chicago when the organization where I worked hired him to teach a training class. We developed a friendship and our families spent time together. Steve always had an interesting story to share and we enjoyed many laughs. A few years later, he offered my first freelance writing job to me. Years later, he was so helpful and insightful as he edited two of my books. I love my friend Steve, and I miss his laughter.

Although I paused writing, I continued to read the Bible, both the Old and New Testaments, and I read some wonderful stories of men and women who faced incredible life challenges. The Lord instructed them not to fear and worked in their lives. As I read these stories, I saw these verses in a new light. I became encouraged and I was reminded that God can be trusted, and He does not lie. He loves men, women, and children, so much that He gave His Son, Jesus for all humanity to have salvation, a relationship with God, and of course to have His peace. He is with us daily, through the good times, in times of uncertainty, and in times of trouble, no matter how fearful and intense each situation is, and He wants us to trust Him in each situation.

I sincerely hope that you find the information within these pages helpful, especially the scripture verses on fear. I share scripture, research and some personal insights along the way. May your heart and mind be encouraged as you read this book, and may the peace of God rule in your heart. Peace to you.

ONE

The Journey

No More!

I quit! No two-week's notice: I resigned. Years ago, I decided I no longer wanted to be the chief executive officer of my life, and I decided to place my trust entirely on the Lord. I realized I could let go of the false idea of the control I thought I had on my life, and I allowed Him to take control because I knew that I could trust Him since He knows what is best for me. Not an easy step for a recovering control freak! Once I surrendered my life to the Lord, I prayed the most incredible, most sincere, the most frightening prayer of my entire life: *Lord, may your will be done in my life.* That prayer opened the door for so many events in my life: some joyous, some funny, some intense, some sorrowful, along with failures and successes. Through each event, I know that no matter how fearful they were, the Lord was always by my side. He encouraged me, listened to me, and accepted my confusion, my questions, my fears, and my tears. As a believer and follower of Jesus Christ, I never, ever, experience anything in this life without Him, and that brings comfort to my heart.

Although I share some personal stories with you, this book is not about me. This is God's story, and I am passionate about sharing this story with you. My journey on fear started as part of my personal

Bible reading. As the learning journey continued, I read insightful information about fear, anxiety, and depression, and I realized I had to share what I learned with others. I try to be a life learner, and I enjoy reading every day, and I was excited to learn so much from the Bible, as well as from the research which mental health professionals have documented. As a former college instructor, I still like to share knowledge with others; I knew that I had to share this information with other people. I truly believe that the Lord paved the way in this endeavor. My motivation for writing this book is to help people who need hope in their lives; to help people who need freedom from the bondage of fear and anxiety, and show them how to place their trust in Jesus Christ.

The pandemic brought fear and uncertainty to our lives, and I knew I had to share everything I learned with as many people as possible. I read that drug and alcohol use increased and that the suicide rate increased too. Sadly, there are a high number of orphans who were left behind because their parents died, and parents who lost children because of the pandemic; this broke my heart, and I knew that I had to share the research and the love and hope of Jesus Christ. My prayer is that you find the freedom to allow the Lord into your life, and find the freedom to release the worry, fear, and the anxiety from your life.

Think fast…run fast!

It was a nice morning as the young girl walked to the elementary school. Up ahead she noticed a man watching her and he smiled at her. She looked around and decided to cross the street. He followed. She walked a few more quick steps and crossed the street again: he followed her. As her heart beat faster, she picked up her pace. That morning, she had left about five minutes later than usual, and she looked around to see if any of the other kids were walking to school, and sadly, the streets were empty. She tried to stay calm and she knew if she could get to the clearing near the major street, she could reach the crossing guard at the opposite side. She crossed the street again, and he followed her. As soon as she reached the clearing, she ran as fast as her short legs could carry her, and he chased after her. By the grace of God, she only looked behind her once and somehow she stayed clearheaded. She was not a very good runner, probably the worst runner in her class; however, that morning she ran as fast as she could. By the time she reached the clearing the man no longer chased her. She was completely out of breath. Her left side ached, she was bent over trying to catch her breath, and after a moment, she was able to continue her walk. She briefly spoke to the crossing guard and let her know what happened before she continued her walk to school.

No Fear

I do not like to live in fear; actually, I loathe it. As a recovering, functioning control freak, I do not like to be out of control. It seems that when I allow fear to creep into my head and into my spirit, I tend to react with my emotions rather than respond with rational thinking. Like many people, when a serious situation happens, I realize that I have absolutely no control; I tend to worry or can become fearful.

I am no stranger to fear. As a child I experienced fear many times. When family issues arose, conflict ensued, and voices were raised by the adults, I was afraid of what would happen to my family. As a child, thoughts of abandonment filled my young mind, and I was afraid my parents would leave me. My heart raced as I ran away from a child molester one day as I walked to school. For you see, that was me in that story, and I ran for my life in order to get away from the man who chased me. When my sister ran away from home, I was very sad and afraid; I was afraid for my parents and I was afraid for my sister, not knowing where she was and if she were safe. I developed insomnia and I did not eat well. As a teenager, I tried to be the peacemaker between my parents and my sister to no avail, and my health suffered horribly. I could not sleep, and I did not feel well. I took public transportation to school and I had to catch the bus to be on time. I was tired a lot, and my heart was broken. My parents took me to see the doctor.

The day my father suffered his first heart attack, I was afraid for the uncertainty of his life. One day while we were out shopping, sadly, my father suffered another heart attack. My mom and I managed to get my father into the car, and I quickly drove to the hospital. I had a driver's license; however, I did not have a lot of driving experience, since we only had the one car which my dad usually drove. I took the responsibility to get my dad to the hospital since my mother did not drive. I was used to driving around our neighborhood and never on the expressway, and trust me, I was very afraid. Not only did my parents depend on me to get my dad to the hospital quickly, they wanted all of us to get there safely. The busy Chicago expressway was a challenge and I was terrified as I merged into the heavy, fast traffic flow. Sometime later, while I was in college, the doctors discovered that my father had severe blockage around his heart and he needed open-heart surgery. He was transferred to a hospital in Milwaukee, Wisconsin for the procedure. The procedure was to be life changing and help him live a better life. The day after his surgery, I stood at the side my father's hospital bed as he took his last breath. The team of nurses ran into the room with the crash cart and I was ushered out of the room. They attempted to save his life and were unable to save him: I was afraid and wondered what would happen to my mother.

When I was in my mid-twenties, I was involved in a car accident. It was a rainy day and I drove down the winding road which ran through the forest not far from my home. As I approached the street light which was red, and I noticed the car behind me as it sped towards me. I assumed the driver would not be able to stop in time or within a safe distance behind me. As my car slowed down to a complete stop, I decided to move onto the shoulder. I figured if the guy behind me was going to smash into a car, it would not be mine, and I thought he would plow into the car which originally had been in front of me. As the car came close to a complete stop, the car hydroplaned to the right side and slammed into my car. For a second, my car was in the air and then slammed down into the ditch on the side of the road. As the car flew off the road, my hands tightly held the steering wheel that I hardly noticed that my neck and my knee were injured. The driver in the car in front of me, pulled his car to side of the road and he was the first person to reach me, and he was able to help me out of the vehicle. I was so frightened, and I was in shock. I had never been in a car accident and I was completely devastated.

When I spoke to the doctor, he asked me what I liked to do in my spare time, and my response was *ride my bicycle, hike, backpack in the mountains, camp.* His response was, *you will never be able to do any of those things again.* I was surprised and devastated by his words, and I was afraid for my future. Will this pain ever go away? How can I ever sleep comfortably again? When will I be able to drive? How can I ever work again? I cried out to God and I asked Him for relief from the intense pain, and I prayed for a miracle in my life. After months of painful, challenging physical therapy, I slowly was able to do simple tasks, like shower and wash my hair, dress myself, and walk from my bedroom to the backyard. Although the intense pain continued, I was motivated to not stay in that condition. Month after month, the pain continued and I knew I could not let the pain stop me from enjoying my life. With my Bible in my backpack, I started taking slow, short walks, and each day, I could go just a bit farther. When I reached my limit, I would sit and read my Bible, and once I caught my breath, I would head back home. Several months later, I was able to drive again, and I would drive to the woods and hike through the forest. I did this twice per week in hopes of regaining my strength and reduce the awful pain. Within one year of the accident, I was doing so much better, and I thanked God daily that He gave me His strength so that I could overcome this terrible situation.

One day, while I was about six months pregnant, I had a map open on my desk, and I stared at it trying to decide where I could move with my new born son after he was born. I wanted to live in peace and thought I could find a small and affordable place to rent near my office. Then when Jeremy died, I felt like my life was so unpredictable. After the loss of my son, I faced the fear of living without him, and living in my relationship. I faced fear as I lived in a dysfunctional relationship. Years later, I was fearful as I stepped away from that dysfunctional relationship knowing I needed the courage to save my life and my sanity.

A few years after Jeremy died, and many counseling sessions, I was pregnant again. This time, I did not fear because I knew God was in control of the pregnancy and the life of my child. The doctor worried, the nurses worried; however, I knew in my heart that if I were to lose this child, the Lord would walk every step of that journey with me. Praise God, my baby was healthy, and my son, Jon was born, the doctor wept tears of joy with us. About one year later, I was pregnant again, and I had a new physician. I was referred to a doctor who was familiar with high-risk pregnancies, and I will say, she was extremely concerned for me, my health, my age, and the condition of my unborn son. She recommended all sorts of tests and cautioned me that we may have to take the baby prior to birth, and my response was, *no*. I agreed to only two of the tests and both were innocuous. I did not want to place any additional stress on my baby or place him in danger. I let the doctor know that no matter the test results, this baby would be born. My son moved around quite a bit, and the day before his birth, he was right side up, and of course, the doctor worried even more for me. The next day, he was ready, and was upside down; however, on the final labor push, the nurse saw that he was not breathing since the umbilical cord was wrapped around his neck. The nurse immediately cut the cord, cleared his airway, was able to get him to breathe, and praise God, my son, Jared was healthy.

Throughout life I have encountered fear due to the loss of a job, the loss of a home, the loss of my children, loss of finances, friends. Each situation brought fear into my heart, anxious thoughts into my mind, and tears to my eyes. Although each situation was a complete challenge, I encountered God's protection, His grace, His mercy, and His never-ending love for me. Each fearful situation taught me so much: I am truly not in control, I am able to trust the Lord for His guidance; I know that He will never leave me. He may have not calmed each storm in my life; however, He calmed my mind and heart so that I could endure the storms.

In the 14th chapter of the book of Matthew, in the New Testament, we read the account of Jesus as He walked on the water. Peter, one of His disciples, asked Jesus to bid him to step out of the boat. For a moment, Peter stands on the water and starts to walk toward Jesus. All around them was a storm, and if you have ever been in a boat on the sea during a storm, you know that the storms can be intense and frightening. While Peter was focused on Jesus, he was able to walk on the water toward Jesus; however, when Peter decided to look around and focused on the storm, he started to sink into the water. That is exactly the same way it is for me; when I focus on the Lord, I am able to get through any storm in life, and when my focus shifts to the situation, I sink. I know that I am able to get through any storm in this fearful life, as long as my gaze and my faith are fixed on the Lord.

I like to read, and I enjoy suspenseful stories which are filled with cleaver clues. I enjoy suspenseful movies and thrillers and I like to solve the mystery of the story; however, I am not a fan of horror films. I do not find them logical, and I quickly lose interest in the weak story lines. In life, it basically is the same, I can chose to be fearful or I can chose to be logical about my situation and not allow my circumstances to overwhelm me. I know, I understand, this is much easier said than done because at times the fear I encounter is so real, so overwhelming, like a giant I must battle, and at times, I feel ill-equipped.

The Bible is filled with many passages which tell us to not be afraid. I find it interesting that God so easily knows and understands our minds, our hearts, and our human condition; He understands that there are situations in life which cause fear and overwhelm us. He knows that fear is not aligned with His way of thinking, and fear is a human condition. The Lord understands our human condition and He knows that fear is our knee-jerk response in many situations in life. Time after time, we are told in scripture *do not be afraid*, and yet some of us live our lives in constant worry, fear, anxiety and depression every day.

As we travel together on this fear fact-finding journey we will talk about fear, the types of fears we face, what fear does to our bodies, and what steps we can take to overcome the fears in our lives. Hopefully, by the end of our journey, we will feel empowered to take control of our thinking, not give into fear, and live in peace as we trust in the Lord.

TWO

Human Emotion

When I Am Afraid

The dictionary describes fear as: *A painful emotion or passion excited by the expectation of evil, or the apprehension of impending danger; apprehension, anxiety, solicitude; alarm; dread.*

Sound like your life? Somedays it sounds like my life. When I face troublesome situations I admit I face life with some apprehension. When facing trials, the unknown of today may cause anxiety and of course, tomorrow is a blank slate and my imagination may fill the pages with my own creative script. I have questions, many questions, and the what-ifs. Those types of questions can take my mind to dark places which were never intended for me to enter. The what-if questions can drive me to think illogical, compulsive thoughts, and have irrational expectations.

When my son Jeremy died, I was physically tired, emotionally spent, and fearful that I in some way may have caused his death. I had trouble sleeping, I had an irregular appetite, and I felt alone. This made a recipe for disaster. My mind raced with questions: How could this have happened? Was I a bad mother and a terrible caregiver? Could I have unknowingly done something wrong? Would I be arrested? No one else in my family had ever lost a child, was I being punished? This was all a mistake, a bad dream. When will the hospital call me and let me know my son was alright?

I cried out to the Lord and I gave all those illogical questions, all my anxiety, all my fears to Him. I knew I had to do something to clear my head and erase all the illogical, compulsive, irrational thoughts from my mind and fill my mind with clarity, logic, and peace. Daily, I sought God' Word for peace, and I made notes in my journal. I found peace in knowing that the Lord is with me through the storms of life, and that I am safe, sound, and can live in peace as the storms surround me. The reality is I had done nothing wrong as a mother or caregiver; I would not be arrested, and the hospital would never call me and tell me my son was alright. This was not a bad dream. The sad reality is that, my son was born with a congenital heart condition which went undetected until his death, and an autopsy revealed the results. Yes, my son Jeremy died, and yet, God's peace washed over me, and He took my pain, sorrow, fears, anxiety, and He replaced all of it with a sound mind, logical thinking, His healing, and His peace.

This experience taught me so much about myself, about the God I love and serve, and about grief. I sought help to travel my grief journey and I met with a therapist. I attended several support groups, and years later, I had the incredible opportunity to share what I learned with others as I facilitated my own support group. Years later, I was able to publish the book, *Surviving Grief, The Little Guide To Cope With Loss* as a way to help others. In *Surviving Grief,* I share practical, tangible ways to walk the journey of healing.

When I lived with fear and anxiety, my body was stressed and it did not do well. I did not sleep well, I over-ate, or at times, I did not eat at all. I occasionally would have a glass of wine with dinner; however, I felt like taking a strong drink, or two and drown my sorrows. Although drinking alcohol is a symptom of grieving, I chose not to start drinking more since I knew it was not logical and alcohol could not return my son to me or heal the ache in my heart. I knew that fear and anxiety could cloud my thoughts and judgment; however, I wonder what all that fear and anxiety did to my body.

I like to read and do research, and when I looked online, I found some insightful information on the topic of fear. Several articles are referenced throughout the book. There are several hyperlinks listed which you take you directly to the pages I mention. I hope you take some time to visit the websites to learn more about each topic, and read the articles. For your convenience of typing the characters into an internet search box, the links have been shortened; however, if you would like to see the entire, long hyperlink, you will find them listed in the *Resource* section at the end of the book.

Fear, worry, anxiety, depression, they each take a toll on the body. Fear can cause our minds and our bodies to respond in very physical ways and when we live in constant or chronic fear, we literally hurt ourselves. Our minds, our bodies are not built to live in constant fear or anxiety. In the state of fear, the heart rate increases, blood pressure rises. We want our bodies to respond to fear when we are in real danger, we want the brain to aware of danger and cause our bodies to move to safety; however, we do not want our bodies to respond like this often because we are in constant fear, especially when no real danger is present.

Neurobiology

Aarash Javanbakht and Linda Saab wrote an article for the *Smithsonian Magazine* in October 2017. In *What Happens in the Brain When We Feel Fear*, they make a reference to the holiday celebration of fear, Halloween which we celebrate every October (rb.gy/nh3wuj).

They explain the fight-or-flight response our body takes when we are faced with a fearful situation. Our minds work to process the fear as real or not, and our brains and body respond to aid us in those situations.

The brain becomes hyperalert, pupils dilate, the bronchi dilate and breathing accelerates. Heart rate and blood pressure rise. Blood flow and stream of glucose to the skeletal muscles increase. Organs not vital in survival such as the gastrointestinal system slow down.

A part of the brain called the hippocampus is closely connected with the amygdala. The hippocampus and prefrontal cortex help the brain interpret the perceived threat. They are involved in a higher-level processing of context, which helps a person know whether a perceived threat is real.

Mind and Body

Did you catch that? When we experience fear, our bodies respond accordingly. When fear is present the body will respond with a fight-or-flight response: either we stand our ground in the battle or we quickly exit the situation. Let me stop here and say, when fear is rational or real and present, such as, the building is on fire, my brain should send a signal to my body so that I exit the building quickly. I want my body to kick in with a flight response such a faster heart rate and breathing so that I am able to walk faster and get to safety. That is a good thing! However, when fear is irrational, such as I made eye contact with the clown in the opera, *Pagliacci*, and now he will kill me, and thus I run out of the opera house: that is not a good thing. That type of thinking is irrational and I do not want my body to respond in the same manner it does when the fear is rational. I do not need my heart rate to increase, or my blood pressure to rise. I want my brain, my hippocampus and amygdala to process the perceived threat as irrational, or not real.

Can you imagine what we do to our bodies when we constantly live in fear, anxiety, and depression? This is why it is vital that we think clearly and rationally through every situation in our lives. When we face fearful situations it makes sense to take all of our fears to the Lord. Prayer and meditation are powerful resources we can use to focus on the Lord. We are able to leave all our fears, anxieties, and depression with Him. We have options to help us overcome our fears. We can seek the help of a professional therapist, a doctor, take medication to help us focus and remain calm. We have resources we can use to help us in our journey of healing and have healthy mental and physical health.

Be Fearless

Jonathan Alpert, has a blog with *Huffpost* where he describes how the body responds to fear. Alpert is a licensed psychotherapist and the author of *Be Fearless: Change Your Life in 28 Days*. In his blog, *What Fear Does to Your Body and How to Handle It*, he described his own personal encounter with fear: (rb.gy/d9sde9).

Alpert takes the approach of thinking clearly in fearful situations, rather than retreat, thrive in the midst of the fear. Here is a brief excerpt of how he thinks differently about the fear responses.

Below are four common physical reactions people have to fear and anxiety and ways to think about them differently:

- *Sweating. Reframe it like this: "Good, my body is ready for this sporting event called life! It will keep me cool under pressure."*
- *Pounding heart. Reframe it like this: I can feel comfortable knowing that my defense against stress is functioning well, including my ability to get a surge of strength and energy.*
- *Shortness of breath. Reframe it like this: My body is getting the oxygen it needs. The increased breath is going to fuel my muscles and brain with oxygenated blood so I will think more clearly and react more quickly.*
- *Dry throat. Reframe it like this: Parts of my body that really need fluids will now get them so that they function effectively under stress. I can always take a sip of water to moisten my throat.*

Impact

Louise Delagran, MA, MEd penned an article, *Impact of Fear and Anxiety*. The *University of Minnesota* has Delagran's article on their page of the *Earl E. Bakken Center for Spirituality & Healing*: (rb. gy/7qagwu). Delagran provides very helpful information to help us understand the impact of chronic fear on the body. She explains how it affects physical health, memory, brain processing and reactivity, and of course mental health. Here is a brief excerpt of the article.

Impact of Fear and Anxiety

Fear is a human emotion that is triggered by a perceived threat. It is a basic survival mechanism that signals our bodies to respond to danger with a fight or flight response. As such, it is an essential part of keeping us safe.

How fear works

Fear prepares us to react to danger. Once we sense a potential danger, our body releases hormones that:

- *Slow or shut down functions not needed for survival (such as our digestive system)*
- *Sharpen functions that might help us survive (such as eyesight). Our heart rate increases, and blood flows to muscles so we can run faster.*

Anxiety

If I were to watch a scary, horror movie and afterword felt anxious, that may be expected. However, if after a serious event or experience, we live in constant anxiety then we may be dealing with mild to severe anxiety disorder which may cause us to alter our lifestyles, such as the person who will not leave their house or someone who experiences chronic anxiety attacks. Sometimes my mind can fill with too many thoughts which can cause anxiety. It is helpful to have a Bible verse like Psalm 94:19: *In the multitude of my thoughts within me, Thy comforts delight my soul.* I also like the New King James Bible version of this verse: *In the multitude of my anxieties within me, Your comforts delight my soul.*

Anxiety is an emotional response which may include worry, tension, recurring or compulsive negative thoughts, and an increase in blood pressure. Anxiety is similar to the what-if questions because it is a future-oriented response, whereas fear is typically present during a specific or certain threat. An additional resource on anxiety is the *American Psychological Association*: (www.apa.org/). They summarize the information on their website based on the *Encyclopedia of Psychology* and the *APA Dictionary of Psychology.*

Anxiety is considered a future-oriented, long-acting response broadly focused on a diffuse threat, whereas fear is an appropriate, present-oriented, and short-lived response to a clearly identifiable and specific threat.

Donald Black, M.D. is the Professor Emeritus of Psychiatry at the *University of Iowa, Carver College of Medicine;* he is also the Staff Psychiatrist, at the *Iowa City Veterans Administration Medical Center.* His article, *Anxiety Disorders,* on the *American Psychiatric Association* website, addresses anxiety: (rb.gy/if9nka). He believes anxiety is a natural response to stress and in some cases be beneficial since it will alert us to danger and help us to pay attention to our situation.

... anxiety disorders are treatable and a number of effective treatments are available. Treatment helps most people lead normal productive lives.

Depression

Millions of people around the globe suffer from depression. Depression is not the same as anxiety; however, at times, we may experience both at the same time. Depression may be short-term, like dealing with the emotion of a serious, emotional event in life or it may affect us in a long-term way which may interfere with our daily activities. Depression occurs when we feel completely discouraged, hopeless, sad, unmotivated or we lose interest in our lives or daily activities. Now, keep in mind, at times when we are sad we may experience all of those symptoms; however, when we experience a serious, emotional event in our lives, these symptoms may be prolonged and we may feel this way for several weeks. When the symptoms we experience disrupt our daily activities, it is time to seek professional help. I recall working with someone who battled depression. They missed lots of work days and sometimes when they returned to the office, it was obvious that they had not showered or washed their hair for many days. Their depression clearly interrupted their daily routine. If you believe you suffer from depression, please be sure to reach out to a therapist, counselor or psychiatrist and get professional help.

The *Anxiety & Depression Association of America, ADAA* has a helpful article, *What Are Anxiety and Depression?* They provide insightful information on the different types of depression we may suffer, and they provide helpful resources on their website, including a peer-to-peer support community: (rb.gy/osvrob).

Major depression is a treatable illness that affects the way a person thinks, feels, behaves, and functions. At any point in time, 3 to 5 percent of people suffer from major depression; the lifetime risk is about 17 percent.

They identified different types of depression such as major depressive disorder, persistent depressive disorder or dysthymia, premenstrual dysphoric disorder; depressive disorder due to another medical condition, adjustment disorder with a depressed mood and of course, seasonal affective disorder, known as SAD, which affects people around the globe especially places where the sun does not always shine brightly.

Not a Good Look

Nothing good comes from living a life filled with worry, fear or anxiety...nothing! When we live with the chains and bondage of fear and anxiety, we do not live the lives which God intended for us to live. We miss out on great opportunities, many good and fun, enjoyable events and activities, and we miss spending time with the people we love and who love us...and worse, we make our selves sick, literally. This is truly no way to live.

The Side Effects of Worrying – What to do instead, is an article written by Emily Holland: (rb.gy/l5nuet) which is on the Chopra website. She shares a list of the unpleasant things we bring into our lives by living with constant or chronic worry.

- *Difficulty concentrating*
- *Difficulty making decisions*
- *Disruptive sleep*
- *Elevated levels of cortisol, the stress hormone*
- *Exhaustion*
- *Headaches*
- *Irritability*
- *Nausea*
- *Muscle tension*

I appreciate her article because she helps us find tangible ways to work through our issues. She recommends to get back on track with our thinking by being mindful, meaning, doing things such as focus on our breathing, observe our thoughts without engaging them, and when we allow our minds to wonder, we can bring our focus back to our breathing. We can make notes to ourselves and find creative ways to find positive solutions to our issues, and remember the things in our lives which we are able to control when we face situations which are out of our control.

Cortisol

There is a very informative and helpful article, *Cortisol,* published by the *Cleveland Clinic*: (rb.gy/ljgwrt). Cortisol is a steroid hormone, a glucocorticoid hormone produced in the body by the adrenal glands which are part of the endocrine system, and is much needed to help regulate the body's response to stress.

- *Regulating your body's stress response.*
- *Helping control your body's use of fats, proteins and carbohydrates, or your metabolism.*
- *Suppressing inflammation.*
- *Regulating blood pressure.*
- *Regulating blood sugar.*
- *Helping control your sleep-wake cycle.*

There are several steps that we can take to help reduce the cortisol hormone levels to reduce the impact on the body.

- Get quality sleep
- Exercise regularly
- Limit the stressful thinking
- Breathing exercises
- Laugh
- Make and take care of healthy relationships

Sometimes cortisol is labelled as the stress hormone; however, it does much more than that since it may affect every organ in the body. When we face too much stress or prolonged stress, the doctor may recommend that we attempt to live a less stressful life along with taking medication to help regulate the levels of cortisol in the body. We must learn to break the habit of negative thoughts which adversely affect our bodies. If you have uncontrollable thoughts of fear and anxiety, it would be wise to speak with your doctor and have them check your cortisol levels so that they can help you manage them.

So, what is the antidote?

There is no magic formula or magic wand to cure fear or five easy steps to find relief for chronic fear; however, there are logical, trustworthy, and possibly challenging steps to help ourselves. There are some wonderful resources available to us to help us overcome the fear and anxiety we face. We do not have to try to overcome fear on our own, and dong this alone is not recommended. We do not need to live in denial and pretend we are not hurting ourselves by constantly living in fear, anxiety, and depression. There are steps we can take to care for ourselves, our minds and our bodies, and overcome fear and live healthy and meaningful lives. We do not need to pretend that we are doing alright or feel fine when we are not; that does not help us nor the people around us. I do not recommend that you share every feeling and thought with everyone you know because that is counterintuitive and unproductive, and may further drag you down into negative thinking since your family, friends or total strangers, may not know how to adequately help you. I do recommend that you take the healthy, tangible steps to take care of the underlining causes for the fear and anxiety. Remember, it is your responsibility to take care of your body and your mind, to care for your physical health and your mental health; no one else is able to live your life for you. This is definitely one area of your life where you are able to take control, your wellbeing. Focus on taking good care of yourself and live a fulfilling life free from the bondage of anxiety, depression, and fear. In the next chapter we will take a look at some of the tangible things we can do for ourselves to defeat worry, fear, and anxiety.

Take the first step, and put up a *no vacancy* sign, as a visual reminder that fear is not welcome in your life. I created one for you, feel free to use it. The next chapter will focus on additional healthy, tangible steps we can take to help us in our journey.

No Vacancy.

Fear You Are Not Welcome Here!

THREE

Tangible

At times, we face overwhelming events, and it may be difficult to think of anything else other than the situation at hand. Our time, our energy, our focus, or lack of it, may be consumed with nothing else but the situation or event which occurred in our life. I think most of us feel this way at times, and it is totally understandable when we are overcome by life-altering situations.

I am the type of person who does not like to sit still for very long. I usually find something to do with my time. I like spend an afternoon outside with my camera as I explore the area; I enjoy gardening and I like to visit the botanical garden, along with different nurseries around town to see what they offer, and then spend time in my own garden. I enjoy good conversation and I keep in touch with the people I love and whose company I enjoy. I like to take walks, hike the mountains; I enjoy cooking and baking and trying new recipes. In the evening, then I like to sit and read, write, color, do word puzzles, or stream a movie. I like doing tangible things to fill my time, and it is the same way when I face an issue, I like to read about what other people experienced and learned, and I read the Bible, and I pray.

After the death of my son Jeremy, I visited the library and found a few medical and anatomy books to gain a better understanding of his heart condition. I made some notes, and I visited the doctor to ask some specific questions. When my step-son Joel passed, I went online and read helpful information about what happens to the body when certain drugs and alcohol are mixed. Rather than feel like I was losing my mind, I wanted to gain as much knowledge as I possibly could in order to help myself process their deaths. Perhaps it is the recovering control freak in me or perhaps it is the logical way I tend to think to find facts, solutions, resolutions, and closure in life, and so I tend to do tangible things to help me during the healing process. The same with anxiety and fear, I like to do tangible things to help me with the process to overcome the negative and pour positive into my life. I want to share some tangible steps which you may take to help reduce worry, fear, and anxiety. My prayer is that you find these things helpful, healing, and will incorporate them in your life.

A. Acupuncture

Acupuncture is an ancient treatment method developed thousands of years ago, to treat illness, injuries, pain, and most recently has been used to treat individuals with anxiety, stress, and drug abuse. Acupuncture uses small needles which are pushed into the body's meridian pressure points, half a millimeter away from a nerve, and help the body regulate naturally.

Why Acupuncture Works for Anxiety Relief is an article written by Maura Hohman where she describes the benefits of this ancient practice: (rb.gy/a3kuj7).

Acupuncturists insert each needle half a millimeter away from a nerve, Dr. Hsu explains. Depending on where the needles go, acupuncture can cause the nervous system to produce painkilling chemicals, jump-start the body's natural ability to heal itself, or stimulate the part of the brain that controls emotions, including anxiety. All of these results, Hsu adds, can help people feel more balanced and treat a variety of illnesses.

Acupuncture works. It help the body heal, and the needles do not cause much pain or discomfort. I had this procedure done once and the needles were placed on the acupressure points on my face. After the procedure, I felt calm and less stressed. If you decide to try this method, then be sure to visit a certified acupuncturist for the treatment.

B. Bible Reading

One of the best things I can do every day is read the Bible and learn about the lives of the people mentioned within the pages. I can use scripture to help me think rationally, encourage my faith, and learn something new daily. The Bible is the inspired Word of God and I am able to read it, learn from it, memorize it, and use it as the moral compass in this life. There are dozens of verses in scripture which deal with fear, and I am able to use those verses as a guide, a reminder, that I do not have to live in fear or be anxious because I am able to place my trust in the King of Heaven, Jesus, and trust Him in every fearful situation in my life.

My favorite book of the Bible is the book of John, in the New Testament. In this Gospel, we see Jesus for who He is: Jesus is the Son of God, the Lamb of God; He is the Way, the Truth, and the Life, the Savior, Redeemer, and coming King. One verse I have clung to in life is found in the book of John, and these are words which were spoken by Jesus, John 14:27: *Peace I leave with you, my peace I give unto you: not as the world giveth, give I unto you. Let not your heart be troubled, neither let it be afraid.*

In the book of John, we also find the story of three siblings, Martha, Mary, and Lazarus from the city of Bethany. They were friends of Jesus. Jesus was out of area when Lazarus became ill. Word was sent to Jesus to let him know about His friend's condition. Days later, Jesus returned to Bethany; Mary and Martha let Him know that Lazarus had died. When Jesus arrived at Lazarus's tomb, He looked at the faces of His friends, and He had compassion for them, and He wept with them. Jesus did not quote a religious platitude or cliché; nor did he search for the right words to say to comfort His friends: He wept. Moments later, Jesus called out Lazarus's name and commanded that he come forth out of the tomb. Family and friends witnessed the miracle of Lazarus come back to life as he stepped out of the tomb. This story touches my heart because Jesus knew Lazarus was dead, Jesus knew He would call Lazarus out of the tomb; however, He wept with His friends whom He loved. He allowed the emotion of loss to touch His heart, and yet, He performed a miracle as He brought His friend back to life. This story comforts me knowing that the heart of Jesus is touched by my losses, and He understands my tears.

In the book of Matthew, we learn of the genealogy of Jesus and His ministry. When you take the time to review His family line, you will see that His family has some interesting people in it. One of the stories in this book contain phrases I like to use when I pray, *speak the word* or *just say the word*. This phrase comes the account of the centurion, the soldier who approached Jesus to let Him know that his servant was ill and asked Jesus to heal him.

And when Jesus was entered into Capernaum, there came unto him a centurion, beseeching him, and saying, Lord, my servant lieth at home sick of the palsy, grievously tormented. And Jesus saith unto him, I will come and heal him. The centurion answered and said, Lord, I am not worthy that thou shouldest come under my roof: but speak the word only, and my servant shall be healed. For I am a man under authority, having soldiers under me: and I say to this man, Go, and he goeth; and to another, Come, and he cometh; and to my servant, Do this, and he doeth it.

When Jesus heard it, he marvelled, and said to them that followed, Verily I say unto you, I have not found so great faith, no, not in Israel. And I say unto you, That many shall come from the east and west, and shall sit down with Abraham, and Isaac, and Jacob, in the kingdom of heaven. But the children of the kingdom shall be cast out into outer darkness: there shall be weeping and gnashing of teeth. And Jesus said unto the centurion, Go thy way; and as thou hast believed, so be it done unto thee. And his servant was healed in the selfsame hour.

This is such a great story and a great example of faith by the centurion. He believed that Jesus could heal his servant without being in the same room as the ill man. The centurion understood the chain of command and he had such great faith in the healing power of Jesus. At times, when I pray for something very important or for someone who is in a bad situation or for someone who needs a miracle healing, I ask the Lord to just say the word so that person will receive His grace and His healing. The Bible is rich with powerful stories and examples for our lives.

After Jeremy died, I asked a friend to write out the scripture verse found in Psalm 147:3 in calligraphy. She not only wrote the verse for me, she framed it and that frame still hangs in home: *He healeth the broken in heart, And bindeth up their wounds.* That verse became the foundation for the support group for grieving parents which I facilitated.

I also like the book of Philippians, because it is such a great reminder to be content in this life, no matter what I experience. When I live in fear or anxiety, I am not content, so it is helpful to read this book as a great reminder of how to be content regardless of my situation. I love the book of Psalms and the poetic way this book brings my focus and dependency to the Lord. Psalm 23 is such a great reminder that I have the freedom to trust and follow the Lord since He is my Shepherd, and in Him, I have everything I need in this life and the next. I also like to read the book of Proverbs; it has 31 chapters, which is awesome since I can read one chapter for every day of the month and find wisdom within those words.

A verse I really love is II Timothy 1:7: *For God hath not given us the spirit of fear; but of power, and of love, and of a sound mind.*

A verse I like to recite in the mornings is Psalm 118:24: *This is the day which the LORD hath* made; *We will rejoice and be glad in it*. I have a pretty, wall print with daisies in a jar and this verse printed on it which hangs in my bathroom so I see it every day and multiple times per day. Such a great reminder to help set a positive tone and posture for my day!

The book of Genesis lays the foundation of creation and humanity. It also contains the account of Noah, the Ark and the 40-day flood which covered the earth. The book of Exodus gives us the account of the Jewish people and how Moses was instrumental in their freedom, and we have a front row seat to the amazing miracles of God. We read about the parting of the Red Sea and how the people crossed over on dried ground to reach safety from Pharaoh's army.

The book of Daniel contains the story of my personal Bible heroes, Shadrach, Meshach and Abednego. These three men were courageous to obey the Lord and suffered the consequence at the hand of the King Nebuchadnezzar and were thrown into the fire of a furnace; ultimately rescued by the Lord Himself. It is an amazing story of how these men trusted God regardless of the earthly consequences and were victorious. Daniel was such a devoted follower of God and Daniel trusted the Lord and prayed several times daily. The king commanded that all the people pray only to him. Daniel choose to obey God's law rather than the king's law, and his civil disobedience could have cost him his life. He was thrown into a lion's den. The Lord shut the mouths of the lions and Daniel survived the night, and was released unharmed the next morning. What amazing stories of faith and prayer we find in this book.

The Old Testament is full of prophecy about the birth and life of Jesus, the Messiah. The books of Matthew, Mark, Luke, and John are the books of the Gospel, the Good News of Jesus Christ. The Gospels teach about Jesus, His life, His ministry, His death, and His resurrection. The book of Luke contains the details of the birth of Jesus, which are the verses referred to as the Christmas story. Luke, the physician, historian documents the life of the early church planters across Asia. In Luke we have the account of the Lost Coin, and the Prodigal Son, and both of these parables are wonderful analogies of how the Lord searches for us. The book of Acts teaches about the early days of followers of Christ, and the book of Romans encourages us to walk the talk of our faith. Chapter three of the book of Romans is very powerful, and some theologians may agree that this chapter is probably one of the most important sections of scripture ever written since it contains the verses of the *Romans Road* to salvation: the straight, narrow, and very clear path which leads to us to God. The eighth chapter of Romans begins with one of the best things for us to know in life! *There is therefore now no condemnation to them which are in Christ Jesus, who walk not after the flesh, but after the Spirit.*

The book of Revelation provides insight to the pinnacle of Christ's return and our future. Do not think for one moment that the Bible is dull or boring! There is so much value in the Bible, and I love it. The Bible is an exciting book to read and as a follower of the Lord, I want to read it, know it, trust it, and share it with others.

I encourage you to read God's Word, study it, know it, and live it. Find verses which speak to your mind, your heart, your spirit, and read them daily. Create wall art or purchase wall art with scripture verses and place them around your home for encouragement. If you have never studied the Bible, start with one verse per day or one chapter per day. I like using the *YouVersion* app on my cell phone and every morning before I get out of bed, I read the verse of the day and I pray. This is such a great way to start my day, and have a positive posture on my day even before I get up and get started with activities. I keep a calendar on my desk which contains a scripture verse for each day, and it is a good thing to read before I start my work day, and sometimes I re-read the verse throughout the day. My leather-bound Bible shows signs of age and use...which is a good thing. Adrian Rogers once said, *If you have a Bible that's falling apart, you'll have a life that's not.*

Sometimes people avoid reading the Bible because they think

they need to have a theology degree to read and understand it, and that is so not true. We can read the Bible, learn from it, memorize it, live it, find wisdom from it, find strength from it, find courage from it, and find the loving words of Jesus who invites us to trust Him today and for all eternity. Find a translation which is easy for you to read and start reading it. This is one of those instances where it is about quality and not quantity. Start with one scripture verse per day or one chapter per day. I recommend starting with the book of John. If you need help understanding passages, then I recommend that you purchase a study guide, attend a Sunday school class or a weekly Bible study group. Call a friend who you know reads the Bible on a regular basis and ask questions and schedule time to meet with them. Attend a church service and gleam truths and practical life applications from the sermons preached by the pastor.

I grew up reading the King James Version of scripture which we will discuss in further detail in Chapter Six; I love it and the old English language, and I trust it. Unless noted, all the scripture verses I share with you are from the King James Version, KJV. One thing I want to be clear about is the Bible is true, and I believe it. The written Word of God is inspired by the Holy Spirit and written by individuals who were guided by the Spirit of God to record His Word. The Bible is inerrant; it is without error. It is not true because I believe it; it is true, and thus I believe it.

C. Breathe

From the moment we are born we have an instinct to breathe. We know that breathing is essential to our daily life. It seems at times, when I face a challenge, for some odd reason, I hold my breath. I realized this as I moved some heavy objects and it dawned on me that the task was more difficult because I had stopped breathing. I noticed I did it again when I worked outside and lifted some heavy rocks as I cleared a patch of dirt to create a new garden. I became more aware of this habit when I faced a stressful time, and wondered why or how I had developed this unhealthy habit. Now I am more aware of my breathing patterns and when tempted to hold my breath during a stressful time, I actually spend focused time to do some breathing exercises.

I do not recall who mentioned this technique to me; however, I routinely practice it when I feel stressed, anxious, or feel overwhelmed. I take a deep breath as I count for five seconds, I hold my breath for six seconds, and I release it while I count for seven seconds. I call it the 5, 6, 7 breathing exercise. I do this exercise two or three times and it helps to reset my thinking. It helps bring me to a calm demeanor, and then I am able to continue with the task I want to complete. Another breathing exercise I like to do is stand, stretch my arms over my head as I take a deep breath and then release it after a few seconds as I lower my arms. I find that when I take cleansing breaths, it helps my body release the negative thoughts and clears my mind so that I am able to function in a healthier way for the rest of my day. One great thing about these breathing exercises is I am able to do them anytime, anywhere, and as often as needed.

When we breathe we use our diaphragms. Therapists may recommend diaphragmatic breathing to help reduce anxiety and improve emotional wellbeing. This exercise focuses on how we can contract the diaphragm, expand the belly, deep inhalation and deep exhalation. Diaphragmatic breathing may be used in meditation, martial arts, yoga, and Tai chi. This exercise is similar to box breathing, used with guided imagery and muscle relaxation.

D. Community

Humans are social creatures, and we were never meant to travel this journey of life alone, and being social is a healthy thing to do for ourselves. It is wonderful to have family, friends, classmates, co-workers, neighbors, and acquaintances, and share experiences with them. I totally understand that there are times when we benefit from time spent alone to recharge our energy and focus on task; however, it is very beneficial to spend quality time with the people in our lives. I like to have a fair balance in life: I like to spend time alone and with my pets, and then there is time I enjoy to chat and spend time with family and friends. You know that person in your group of friends who calls and ensures that you get together with them? That is me with my friends; I am the cruise director in life and I call my friends and invite them to spend time with me. I know that my friends are busy with work, kids, and life, and I invite my friends to hike with me, go to dinner or see a movie together, or simply meet for coffee and chat. Last year, I decided to spend time with a former colleague; we meet on a regular basis to cook, converse, and of course eat. We find interesting and foreign recipes and we cook, chat, laugh, and enjoy a delicious meal together. Anytime I spend an enjoyable time with friends and family, I feel lighter, I am happy to see them and spend quality time with them.

Day Designer has an article online: *Why It's Important to Spend More Time with Friends and Family:* (rb.gy/oyc8pj). They share some insight on the benefits of spending time with others.

1. *Spending time with family and friends relieves stress: Individuals who spend more time with family and friends tend to have better coping mechanisms when it comes to handling stress.*
2. *Helps your overall well-being: Social groups provide emotional support, which helps you feel better about yourself.*
3. *It's great for heart health: A study found that when individuals have the support of family and friends, they actually have a lower pulse and blood pressure which, in time, helps to lower the risk of cardiovascular disease.*

I know some of you may be thinking, spend time with my family? No way! It may be difficult to get along with your family, and sadly, in some cases it may not be safe for you to spend time with them. I do recommend that you make time to visit with friends. If your friend pool is not very supportive, then I highly recommend that you find new friends whom you trust and are supportive. A few years ago, I wanted to do some activities around town; however, due to schedule conflicts and family obligations, most of my friends were not available. So, I went online and found a social adult group whose focus was cultural outings in the valley. It was a fun group and I was able to meet some new people. I enjoyed the activities we did together: we visited the art museum, the botanical garden, attended a lecture at the Audubon society, and we would get together for dinner. I was able to meet new people, and spend enjoyable time doing things I like, and also, I did not have to feel alone doing these activities. Due to schedule conflicts I was not able to attend all the meetings, and then the group took a break during the pandemic. I need to see if the group is active again and get going on doing some fun things with new people.

One great way to have community is to attend church and get involved in the programs they have available and participate or volunteer. Most churches have Bible study classes on the weekends, and some also during the week. There are classes for men, women, mixed groups, couples, single people, as well as specific topic classes, and small group gatherings during the evenings. Over the years, I have met many people through Sunday school classes and small group gatherings. Since high school, I sang in the church choir. I was also part of a worship team, a smaller group which led the congregation in singing, and I met many people this way. One group which was fun, was a women' group; we spent time chatting about a Bible verse, we prayed, and then we worked out together; very fun. I have facilitated classes and met lots of new people and have made new friendships. I have friends from church, here in the area and even some from Chicago with whom I still keep in contact. Make new friends, and find people with whom you have things in common. Spend time with people who can teach you something new. One person I met at church creates beautiful quilts and she invited me to join her group one evening to see their projects; they made beautiful quilts to give to church families who had their children dedicated to the Lord. Although, I have no talent for quilt making, it was fun to learn about sewing, to meet new people, and of course, laugh together.

If you are not a church member or do not attend church on a regular basis, I encourage you to find a local church to visit and join. When I moved, I wanted to find a new church, and I opened a search page on my computer and I looked for non-denominational churches near me. I visited several church websites, I read about their staff, their vision, their statement of faith, and their ministries. I made a short list of church names with addresses, and I visited them. As I sought for a new church, I did not take a consumer approach. I took a supportive approach. I want to be able to say that I am supportive of the pastor and the church's mission and ministries, and able to speak confidently that the Lord led me to the right place. A place where I can learn and be part of the community, and of course where I am able to freely and happily support financially. I want to worship with like-minded individuals, and I want to be part of a church which is Bible-centric and teaches about salvation in Jesus Christ alone.

Ask neighbors and friends for recommendations about where they attend, this is also a great way to find a good church, so ask! It is so important to value the gathering of believers and be excited to reach the community for Jesus. Do not attend church to simply attend a weekly service and be a pew-warmer; instead, be active, get involved and be part of the church reaching the world in your community. There is always room for one more person to join the teams at church, so find a church and get involved.

One thing I want to mention, in your search for a church, do not look for the perfect church because it does not exist. The church consists of people just like me, sinful and imperfect. If you find yourself being critical of the pastor and the members, keep in mind, we are all fellow servants of Christ, and we are all sinners saved by grace. God does not appreciate us when we become wise in our own eyes or proud or arrogant, and He wants us to have a humble heart and spirit with Him and with others. If the church you visit does not teach from the Bible or encourage you to live in the power of God, then by all means visit another church. If the sermons include Jesus plus for salvation, then head for the door, because there is only one way to salvation. If the sermons do not include Bible teaching, then get out of there quickly!

I recall a few people mentioned to me that when they visited a church for the first time, they thought the people were not friendly. So, I asked these questions: *How many people did you say hello to that morning? Did you extend a warm, kind, friendly greeting to someone that day? Did you introduce yourself to the pastor?*

My friend, Joel Thurston, M.Div., J.D., Esq. is a brilliant attorney and he is part of the *Journey Church*: (www.journeychurchaz.org/). He is the Vice Chairman of their Elder Board, and occasionally he preaches at the church. One of the times he preached, he invited me to visit *Journey* and hear his sermon. Joel's sermon was great and timely since his message was about suffering together. His message is based on I Peter 5:1-14 and is entitled *Strong, Firm, Steadfast*. The four major points or outline of his message were:

1. *We suffer Together*
2. *We suffer Humbly*
3. *We suffer Vigilantly*
4. *We suffer Trusting*

After the service, I approached Joel to thank him for his invitation to visit his church, and let him know that I appreciated his sermon. I told him I took some notes that morning to use in the book I was working on at the time. I was surprised when without thought or hesitation, Joel graciously handed his sermon notes to me! I let him know how very grateful I was for his willingness to share his notes with me. What a wonderful act of community: Thank you Joel! With his gracious permission, I am happy to share some of the insights he preached on that morning. I used excerpts from the message and not the entire message.

If we are going to suffer in such a way that it makes us strong, firm and steadfast, we must suffer together. We have to suffer in community. Look at 5:1-5a. Notice that Peter assumes there will be leaders in the church. He doesn't discuss their duties, their motives. What metaphor does Peter use to describe the church leadership? Shepherd. Throughout the Bible, God is the shepherd of his people. He extends the metaphor to the apostles. Remember in John 21 when the apostle Peter is restored after he denies Jesus, Jesus asks Peter several times if he loves him. Peter responds each time with yes. Jesus says, then feed my lambs. Take care of my sheep. Then the apostles apply the metaphor to the church leaders more generally, as Peter does here. God wants his church leaders to care for his people in the same way that a shepherd cares for sheep.

Friends, if we aren't careful our ever changing and evolving desire for individual happiness fueled by social media and our cancel culture can lead us to silencing and getting rid of people in our lives we disagree with, but who may have our best interest at heart, particularly those in the church, our family of faith. This is a real danger that we would approach church as consumers. Like any other consumable we purchase, church has become disposable for many American Christians. When the sufferings of life come our way, Peter reminds us that if we want our suffering to result in making us strong, firm and steadfast, we cannot do it alone. Church is not a building, it's a family. We may be a dysfunctional family, but we are a family. We need each other. We are meant to suffer together. You may have heard us say at our Town hall meeting that you don't have to be a member to participate in the full life of Journey church. While true, we aren't going to exclude you, the statement is incomplete. If Journey is your church home, you should become a member. It's not about joining a club or organization. It's about committing to a family. We want your commitment. We need your gifts and encouragement as we suffer. And you need our commitment to help you stay the course and hold you accountable.

Peter goes on to describe what kind of community we are to be. Look at 5:5b -7. All of you, clothe yourselves with humility toward one another, because God opposes the proud but shows favor to the humble. Humble yourselves, therefore, under God's mighty hand, that he may lift you up in due time. (Humble yourselves by) casting all your anxiety on him because he cares for you. If we are going to be strong, firm and steadfast, we need each other, and we need each other to be humble. I must be willing to submit to you and you must be willing to submit to me. Together we must submit to God. We must suffer together, humbly.

God does not bring trials into our lives so that we'll fall. No, we fall when we believe the lies of Satan in the midst of our trails. The two words used for Satan here is enemy and devil. Enemy is the same Greek word used for legal opponent in a lawsuit. Devil means slanderer. Together they are used to indicate that Satan is the malicious prosecutor bringing false charges against us.

We resist Satan, we overcome evil by standing firm in the faith. Peter is not talking about finding strength in the act of believing. He's reminding us that we resist our false accuser by drawing strength from what we believe.

E. Counseling

If you and I were taking a walk and I fell down and broke my leg, you most likely would call emergency services for help. If I told you, *oh, no worries, I am fine,* you would think I were silly, delusional, and not aware of my situation. Let's say, my leg broke and the bone was sticking out of my leg! Yikes. You would not argue with me and you would simply call for help for the compound fracture, right? Sure you would, you would not let me attempt to get up and walk on my own. Well, when we are injured, it is best to seek medical treatment. But what about when no one can see the injury? What about when the injury is to my mind or my spirit? What about when we need the help of a pastor, a mental health counselor, a therapist, a psychiatrist? Sadly, some people feel the social pressure or the stigma about seeing a therapist. Perhaps they had a negative experience in the past with one therapist and assume they are all the same, and they do not trust them. Some individuals may worry about what other people might think about them and perhaps that they are weak. In reality, seeking the help of a professional therapist is a strength. When we realize that we cannot fix ourselves or have all the answers and seek help, we are doing what is best for ourselves regardless of what others think about us. If after a fall, what would it matter what others thought about me going to the hospital to get help for a broken bone? In that same manner, why should I care about someone else's opinion of me, if I need to see a mental health provider? Do not let fear or pride stand in the way of getting help for your situation; do what is best for your own mental health.

To seek professional help when we need it is a wise thing for us to do. There have been several occasions when I sought the help of a professional therapist: after my son Jeremy died, when my marriage started to fall apart, when my step-son came to live with us, and after his death. There is no shame in needing help, in getting help, and getting better. The real shame is never getting help when we truly need it. Do not let anyone or anything stand in the way of doing the right thing for yourself. Get help and work through the challenging issues of life, especially when fear, anxiety, and depression gets in the way of healthy functioning through life and living a fulfilling life.

David Hoy & Associates have an article online: *5 Long-Term Benefits of Therapy*, which describes the benefits of getting professional help: (rb.gy/qu6bch). It is very important for us to learn how to manage the emotions, and aftermath of the events in our lives, and therapy provides the opportunity to learn how to cope and move forward.

1. *Therapy can help you learn life-long coping skills.*
2. *Therapy can change how you interact with people in your life – in a good way.*
3. *Therapy can make you feel happier.*
4. *Through its link to happiness, therapy leads to more productivity.*
5. *Therapy can help improve chronic stress.*

F. Exercise

For many of us, this is a bad word; yuck, exercise; however, exercise is so great for the body, the mind, and the spirit. There are so many physical things we can do to lift our spirits and take the focus off of our fear, anxiety, and depression. Rather than sit around and consume your time, energy, and mind with negative thoughts, invest in your health and move your body and heal your brain.

Bronwyn Griffiths has an interesting article on the *Polar* website (rb.gy/yzuxxv) entitled, *How Exercise Affects the Brain: Does Your Workout Make You Smarter?* Griffiths describes the four key areas of the body affected when we exercise: molecular and cellular changes; changes in neurotransmitters; functional and structural brain changes; socio-emotional changes. Take a moment and read the article, it is worth the time and hopefully the information will motivate you to start moving and moving towards a healthier you; exercise the body and heal the brain! If you have a medical condition and not sure what exercise works best for you, be sure to speak with your physician before you start any exercise program and tailor your exercise routine on what is best for you.

I enjoy taking my dogs for long walks; I get exercise and they get exercise! When we walk together, the dogs are able to burn much of their energy, and although all three of them are senior dogs, you would not know it to look at them since they are very spry and still have lots of energy. After a long walk, they sleep better and through the night, and I get some good sleep too. I love to hike in the mountains, and that is so therapeutic. I am able to see the beauty of the mountain, the cacti, the desert plants, and the rocks, which I like to stack to mark the path for others. When I hike, I am able to spend time alone, with a friend, or with one of my dogs, and not think about much else. I typically start the trail thinking about the challenging things in my life and I pray; soon after, I allow my mind to wonder and I focus on the beauty which surrounds me. Sometimes I sing aloud, or I will stop along the path and sit and read my Bible. After 60-90 minutes of hiking, I feel so great and I find that this activity is so therapeutic. My spirits are lifted, my head is clear, and of course, my clothes are sweat soaked; hiking is so beneficial.

I am a big fan of dancing, so that is one thing I enjoy and one thing which helps me feel and think better. I play music, I sing along, and dance like nobody is watching. I enjoy Zumba since it is dancing with a purpose. I appreciate yoga; although, I am not great at it or very graceful, I know it is good for the body. I received a gift of boxing gloves and I like to use a punching bag to work out and get the blood flowing. It is fun, and fun is good, exercise is good, and I know my body and brain need it! Find the activity which you enjoy and do it! Go to the YMCA, a health club, talk with a personal trainer, take an exercise class, go for a walk outside or on a treadmill, ride a bicycle, take a swim, lift weights, or a kettle ball; whatever you can physically do, do it. Set your mind on taking healthy action and take the first step; that one is the hardest one to take, and then follow it with the second step. If you do not like to do things alone, then ask a friend to join you; however, if you must go alone, go alone, attend a class, and meet new friends. Do not use going alone as the cop-out or an excuse to take care of yourself. There are so many workout videos online which allow us to work out alone or with friends in the comfort of our own homes. Find a helpful video online, get the coffee table out of the way and move, and have fun. Be sure to check in with your physician before you start any exercise program and then get moving! You are responsible for your health, so be responsible! I wish you good physical health and good mental health.

G. Gratitude

I find it easy to be a grateful person because I am very blessed regardless of the amount of money in the bank, the stack of bills needed to be paid, or the amount of food in the pantry, or when I am able to barely make ends meet, I am blessed. When I help others and they thank me, my response usually is, *my pleasure* since helping others is one of the ways I show love and respect. I appreciate it when someone gives a helping hand with a task, a project, spends time with me, or when someone gives a gift to me. I believe it is important to be grateful in life and when I face challenges, I find that I must focus more on all of God's goodness. Scripture teaches us to go before God with a posture of thanksgiving, and I want to always be a grateful person regardless of my possessions. This does not mean that everything in my life is a beautifully paved, yellow-brick road and that I never experience challenges, it simply means that in those challenges, I am able to take time and thank the Lord for all of His goodness.

I like to write things down on paper, and one habit I incorporated in my life is to write down my blessings, especially the blessings during the storms of life. When my boys were young, we had a bedtime ritual. They would recite the Bible verses which hung on their bedroom wall, and then climb into their beds. We would all share one or two things for which we were grateful that day and I wrote it down in our gratitude journal. I would write down the things they shared in hopes of getting them in the habit of being grateful to the Lord for everything in their lives. Then of course, I read a brief story to them, we prayed together, and then lights out for the night. Those are fond memories and I appreciate that the Lord created a grateful heart in each of them and today, they continue to praise God for His goodness to them in spite of the trials they each face.

I encourage you to look past the challenges you face today, and grab a pen or pencil, a piece of paper, a journal, or keep an electronic document and write down one or two things for which you are grateful every day. In spite of the problems, the fears, the worry, the anxiety, you can look around and be grateful for something in your life. I know that it may be difficult to look past your situation; however, take a deep breath, clear your mind, and focus on the important things and the blessings. If your conclusion is that you have nothing – here are some of the things on my list:

- Breath: I am grateful to the Lord that He gives the very breath I need to live.
- Bible: I am grateful that I have God's Word available to me daily, and have access to read it any time, any day, anywhere.
- Salvation: I am so very grateful that the good news of salvation was presented to me and by faith, I trust in Jesus as my Savior and have eternal life.
- Prayer: I am grateful that I am able to speak with God about everything daily, any time, any place, and all the time.
- Children: Although they are not perfect and need lots of prayer daily, I love them and I am grateful for the gift from God for their lives. I know He is with them every day and in every challenge. They need wisdom with their faith walk, the decisions they make, their relationships, their careers, and I know that the Lord will provide that to them so that they depend on Him and not their own wisdom.

I am grateful to God for so much in my life: my home, my car, my mental acuity, the ability to work, my pets, my friends, my family, my health, my church, my pastor, my flower garden, the birds in my yard, the butterflies in my yard, the bees in my yard, the sunshine, the trees, mountains I can see every day, the food I eat daily, the clothes I wear. Let's face it, at the end of the day, I rather count my blessings instead of my troubles or burdens. In spite of life's troubles, I can always find something to be grateful for each day, and I encourage you to make a list daily of all the things in your life for which you are grateful and see God' goodness in your life. Take a break from worry, fear, and anxiety and be grateful.

There is scientific evidence to the benefits of gratitude. Courtney Ackerman, MA, has an article: *28 Benefits of Gratitude & Most Significant Research Findings* is available on the *Positive Psychology* website: (rb.gy/tuiuye). It is interesting to read how a simple act of gratitude can benefits our lives in so many ways.

Gratitude and Emotional Benefits

1. *Make us happier*
2. *Increase psychological wellbeing*
3. *Enhance our positive emotions*
4. *Increase our self-esteem*
5. *Keep suicidal thoughts and attempts at bay*

Gratitude and Social Benefits

6. *Make people like us*
7. *Improve our romantic relations*
8. *Improve our friendships*
9. *Increases social support*
10. *Strengthen family relationships in times of stress*

Gratitude and Personality Benefits

11. *Make us more optimistic*
12. *Increase our spiritualism*

13. *Make us more giving*
14. *Indicate reduced materialism*
15. *Enhance optimism*

Gratitude and Career Benefits

16. *Make us more effective managers*
17. *Reduce impatience and improve decision-making*
18. *Help us find meaning in our work*
19. *Contribute to reduced turnover*
20. *Improve related mental health and reduce stress*

Gratitude and Physical Health

21. *Reduce depressive symptoms*
22. *Reduce your blood pressure*
23. *Improve your sleep*
24. *Increase your frequency of exercise*
25. *Improve your overall physical health*

Gratitude's Role in Recovery

26. *Help people recover from substance misuse*
27. *Enhance recovery from coronary health events*
28. *Facilitate recovery with people with depression*

In preparation for the Thanksgiving dinner we hosted for family and friends, I started thinking about the people we invited, and of course the meal preparation. For several days, I prayed for each person, and for those who could not attend, and asked the Lord to bless everything, the food, the fellowship, and that everyone would have a wonderful time as we celebrated my favorite holiday. I keep a folder in my desk of readings and games for the holidays and when I opened the file last year, I found a sheet of paper with the words

I had penned several years ago which I had shared with our guests, and I decided to read it before we prayed. I share it with you here, and I believe it sums up a great reason to be grateful every day.

A Thanksgiving Thought

At this time of year, we pause to think about all the things and people in our lives for which we are grateful. I wonder what our lives would like if we took quality time every day of the year to be thankful to God.

Think about all the times you prayed this year and most importantly, when you prayed earnestly. Do you recall the difficult, challenging, frustrating times or the issues, or perhaps an illness that brought concern? Did you reach out to others in your life and ask them to pray and join you in your quest to find God's will in the situation? Do you remember where you were when God answered your prayers?

Did you take time to praise Him and thank Him for reaching down from the vastness of Heaven and visit your life and situation? How much time did you spend in thanking Him for answering your prayer requests? Did your time of gratefulness equal the amount of time you spent in prayer? Did you let others know that God so graciously answered your prayer, even when His answer was no?

Think about what our lives would like if we spent the same amount of time, energy, and emotion in praising God for His answer to prayer as we do as when we are on our knees begging Him for His help. What would our lives look like if we decided to express our joyous thanksgiving to God every day and live our lives in daily gratitude?

In this season of thanksgiving, ask God to touch your heart. Ask Him to give you a grateful heart and of course, be thankful for it. Take time to express your gratitude to God and live and enjoy the richness of being in His presence.

H. Healthy Eating

You most likely have heard the phrase, you are what you eat, and let me add, most importantly, *we are what we eat eats*! If I decide to eat red meat, I enjoy grass-fed lamb. I rarely eat red meat; however, I enjoy turkey, chicken, and duck, which are allowed to roam farms and not filled with hormones. I like fish which comes from natural waters, and not filled with antibiotics like farm-raised fish. I like eggs from chickens which are raised without cages and able to roam outside. I like to eat organic fruits and vegetables. Sadly, like most people, at times, my appetite is affected by my emotions and when I feel out of sorts, I crave comfort food. I love mac and cheese, and when I feel sad or depressed, I can eat more of it than I care to admit. Who does not like a fresh baked chocolate chip cookie, or six, or two (huge) slices of chocolate cake? On the other hand, at times, I do not eat anything. I drink lots of water or lemon water with apple cider vinegar; and sometimes I am not interested in food, and the thought of food makes me feel uncomfortable. That is not good. Some days, I forget to eat. I focus on a task, a project, or my mind is filled with thoughts, things I wonder about and things which concern me. Overeating or not eating, neither is a healthy thing for our minds and bodies.

Our bodies need protein from dairy, meat, chicken, eggs, fish or if vegan, fresh fruits, nuts, and vegetables; two to three meals per day, and plenty of water. When our focus is worry, fear, anxiety, depression it becomes difficult to eat properly. Be sure to take time to eat, and eat healthy foods which will give you the strength your body needs and helps your brain. Today it is so easy to prepare healthy meals with the help of a grill, a crock pot, a pressure cooker, a roaster, conventional oven, and an air fryer. There are thousands of recipes online on how to prepare healthy meals which are flavorful and good for you. I like to view recipes on *All Recipes*, (www.allrecipes.com/) or on *YouTube: (www.youtube.com/)*. Do your research and find the foods which are best for you to eat and of course avoid fast food and the greasy, and sugar-filled foods which are not good for you!

Be mindful of your alcohol and caffeine intake and find ways to reduce the amount you consume since both alcohol and caffeine may make your make your symptoms worse. Start slowly and cut back on one cup of coffee or tea, and then increase the number to two cups per day the following day, especially if you consume many cups of coffee or tea or sugary power, energy drinks daily. Limit your intake of alcohol as well to reduce the risk of overstimulating the nervous system and reduce anxiety and panic attacks.

Uma Naidoo, MD has a great food guide on the *Harvard Medical School* publishing site and shares information on healthy eating. The article is *Nutritional strategies to ease anxiety*: (rb.gy/1rsjzq).

Anxiety is thought to be correlated with a lowered total antioxidant state. It stands to reason, therefore, that enhancing your diet with foods rich in antioxidants may help ease the symptoms of anxiety disorders. A 2010 study reviewed the antioxidant content of 3100 foods, spices, herbs, beverages, and supplements.

She recommends that we drink plenty of water to avoid dehydration, and add foods high in antioxidants to our diet: Pinto beans, black beans, red kidney beans; Gala apples, Granny Smith apples, Red Delicious apples, prunes, sweet cherries, plums, black plums, blackberries, strawberries, cranberries, raspberries, blueberries; walnuts, pecans; artichokes, kale, spinach, beets, broccoli, and spices such as ginger and turmeric since they contain antioxidant and anti-anxiety benefits.

I. Journaling

Even though we live in a digital age, I still love stationary products: I am a pen snob. I like fountain pens and I like a heavy weight pen which writes smoothly, and I have a few favorites which I use on a daily basis. I like personal stationary to write letters; I take lots of photos and I use my photographs to make blank cards, and one of my favorite things is a blank journal. I also use my photographs to create journals. This way, I use my creative skills even before I write one word on the blank page.

I have several journals filled with the words of my thoughts and prayers and of course, I have a nice collection of blank journals waiting to be filled with words of the reflection of my thoughts. When I am in a store and see that journals are on sale, I typically grab one or two for myself or to give to others. After Jeremy's death, I learned the value of writing down words in a journal to express my thoughts. My personal journals are filled with words of serious thoughts, funny thoughts, random thoughts, prayers, and words which I was not able to utter to another human being. Lots of days, I would sit outside with my dogs and I would write. After walking the dogs, it was nice to be outside together and I wrote about what I thought, what I felt, my prayers, wishes, and how insecure I was in my relationship. The fall weather was crisp and I spent a lot of time outside to help clear my mind, read the Bible, pray, and write words, private words without care or concern that anyone else would read my journal.

In the support group I facilitated, I talked about the value of using a journal to write down the things we want to say to our children, the thoughts we have about them, how we miss them, and the prayers for healing we raised up to the Lord on our behalf. I wanted to ensure that everyone who came to the meetings had a journal, so I had plenty on hand to give away to anyone who wanted one. I also had Bibles available if anyone wanted to take one, and I recommended that they use the Bible and the journal together so they had a place to write down things they gleamed from reading scripture.

Years later, I read articles about the therapeutic value of using a journal and how therapists were recommending it to all their patients. I smiled thinking that I was ahead of the game per se on the notion of the value of the personal written word. A journal is a great tool to use and it is powerful when we come to terms with the emotions we experience: challenges, sadness, sorrow, fear, anxiety, depression, healing, and joy. Journaling is so beneficial, not only do we use our creative skills and communication skills, it actually helps us physically, mentally, and emotionally. Hand writing may help to stimulate the brain in a way that typing on a keyboard does not. Hand writing is helpful as we capture our thoughts into the written word, it helps us to be creative, and it helps us with our communication skills. The journal you chose can be inexpensive, softbound, hard cover, or one that you make yourself. The journal itself is not the focus, the focus is pouring your uncensored words onto the pages of the journal. As a technical writer and author, correct sentence structure is important to me, along with correct punctuation, spelling, and grammar; however, when I write in my journal, all structure goes out the window. Sometimes, thoughts flood my mind, and then I fill the journal quickly as the thoughts occur to me. My journal is private and not for sharing with anyone or open for critique. So when you use a journal, there is no need for fancy hand writing, unless you really care about it; no need to focus on grammar or punctuation, unless that is important to you. Find freedom in not having to follow writing rules when expressing yourself in a journal. Feel free to draw a picture to help you express your thoughts. The practice of using a journal is for a healing process, not to create a Pulitzer Prize winning document.

If you are not familiar with the use of a journal or know where or how to start, do some research. Kasee Bailey has an article on the *Intermountain Healthcare* website which focuses on the benefits of journaling for better health and it contains a list of the benefits: *5 Powerful Health Benefits of Journaling*: (rb.gy/ak57jz).

1. *Reduce Stress.*
2. *Improves Immune Function.*
3. *Keeps Memory Sharp.*
4. *Boosts Mood.*
5. *Strengthens Emotional Functions.*

The *Kaiser Permanente* website also has an article online and they include the seven benefits of journaling and share a different perspective on their research: *Why everyone should keep a journal – 7 surprising benefits*: (rb.gy/5evyza).

1. *Achieve goals*
2. *Track progress and growth*
3. *Gain self-confidence*
4. *Improve writing and communication skills*
5. *Reduce stress and anxiety*
6. *Find inspiration*
7. *Strengthen memory*

Sometimes a guide or structure may help us as we stare at a blank page uncertain on where to start with a journal. The blank page is exciting to me; however, it may be a daunting, overwhelming, challenge to others. Here is a format that you may follow as you begin your journal writing experience. Find a scripture verse for the day and place it at the top of the page. Use the thought provoking questions as you identify where your thoughts or feelings lead, and end with a prayer request for the day. Here is a template; feel free to use it or modify it as you please.

Day One
The LORD is my shepherd; I shall not want. Psalm 23:1

Today I feel, think or believe:

_____

_____

_____

Is what I experience today rational or irrational? Why or why not?

_____

_____

_____

What tangible, healthy steps am I ready to do to help myself?

_____

_____

_____

Today I am grateful for the following:

_____

_____

_____

Today my prayer request is:

_____

_____

_____

J. Laughter

When I feel overwhelmed, one of the things I like to do is make time to laugh. Sometimes, it may take a few minutes for me to be able to laugh about most situations; however, I do try to find a reason to laugh and trust me, I love to laugh. I have a good sense of humor, and I think I am one of the funniest people I know! Some years ago, I took a bad spill and while I was on the ground in pain, I laughed thinking about the horrible, ungraceful way I fell. I was in terrible pain and yet I was laughing. Actually, I can still laugh about it today. Another time, while hiking with friends in Hawaii, we were in caves and natural mountain tunnels, and the soft, wet ground gave way and down I went. I laughed, and yet so upset that I was on the ground in the mud, and my backpack strap ripped, and all I could do was laugh. As I got up, someone behind said they had a good laugh due to the funny way I tried to not fall, and the entire group laughed. I like to laugh every day and I try to find a reason to laugh because it is such a great way for me to release stress.

I still enjoy the television shows, *Frasier*, and *Seinfeld*, two programs which ran years ago. I am very fortunate that I am able to stream several episodes during the week and I laugh. I also enjoy clean, stand-up comedy. I seek out funny movies to watch and eat popcorn and take a mental break to forget about the cares of the world. I like to play board games and laugh and have a great time. Sometimes my silly dogs make me laugh too. I think it is good to have a positive outlook in life and laughter helps me.

I think most everyone enjoys laughing, and it is so helpful for our brains and our bodies. I have a silly, comedic response to some of life's situations and the people I have encountered. I like to listen to detailed, funny stories people share or a clean or clever joke with a great punch line. There are a few stand-up comedians I enjoy like Jerry Seinfeld; however, I truly prefer clean comedy which is free of the profanity most comedians chose to use. If you are not familiar with stand-up comedy, or if you enjoy stand-up comedy and need some variety, here is list of comedians you may appreciate...and laugh! Keep in mind, I do not control the context these comedians use! If they changed their material or you are offended by something they say, there is no need to let me know!

Anita Renfroe	Justin Fennell
Anjelah Johnson	Kellen Erskine
Bob Cates	Ken Davis
Brad Stine	Lisa Mills
Brian Regan	Matt Jernigan
Chonda Pierce	Mark Lowery
Daren Streblow	Max Winfrey
David Dean	Michael Jr.
David Ferrell	Nate Bargatze
Denis Regan	Paul Aldrich
Dustin Nickerson	Rex Havens
Greg Hahn	Rik Roberts
Henry Cho	Robert G. Lee
Jeff Allen	Ron Pearson
Jenna Kim Jones	Ryan Hamilton
Jim Gaffigan	Taylor Mason
John Crist	Thor Ramsey
Jonnie W.	Tim Hawkins

Allow yourself time to step away from the cares of this world, the fears and anxiety from which you suffer, and laugh; laugh big! Give permission to yourself to release the troubles of fear, anxiety, and depression and enjoy yourself. You will benefit from a good, hardy laugh or two. There is an old saying that laughter is the best medicine and I agree. When I laugh it does my mind good and my brain is happy with endorphins. Proverbs 17: 22 tell us, *A merry heart doeth good like a medicine.*

There are two informative articles online on laughter: *Help Guide: Laughter is the best medicine*: (rb.gy/uxqwx4) and *Mayo*

Clinic: Stress Relief from Laughter? It's no joke: (rb.gy/ciicna). Both articles have some helpful information and are good reminders why it is so important to take time every day and laugh. *Help Guide* authors, Lawrence Robinson, Melinda Smith, M.A., and Jeanne Segal, Ph.D. tells us that laughter is good for our health. If you do not have a healthy sense of humor, be sure to read the article for tips on how to develop one!

- *Laughter relaxes the whole body.*
- *Laughter boosts the immune system.*
- *Laughter triggers the release of endorphins, the body's natural feel-good chemicals.*
- *Laughter protects the heart.*
- *Laughter burns calories.*
- *Laughter lightens anger's heavy load.*
- *Laughter may even help you to live longer.*

After a fun time of laughter, I usually feel much better and I have a renewed sense of balance with my thinking and mood. I once watched a movie which had me laughing for days; seriously. I watched the movie in the evening, and the next morning I literally woke up in laughter thinking about the movie. For a few days, I laughed again thinking about the satire I watched days earlier. My mood was basically upbeat that entire week even though I encountered some stressful situations, the impact was not as serious or severe as in other times. The *Mayo Clinic Staff* tells us that laughter has long term health effects.

- *Improve your immune system. Positive thoughts can actually release neuropeptides that help fight stress and potentially more-serious illnesses.*
- *Relieve pain. Ease pain by causing the body to produce its own natural painkillers.*

- *Increase personal satisfaction. Make it easier to cope with difficult situations.*
- *Improve your mood. Laughter can help lessen your stress, depression and anxiety and may make you feel happier.*

K. Learn!

In the early days of the pandemic, I ventured out to the neighborhood supermarket. Instead of wearing my contact lens, I decided to wear my glasses. Like most people, I wore a facemask and gloves. I took my time in the store and walked every aisle to see what was available. I was able to purchase most of the things on my shopping list, and I was amazed at the sight of several empty shelves throughout the store. At first, I gave a chuckle and said, *wow!* I stopped in one area and stared at the empty shelves for a few seconds, and then I prayed. I asked the Lord to help be calm, and I let Him know about the items on my shopping list and asked Him to provide what I needed during this time.

The sixth chapter of Matthew are words of Jesus, which I read and re-read during the pandemic as a reminder that God loves me and cares for me. He takes care of the birds, and the lilies, so why would he not care about me?

Therefore I say unto you, Take no thought for your life, what ye shall eat, or what ye shall drink; nor yet for your body, what ye shall put on. Is not the life more than meat, and the body than raiment? Behold the fowls of the air: for they sow not, neither do they reap, nor gather into barns; yet your heavenly Father feedeth them. Are ye not much better than they? Which of you by taking thought can add one cubit unto his stature? And why take ye thought for raiment? Consider the lilies of the field, how they grow; they toil not, neither do they spin: and yet I say unto you, That even Solomon in all his glory was not arrayed like one of these. Wherefore, if God so clothe the grass of the field, which to day is, and to morrow is cast into the oven, shall he not much more clothe you, O ye of little faith? Therefore take no thought, saying, What shall we eat? or, What shall we drink? or, Wherewithal shall we be clothed? ... But seek ye first the kingdom of God, and his righteousness; and all these things shall be added unto you.

Praise God, once again, His Word brought wisdom and comfort, and with His help, I was not afraid during the pandemic, and I thanked the Lord for His provision daily. Many times, I visited the market, I saw empty food shelves. This does not mean that I did not experience fearful times during the pandemic, this means that in spite of the fearful times I was able to experience God's perfect peace knowing that the Lord was with me every step of the way.

Once home, I planned my menu for the week, with the items I had purchased and the items I already had in the pantry. Then I had an epiphany! Make the uncertainty of pandemic into a culinary adventure, and I created some new recipes. Some meals contained items I typically did not pair together and I discovered that they complemented each other, and the meals were delicious. I went on another adventure and I watched cooking videos online and discovered the world of canning. I learned how to make beet jelly, strawberry jelly, blueberry jelly, and I also learned to make beet juice and almond milk. Several months later, I learned how to make vinegar. This process was so interesting, so I decided to purchase dehydrated fruit and I made mango vinegar, blueberry vinegar, grape vinegar, strawberry vinegar, and fig vinegar. My curiosity and love of learning, took me in another direction, and I learned to make pickled onions, pickled vegetables, and spicy serrano pepper pickles and spicy habanero pickles. I know eating fermented foods is great for gut health and I enjoyed making and eating everything!

I do not own a sewing machine and I decided to do some new sewing projects. I am not a seamstress, and I am only able to do simple tasks like sew a button on a shirt, repair a hem and close a hole on a shirt or pants. I purchased some beautiful material and I reupholstered my four dining room chairs. With the material left over, I made two hand stitched small pillow covers and covered two pillow forms. I was pleasantly surprised with both projects, and the pillows sit on my loveseat.

This may be a good time for you to learn more about the fears you encounter to help you gain a better understanding of the person, place, or object, which causes the fear and anxiety you face. Learn about the ways to cope with the fears by finding articles or books to read, attend a class or a lecture, or contact a therapist to discuss. Knowledge truly is power and having knowledge may be the very thing you need to overcome the fears you face.

If you are anxious, I highly recommend that you take time to learn something new. It can be something simple like a new board game, a craft, or new hobby, find a new recipe to cook, or focus on solving puzzles, read about a new topic, learn a new language. There are countless free classes online, find a topic which interests you and take the time to learn, it may be something fun or something to enhance a skill or your career. Do something to stimulate your brain and enjoy the process as you implement something new in your life. Take a mental break from anxiety; use that energy in something new, something fun, and something tangible.

L. Light Therapy

Light therapy or phototherapy has been used for several decades to help treat patients who suffer from physical health problems to mental health issues. Seasonal affective disorder, small pox, lupus vulgaris, anxiety, depression, cancer, and bipolar symptoms have been treated by phototherapy. One great thing about phototherapy is that there are no harmful side effects related to the treatment. Phototherapy or light therapy may be an option for you and may help lower your anxiety levels as well as help with depression. Check your local area and see if this service is available.

Science writer, Shannon Palus's informative article: *Light Therapy May Work on Chronic Mood Disorders, Too,* explains how the artificial light works: (rb.gy/ehayly).

Two dozen veterans exposed to a bright light treatment saw a decline in depression and bipolar symptoms. There are also positive anti-depressive effects of light therapy.

M. Massage Therapy

When I feel stressed and overwhelmed, I make time to get a full body massage. The therapist I see is really great at her job and after the appointment, I feel so much better. The tightness around my shoulders, neck and back disappear while the therapist uses her skilled hands to help reduce the pain I experience. I suffer from chronic pain and the massage is very therapeutic, not only for my body but for my mind.

James Lake, MD penned the article, *Massage Therapy for Anxiety and Stress* which discusses how massage therapy can reduce stress and anxiety with a successful track record: (rb.gy/kh7mwy).

The anxiety-reducing and mood-enhancing benefits of massage are probably related to changes in EEG activity, decreased levels of cortisol, and increased activity of the parasympathetic nervous system, which acts automatically to calm the body and brain during stress.

The clinic near me offers a discount price when three appointments are scheduled and used within three to four months. Check the pricing in your local area. You may think that you are not able to afford a massages; however, the cost is probably less than you spend daily on a fancy coffee drink for an entire month! Another option is find the local massage therapy school and be available for the students to earn credit hours and the massage is of no charge to you. Another option is to barter. If you know a massage therapist offer a service in exchange for their service, such as cook, clean, walk their pet, pick up dog waste in their backyard, clean their pool, do their shopping, laundry or ironing. Be creative. I recall someone wanting a copy of one of my books and they asked if they could give a book to me in exchange. Someone I know asked if I would write a new resume for them and they could not afford my fee so they helped me by doing some tasks on a project.

N. Medication

I will tell you that I am not a big fan of medication; never have been; however, when the medication is for life support, mental health, and things I am not able to control with diet and exercise, then I will be a good patient, be quiet, and I will take the medication. I will admit, before I head to see the doctor and their prescription pad, I typically look for natural treatments, holistic treatments for whatever I experience. I like natural, organic, healthy options to take care of my body; however, I understand that there are situations or conditions which may require conventional treatment.

I understand that at times, medications are seriously needed, and I say this because you may or may not know that you need medication to help you focus or think clearly and rationally. You may be living in constant fear, anxiety, and experiencing depression, so I can safely tell you, get professional help from a physician. Tell them what is going on with your mind and body so they can effectively diagnose you and recommend the medications you need. You only have one mind and one body, and you owe it to yourself to take good care of yourself; make an appointment today.

You probably already know this, however, I feel much better about saying it. Stay away from prescription medications and illegal drugs which are available on the street from the local drug dealers. You have no idea what those drugs contain or whether they have been tampered or laced with other harmful drugs. Street drugs may not be what your body needs and the stuff you buy on the street is most likely doing more damage than good to your body and to your mind. Do not self-medicate to numb the anxiety you experience. Do not mix drugs with alcohol because nothing good comes from it. Do not take an excess of drugs which may cause you to become addicted to them or worse, kill you. Please seek professional help. If you suffer from drug or alcohol addiction, please take action and get the help you need. Contact the helpline at the *Substance Abuse and Mental Health Services Administration, SAMHSA* at **800.662.4357 or TTY 800.487.4889.** This is a confidential treatment referral service: (www.samhsa.gov/).

Adult & Teen Challenge USA is an amazing organization which helps individuals with substance abuse: (teenchallengeusa.org/). They have a high success rate with their *Christ-centered model of drug and alcohol recovery*. I have spoken to a few people who went through their program, and now lead substance-free lives. When you visit their website, you will be able to search for a location near you and you will see the option to send an email to them and you may call them at **417.581.2181.**

Alcoholics Anonymous: (www.aa.org/). They offer a 12-step program to guide you through the healing process. They offer regular meetings throughout the community. They exist to help alcoholics achieve sobriety. They offer many resources to help individuals who are committed to change their lives.

Celebrate Recovery: (www.celebraterecovery.com/) is a faith-based, 12-step program to guide you through the healing process. Their 12-step process includes admitting powerless in actions, the belief in a greater power, surrender to God, take inventory of lives, confess, ask God to remove the addictions, create a list of anyone they have hurt, make amends with others, admit when they are wrong, prayer and meditation, carry the message with ongoing interactions. They help individuals find freedom from life challenges such as hurt, anger, sexual addiction, codependent behavior, and freedom from addiction. They offer in-person meetings and weekly online sessions.

Re:generation is a faith-based recovery group: (www.regenerationrecovery. org/). Their focus is to help individuals find freedom from addictions, past hurts and destructive patterns. They host weekly meetings, and there is daily course work to be completed in the *Groundwork* guide.

Both *Celebrate Recovery* and *Alcoholics Anonymous* use Reinhold Niebuhr' *Prayer for Serenity:* (rb.gy/lflgfu) which I truly appreciate. It is such a wonderful reminder to ask for wisdom and to live life daily. I shared this prayer with the support group I facilitated to remind them that it is best to relinquish control to the Lord in everything in life. I want to share part of it with you.

Prayer for Serenity

God, grant me the serenity
to accept the things I cannot change,
the courage to change the things I can,
and the wisdom to know the difference.

If the medication of your choice is alcohol, I can confidently tell you that self-medicating with alcohol does not bring anything good to your life, quite the opposite. When you numb your suffering with drugs and alcohol it further clouds your thinking, it impairs your mental acuity, and neither is a solution to your problems. You may think, well, I only occasionally get high or drunk, well, occasionally is not a blanket approval for your negative behavior. You could think, well, even when I am high or drunk, I am able to function at school or work. So rest assured, that in no way justifies your negative, unacceptable, and most likely illegal behavior which your professors nor your manager would appreciate. You run the risk of dismissal from school, you may lose your career, your driver's license. If you were to be involved in an auto accident, you will be charged with driving under the influence of alcohol or drugs, and face imprisonment. Is it worth it? You need help to learn coping skills with life issues rather than avoid them with substance abuse.

Prayer for Serenity

God, grant me the serenity
to accept the things I cannot change,
the courage to change the things I can,
and the wisdom to know the difference.

Recovery Resources:

- *Adult & Teen Challenge USA*: https://teenchallengeusa.org/, **417.581.2181.**
- *Al-Alon* and *Alateen*: https://al-anon.org/
- *Alcoholics Anonymous*: https://www.aa.org/
- *Celebrate Recovery*: https://www.celebraterecovery.com/
- *Re:generation*: www.regenerationrecovery.org/
- *Substance Abuse and Mental Health Services Administration, SAMHSA*: https://www.samhsa.gov/, **800.662.4357 or TTY 800.487.4889.**

What if your anxiety with substance abuse is not because of you but someone who you care for and love? What happens when the person who has the problem is your parent, your sibling, your grandparent, your spouse, your grandchild, or your close friend? What can you do? You are not alone since countless people are affected by the substance abuse problems of people they love and care about in life. I am happy to know that there are resources available to help you cope and move forward in your life in spite of the issues others face. *Al-Alon* and *Alateen*: (https://al-anon.org/) are available to help you. They offer a 12-step program for those whose lives are affected by the negative behavior and poor choices of the people in their lives.

A book I want to recommend to you is *Boundaries: When to Say Yes, How to Say No to Take Control of Your Life,* by Drs. Henry Cloud and John Townsend. This book was life changing and helped me understand the difference between helping another person and enabling them to continue their negative behavior. There is a workbook which complements the book, which is filled with thought-provoking questions which may help you identify key areas in your life where you need help in setting healthy boundaries in life, and focus on the things you are able to control.

Changes That Heal, is another amazing book by Dr. Henry Cloud. This book too was life changing and help me realize that the people who had the most influence in my life, were flawed and did the best they could in life with what they had. And, if they did not have it, they could not give it, like love. Yes, mistakes were made; however, I do not condone their behavior; I am able to forgive them and maintain a good relationship with them and have healthy independence from them.

O. Meditation

If you are familiar with meditation, you know that it teaches us to empty our minds and focus on one thing, our breathing. Meditation is simple to do. Find a quiet place where you will be uninterrupted, sit comfortably, close your eyes and focus on your breathing. When you find that your mind has wondered off to think about other things, redirect your thinking back to your breathing. Meditation is a very healthy way to stop our minds from focusing on the busyness of our day. We take time to let go of our fears, anxiety, and slow down, and take time to not make those thoughts the focus of our meditation time. If you are not familiar with meditation, and would like to explore this as an option to release the stress of fear, anxiety, and depression you experience, I highly recommend this article by *Mindful, healthy mind, healthy life*: *How to Meditate*: (rb.gy/brkkio).

This is a good resource since it provides step-by-step instructions on how to start meditating and the benefits of this ancient practice.

Here are five reasons to meditate:

1. *Understanding your pain*
2. *Lower your stress*
3. *Connect better*
4. *Improve focus*
5. *Reduce brain chatter*

In Philippian 4:8, in the New Testament, we are encouraged to think about things which are *honest, just, pure, lovely, good report*. What a great recipe to use for meditation, and fill the mind with positive things and focus on good things rather than dwell on fear, anxiety, and depression. Here are some good reminders from scripture about meditation.

This book of the law shall not depart out of thy mouth; but thou shalt meditate therein day and night, that thou mayest observe to do according to all that is written therein: for then thou shalt make thy way prosperous, and then thou shalt have good success. Joshua 1:8

But his delight is in the law of the LORD; And in his law doth he meditate *day and night.* Psalm 1:2

When I remember thee upon my bed, And meditate on thee in the night watches. Psalm 63:6

I will meditate in thy precepts, And have respect unto thy ways. Psalm 119:15

Give ear to my words, O LORD, Consider my meditation. Psalm 5:1

Finally, brethren, whatsoever things are true, whatsoever things are honest, whatsoever things are just, whatsoever things are pure, whatsoever things are lovely, whatsoever things are of good report; if there be any virtue, and if there be any praise, think on these things. Those things which you have learned and received, and heard and seen in me, do: and the God of peace shall be with you. But I rejoiced in the Lord greatly, that now at the last your care of me hath flourished again; wherein ye were also careful, but ye lacked opportunity. Not that I speak in respect of want: for I have learned, in whatsoever state I am, therewith to be content. Philippians 4: 8-11

P. Music

Besides playing music to dance, I listen to music for encouragement, and to remember that I am not alone in this life, God's Spirit is always with me. After the death of my son, I recall the days when I would sit in my bedroom alone and I would listen to the *Winter* album by George Winston. If you are not familiar with his music, he plays the piano beautifully. The days my heart was so heavy with sorrow, I knelt next to my bed, I listened to the music and I wept. I wept so hard that my body shook. My heart was so broken, my future seemed bleak, and I wanted to die and be with my son. If the floor opened at that moment and took me, I do not think I would have cared. I was not suicidal, and God willing, would I ever consider taking my life; however, I felt so alone, so sad. My heart was filled with sorrow that it was difficult for me to focus on much else: I love my son, I miss my son. As the music flowed, so did my tears, along with a heavy weight of sorrow. This was a safe place for me to process my grief alone. Back then I did not know the term music therapy; however, I will tell you that the music allowed me to experience the grief I needed to process. The music stirred the emotions I needed to release the tears which needed to flow. The tears which I could not shed in front of others. It gave me the courage I needed to grieve and start the process of healing. This was very therapeutic and healing for my mind, my body and my spirit.

Since then, on several occasions I have listened to *Winter* and while the memories flood my mind of a less fortunate time, now I am able to enjoy the music for its artistic value. It had been some time since I last heard George Winston, and I decided to listen to *Winter* as I wrote this chapter. I am happy to report that the pain is not the same and my emotions do not stir as they did in the past; the tears no longer flow as I listened to these beautiful pieces. As I listened, I enjoyed the music and I did not re-live the pain. I see this as growth, as therapeutic progress. I am grateful to the Lord that years ago, He provided music as a way for me to deal with my emotions and grief.

Music is so beneficial for our lives, and today music therapy is used around the world to help patients with anxiety, physical conditions and mental health issues. There is a helpful article online by Heather Craig, BPsySc, *What are the Benefits of Music Therapy* which details the benefits of music with patients and she quotes Jillian Levy: (rb.gy/u9kjwh).

1. *Music therapy reduces anxiety and physical effects of stress*
2. *It improves healing*
3. *It can help manage Parkinson's and Alzheimer's disease*
4. *Music therapy reduces depression and other symptoms in the elderly*
5. *It helps to reduce symptoms of psychological disorders including schizophrenia*
6. *Music therapy improves self-expression and communication*

There are several songs I like which remind me to not live in fear and these songs remind me to trust the Lord with everything. Some days I play the same song three to five times consecutively and loudly. I sing, I close my eyes, and I lift my hands towards heaven since I use some of lyrics as prayers. The song, *Lord I Need You* by Matt Maher, is like the anthem for my life. I depend on the Lord every day, for everything in my life, and I am willing to humbly approach Him with a grateful heart. Maher is one of my personal favorite Christian music writers and singers, and it was great that he was a local for many years before he moved out of state. It was nice to be able to attend his concerts and chat with him. I hope this song touches your heart as it has touched mine and encouraged me.

I am excited that I am able to share encouraging songs with you! These songs encourage me, and I hope you take the time to listen to the words of these songs and be encouraged as well. If you are not familiar with these songs or artists, take a visit to your favorite online music application store and listen to these songs of praise. James 5:13 encourages us: *Is any among you afflicted? let him pray. Is any merry? let him sing psalms.*

My prayer is that these songs will touch your heart, encourage you, and give you the courage to move forward without fear as the focal point of your life. The list contains the names of the artists, the song titles and the shortened hyperlink to the songs with the lyrics. Enjoy!

All Sons & Daughters: *Great Are You Lord*: rb.gy/njv7cg

Casting Crowns: *Oh My Soul*: rb.gy/x9ui6n
Casting Crowns: *Praise You In This Storm*: rb.gy/ospfkf
Chris Tomlin: *Good, Good Father*: rb.gy/ypyvz3
Chris Tomlin: *Our God*: rb.gy/zjwcby
Chris Tomlin: *Whom Shall I Fear*: rb.gy/rxm2tr
Cory Ashbury: *Reckless Love*: rb.gy/4teujc
Danny Gokey: *Tell Your Heart To Beat Again*: rb.gy/fsg29r
Jasmine Murray: *Fearless*: rb.gy/mdf0bz
Jason Gray: *Sparrows:* rb.gy/qsj4hx
Jonathan David and Melissa Helser: *No Longer Slaves:* rb.gy/lslqbf
Matt Maher: *Lord I Need You*: rb.gy/jy8kxk
Matt Maher: *Run to the Father*: rb.gy/fx9dmg
Matt Maher: *Your Love Defends Me*: rb.gy/apklls
Mercy Me: *I Can Only Imagine*: rb.gy/k4q2om
Rend Collective: *Boldly I Approach*: rb.gy/egtk0d
Rend Collective: *Every Giant Will Fall*: rb.gy/3m73yo
Ryan Stevenson: *Eye of the Storm*: rb.gy/cmqgze
Ryan Stevenson: *No Matter What*: rb.gy/hyoh7l
Tasha Cobbs: *Break Every Chain*: rb.gy/cneavm
Tauren Wells: *Hills and Valleys*: rb.gy/alacxg
Tenth Avenue North: *Afraid*: rb.gy/g2ik7b
Tenth Avenue North: *Control*: rb.gy/ateqbg
The Afters: *I Will Fear No More*: rb.gy/1zf3ng
Zach Williams: *Chain Breaker*: rb.gy/40blub
Zach Williams: *Fear is a Liar*: rb.gy/yyckpt

Q. Positive Reinforcement

When we spend a considerable amount of time to focus on fear, anxiety, and depression, we usually do not speak in a positive manner about ourselves, our situation, or to the people around us. The next time you hear yourself being negative, (or someone brings it to your attention) stop, step away, pray, and speak positive, encouraging words aloud to yourself. One of my favorite phrases in scripture is, *And it came to pass,* which is from the book of Esther in the Old Testament, and a phrase used throughout scripture. I say this to myself because it is a great reminder that whatever challenge I face today, it did not come to stay! This helps me to keep things in perceptive and I know that whatever challenge, fear, anxiety, I experience today will not last forever, and with the Lord's help, I will get through the situation.

I recall years ago, the television program *Saturday Night Live* had a vignette or scene where a man looked in the mirror and told himself daily positive affirmations, such as *I am good enough, I am smart enough, and dog gone* it, *people like me.* The comedy routine was called *Daily Affirmations* with Stuart Smalley: (rb.gy/sxe7zt). This routine was started in 1991 by the comedian Al Franken. Stuart, the fictional character was a member of five different self-help groups. In each episode, Stuart Smalley would talk aloud to himself while he looked in the mirror and this helped give him confidence for his presentation. It was a funny comedy routine; however, I like positive self-talk, and I use this technique, and I have recommended it to others. Positive verbal affirmations are used by professional athletes, performers, and we may all be familiar with the phrase, *you got this.* Positive verbal affirmations are helpful; however, I do not repeat Stuart Smalley' words, I use words with a bit more substance for my life!

Here are some of the phrases I use for positive reinforcement.

- God has not given me the spirit of fear, but of a sound mind.
- The fear I experience is such a waste of time because God has everything under His control.
- I cannot solve this problem, so why am I wasting so much energy on it?
- I do not control other people or their actions, and therefore, I cannot change them; only God can.

- I prayed about the thing or person who is causing the fearful or anxious situation in my life and I must allow the Lord to work His will in their lives.
- I depend on the Lord for my joy, and therefore, I cannot allow anything or anyone to rob me of my joy.

I encourage you to find scripture verses which you like and empower you to live a fearless life. Use those words as daily affirmations of God's truth in your life; say the words aloud so that you can hear yourself say them. If you would like to borrow the statements I use, feel free and say these words aloud to yourself. If you have specific areas to work through, then I encourage to write your own affirmations in your own words so the words are meaningful and impactful. If you want to be like Stuart Smalley and look in the mirror, do it, and say the words of positive reinforcement and encouragement to yourself!

R. Prayer

Prayer is life changing and prayer changes everything. I love prayer and as a believer in Christ Jesus, I am able to boldly approach the throne of God. I am able to pray every day, several times per day, any time of the day, anywhere I am. I do not need to go to church to pray, although I do pray when I am there. I do not have to find a priest, rabbi, or pastor to pray, although I can contact them to pray with me and for me. I can pray alone, I can pray with family, and I can pray with friends, anytime, anywhere. Prayer is so vital to my life, and I am not able to have a successful day without it, seriously. So, when I feel anxious, when I feel afraid, I pray more often and I take my gratitude and petitions to the King of Heaven. If I want someone to pray with me and for me, then I will contact someone, a pastor, a counselor, a trusted friend and ask them to join me in prayer. They are able to pray with me and pray for me.

There are many powerful stories in the Old Testament which tell us about the prayer life of the people who lived during that time, such as Job, Moses Abraham, Daniel, King David, to name a few. One story in particular which teaches the power of prayer is the beautiful story of Esther. The book of Esther contains ten chapters and can be read all in one sitting or within a few days of study. Let me share the setting with you. King Ahasuerus lived in the palace of Shushan, and he wanted a new wife. He ruled over a vast area and he appointed his people to seek out young virgins within his territory and bring the women to the palace. One of the king's scribes was Mordecai, who raised his relative Hadassah, who was called Esther, after the death of both of her parents. Esther was among the women taken to the palace for the king to choose a wife, and after due process, the king selected Esther. King Ahasuerus loved Esther.

The story continues with political unrest within the king's court and his life was in danger, and thanks to Mordecai and Esther, the men who sought to kill the king were captured. Later, a terrible plan was presented to the king by a man named Haman, the king's chief minister. He had convinced the king that the Jewish people were rebellious and should be slaughtered. The terrible news reached Esther, and she knew she had to speak to the king; however, no one was allowed to stand in the king's court, without his request or approval. Although she was married to the king, although she was the queen, she was not allowed to approach the king, and risked death if she dared. Esther was afraid for the lives of the Jewish people which included Mordecai and herself; however, she knew that she had to get word to her husband. She prayed, and she asked the people to pray with her. She needed the courage to enter the king's throne room unannounced, and the courage to lose her life in the process. The message Esther gave to Mordecai was, *Go, gather together all the Jews that are present in Shushan, and fast ye for me, and neither eat nor drink three days, night or day: I also and my maidens will fast likewise; and so will I go in unto the king, which is not according to the law: and if I perish, I perish.*

If I perish, I perish…these were not easy words to say, and yet she chose to risk her life to save the lives of her people. Esther was prepared to die to save the Jewish people; however, she knew the people prayed and fasted along with her. After the three days, she found the courage to risk her life and enter the king's throne room unannounced. It was amazing that when the king noticed Esther in his court, he extended his golden scepter to her, which symbolized that she was able to approach the king! Esther was able to speak to the king and arranged to have Haman attend a dinner with them. Within days, the truth of Haman's plan was revealed and foiled. The Lord answered Esther's prayer, the Lord answered the prayers of her Jewish community. Not only was her life spared but the lives of the Jewish people in the king's territory. The Jewish people celebrated, their prayers were answered! Esther knew that she was there for such a time as this, to be used by God to save her people. Thousands of years later, the celebration is memorialized with the holiday of *Purim* which honors Esther's bravery and the power of prayer and the saving of lives.

The story of Esther paints a wonderful picture of prayer and how God used her prayers and the prayers of her Jewish community. This story is also a great analogy of how we can enter God's throne room unannounced and He will always accept us. We have the freedom to speak to the Lord any time, any day, anywhere we are; we can approach the throne of God freely. We do not have to fear, we can speak to our God any time, and He will always accept us, He will always have time to listen to us. We are so privileged to be welcomed into His court as many times as we need to enter and meet with Him. The story of Esther is also a great reminder that we are here, with the people in our lives *for such a time as this* and that the Lord has a wonderful plan for each of us. We may not understand His plan, we may not agree or like His plan; however, we need to trust that He has a purpose for our lives. He will accomplish great things when we allow ourselves to be used by Him, and take on the challenges we face with courage, just like Esther.

The New Testament contains several examples of how Jesus prayed. He would get up very early in the morning, take a walk alone and spend time in conversation with God, His Father. Daily Jesus spent time in prayer, and sometimes, He prayed until the wee hours of the morning. When He asked his disciples to go with Him to the Garden at Gethsemane, Jesus asked them to pray. Jesus spent 40 days in the desert and was in constant communication with His Father, God. Clearly, prayer was very important to Jesus, and I believe it is just as important for me and for you. Prayer was a daily activity for Jesus and it was non-negotiable: He prayed daily and several times per day. This may also seem counterintuitive, that Jesus the Son of God needed to pray. Somehow, we may think that if anyone did not need to pray, it would be He; however, it was the opposite. For Jesus, prayer was essential, like breathing, the same way it is essential for us. Scripture teaches that as believers we are able to enter into God's throne room and boldly come before Him. We do not need to be afraid, or beg, or ask permission to go to Him in prayer. Prayer involves dedicated time to speak to God, in a quiet place and spend uninterrupted time to speak with Him. In that conversation I let Him know that I am grateful for the people and things in my life, I am grateful to Him for all I have, then I ask Him to bless me and those I love, I can even ask Him to bless my enemies, as odd as that sounds. I can seek His wisdom for my daily living. I am able to leave my cares, burdens, heartaches, and fears at His feet, and in turn He is able to give me His peace.

Right Now Media: (www.rightnowmedia.org/) has the video devotional study on prayer by J.D. Greear called *Just Ask*. He shares that it is very interesting that the disciples did not ask Jesus to teach them how to preach, or how to heal; they asked Jesus to teach them to pray. They watched Jesus step away from them and the crowds and pray, and they most likely saw the value of prayer in His life. Jesus taught His disciples to pray and we can use that same prayer in our daily lives too. We call Jesus's prayer, the Lord's Prayer; however, this was not His prayer, this was the example or the model prayer for the disciples and for us. If you do not know how to pray or not sure how to start, let me help put your mind at ease, praying to God is simply having a conversation with Him. He knows who you are, He knows your name. Simply start speaking to Him. I typically like to start praying by saying, *Heavenly Father* or *Lord* and then speak to Him about what is on my heart. I end my prayers *in the name of Jesus Christ, Amen*. It is so wonderful and comforting to be able to speak with the Lord about everything, knowing that He hears me and cares about me.

Let me share the verses where Jesus taught His disciples to pray. I like these verses because they drive home the point about daily living. I cannot relive yesterday, and I am not able to bring tomorrow into today. He taught them to ask for daily bread, not for weekly bread, and of course, He taught them about forgiveness. Matthew 6: 9-13, we find The Lord's Prayer:

Our Father which art in heaven, Hallowed be thy name. Thy kingdom come. Thy will be done in earth, as it is in heaven. Give us this day our daily bread. And forgive us our debts, as we forgive our debtors. And lead us not into temptation, but deliver us from evil: For thine is the kingdom, and the power, and the glory, forever. Amen.

Our Father which art in heaven, Hallowed be thy name.
Thy kingdom come.
Thy will be done in earth, as it is in heaven.
Give us this day our daily bread.
And forgive us our debts, as we forgive our debtors.
And lead us not into temptation, but deliver us from evil:
For thine is the kingdom, and the power, and the glory, forever.
Amen.

If you have never prayed, or it has been a long time since you last prayed, please know that you are able to start today, right now. It is not a problem if you find it a bit challenging; you are human. Prayer is simply a sincere conversation with God, it is not a conversation to impress Him. Simply find a quiet room, sit, stand, or kneel and start a conversation with Jesus, the King of Heaven. He is waiting for you and He has time to listen to you because He cares about you; actually, He loves you. God is never too busy to listen to our prayers; He pays attention to us and He wants us to come to Him and speak with Him. Tell him about the things for which you are grateful, and then ask Him to take away your fears, anxiety, and depression. Ask Him for wisdom so that you know the difference between rational and irrational fear, and ask Him to give you His strength, His mercy, and His grace for the daily journey of life. Ask Him to lead you to people who can encourage you, ask Him for new friends if needed, and ask Him to help you find a good church. Ask Him for the wisdom to find a reputable therapist or pastor to meet with on a regular basis or a good and reputable doctor to help you find the medication which is best for you. Prayer changes everything, it really does. Prayer takes what looks like a hopeless situation and the Lord gives hope. Prayer takes the cares of the storm to the Lord, and He brings peace. Many times, He calms the storms, and often times, He calms my heart and mind to allow me to walk through the storms of this life.

Olivia Muenster's article on prayer: *18 Calming Prayers for Anxiety That Offer Instant Stress Relief, These soothing words will bring comfort and inner peace to your heart,* was published by *Woman's Day*: (rb.gy/taqgok). The article includes several prayers which you are able to use for your personal prayer time and help get you in the practice of praying silently or aloud. Once you feel comfortable with the written prayers, I trust that you will use your own words to speak to God. Go to Him with a sincere heart, your personal needs and burdens, and talk to Him about what is on your mind; He will listen to you.

I pray every day and many times per day. I pray for my family, my friends, and for the situations we each face. I have prayed to the Lord regarding specific situations, specific decisions I needed to make, specific people, and specific needs. Each time I went to the Lord with my requests, my petitions, I know that He heard my cry for help. It is always incredible when I see His response to my prayers. Situations have cleared or been resolved, a person has been healed, a job opened for me for someone I know, someone surrendered their life to God; I have seen numerous prayers been answered by God. Prayer works and prayer changes everything. I have two little signs in my home, both anonymous: *Remember the days when you prayed for what you have now*, and *When life gives you more than you can stand...kneel*. Both are good reminders for me to see daily.

George Mueller was a pastor in England who relied heavily on the Lord and the power of prayer. When he needed money for his college tuition, he got on his knees and asked God to provide the funds he needed. Within the hour, there was a knock at the door and the gentleman at the door offered to pay for Mueller' education! Mueller was asked to take the pastoral position at a church, and they planned to pay his salary with money which had been collected unfairly, and he refused to take a salary and he trusted the Lord to care for him and his family, and God supplied all their needs. When he saw so many orphaned children in the area, he asked the Lord to supply a place and the means to care for them, and the Lord answered his prayers. With the generous gifts and donations he received, he started the Ashley Brown Orphanage: (rb.gy/npwefg).

My favorite George Mueller prayer is when he prayed for food for the children in his care. One day there was no food at the orphanage and they had 300 children to feed. At the meal time, he asked everyone to gather in the dining room as they normally did for meals. Although there was no food available for lunch, he prayed for the blessing of the food they were going to eat! Within minutes, there was a knock at the door and a baker delivered free bread to them; there was another knock at the door and a milkman brought free milk for all the children!

John Wesley was a preacher, a composer, an author, and he had great compassion for the poor. Although he accomplished so much in life, he is famous for his devotion to prayer. There are several books written about Wesley's life, prayers, his ministry, and when you read them you will gain a sense of his love for God, and the wisdom he experienced from walking closely with the Lord every day. You may find many of his quotes on *Good Reads*: (rb.gy/lywtk3).

Think about all the things which you have accomplished in this life. How you do want people to think about you and remember you after you leave this life? Where is your devotion? I would be humbled and honored to be remembered as a person who prayed earnestly to the Lord, and I would love to live a life completely devoted to prayer and constant sincere communication with God.

Here are excerpts of the John Wesley quotes I appreciate:

- *O praise God for all you have...*
- *Prayer continues in the desire of the heart...*
- *God only requires of his adult children that their hearts be truly purified...*
- *Lord, I am no longer my own, but Yours. Put me to what You will, rank me with whom You will. Let me be employed by You or laid aside for You, exalted for You or brought low by You...*

That last prayer is probably the most powerful modern-day prayer I have ever heard in my life. John Wesley is one of the most courageous people I have ever studied. He was so willing to surrender everything in his life to the Lord regardless of the consequences, because he completely trusted God. This prayer is the epitome of what God asks of us when we surrender our lives to Him. What a great reminder that God is in control of our lives, and this brings comfort to my heart knowing that I am able to trust the Lord with every detail of my life.

Lord, I am no longer my own, but Yours.
Put me to what You will, rank me with whom You will.
Let me be employed by You or laid aside for You,
exalted for You or brought low by You…

You may be thinking *oh sure, prayer does not work*. Perhaps you prayed in the past and the Lord never answered your prayers. I understand. I also understand that when I pray to the Lord, I need and want to be persistent in the asking. Very rarely, do I ever pray only once for something or someone. For example, when friends or family let me know that they will undergo surgery, I start praying for them from the day they mention it to me, even though their appointment may not be for one week or more. I pray with them and I pray for them, several times during the day and up to the day of the surgery. I ask the Lord to be with the surgeon, and the surgical team. I pray for safety while in the hospital, a successful operation and a successful healing and recovery time. I know that the Lord hears all my prayers and He knows what I need before I come to Him in prayer; however, I take the child-like posture of, *are we there yet* when I pray. I pray often, I pray several times for the situation or the person who needs help, and even though many times it is I who need the help or the blessing.

As a child, I learned that God always answers prayers with one of three responses, *yes, no*, or *wait*. I also need to keep in mind that God is not my personal short-order cook or my personal genie who will grant my every wish. He is a sovereign God, who knows what is best for me and I am able to trust Him, even when His response is no. Perhaps the prayer request is premature since I am not ready to receive His response, and then I find that I am in God's waiting room where I am able to continue to wait on Him. Oh trust me, the waiting is never fun; however, I believe that many times I am able to learn more about myself, my dependency on the Lord, and more about Him during the waiting. Perhaps the prayer is selfish or my motivation may not pure, and God's response is no. So do not be discouraged if you do not immediately see a response from the Lord and remember to check your motivation in the prayer and ensure that it is in line with His will. Pray, and pray again, and look for the yes or no from God, or wait on the Lord.

In *Just Ask*, J.D. Greear refers to prayer as being in the correct posture: the posture of trust, the posture of worship, the posture of surrender, and the posture of dependence. He explains that no one needs to remind me to breath every day, breathing is instinctual since my body craves oxygen. Likewise, when I understand the gospel, it will motivate me to crave prayer.

I recall one year the church ran a prayer campaign, and wanted our church family to be covered in prayer for one full week, 24 hours per day. We were able to sign-up for one-hour time slots, and this way, someone was in prayer every hour for 24 hours that entire week. When I initially put my name on the list, I wondered if I could pray uninterrupted for 15 minutes. I recall, my time slot was 9 p.m. and the first night, I went through my list and when I finished, I looked at the clock and saw that I had prayed for about five minutes! Five minutes? Oh goodness. So, I decided to make a list of specific things: things or people for which I was grateful, the people and things in my life. I prayed for people by name, for family and friends, the challenges in their lives and mine, work, relationships, healing for others and so forth. I got back down on my knees and prayed for well over one hour. I realized that when I focused on everyone who needed healing, my family, my friends, my church, the pastors and staff, and everything else I had on the list, it was so easy to spend quality time as I spoke to the Lord. The next evening and the remainder of the week, when it was time for my appointment time to pray, I had absolutely no problem praying for the entire hour. I realized that I truly had lots of people in my life who needed prayer at that time, and lifting each name to the Lord was powerful. The focus was talking to the Lord about each person, each situation, and I knew that He listened and He would answer each prayer as He saw fit to respond. It was not my responsibility to concern myself with His response, it was my responsibility to pray. I can pray about everything and surrender all my cares to Him and allow Him to be the sovereign God that He is.

Have you ever been in a conversation with someone and they

share something personal which is happening in their life? They share the details with you and ask you to pray with them about the outcome. You tell them, I'll pray for you and then the week goes by and you realize that you completely forgot to pray for your friend! I hate when that happens: seriously. On several occasions this happened to me and I felt so horrible for letting down my friends. So, now when anyone asks me to pray for them, I do two things: I make a note on my smart phone about their situation and use that as a reminder to pray for that individual. The second thing I do is ask them if I am able to pray with them while we are together in person or while we chat on the telephone. This way I am able to share their burden and carry it to the throne of God, and this too is a good reminder for me to continue to pray for them in the coming days.

S. Read

I like to read and do research. Ever since grade school, and I spent a considerable amount of time at the library in Chicago and read. I enjoyed doing book reports because it gave me an opportunity to explore, gain new knowledge and document. One year, I read a book on hockey and learned about the players and the game. I fell in love with hockey and enjoyed the excitement of the Chicago Blackhawks games. I still recall the high energy, loud, standing-room only games in the old hockey stadium. To date, I still enjoy watching the games and attend games.

When I was in the last year of my undergraduate program, I was in an accelerated program, and I read lots of textbooks, did research and created a survey to support the thesis I wrote to complete the program. I like to read and gain new knowledge about topics which interest me. After Jeremy died, I read several books about his heart condition, and about other parents who experienced the terrible loss of their child. Reading about their experiences helped me to realize two things. One, I was not alone in this world with the trauma I suffered; there are countless number of parents with empty arms in this world. Second, I read how they dealt with their loss and what they learned from their experiences. When it comes to fear and anxiety, I like to read faith-based books by authors who have experienced and overcome the same emotions.

You may want to subscribe to *365 Fear Nots* and receive daily encouragement: (www.365fearnots.com). You will receive an email which contains Biblical truths on fear and worry. The email will include the verse of the day and a brief summary or explanation of the verse. I encourage you to read the daily email and search the verses in your own Bible to become familiar with the passages where each verse is found and the setting.

Louie Giglio has penned several books for adults and for children. I want to mention a few of his books: *Winning the War on Worry*; *Putting an X Through Anxiety*; *Goliath Must Fall*. He also offers an impactful video series and study guides. I enjoy his books and occasionally I watch his sermons online. I appreciate his sincere, conversational style of communicating as he preaches, and his style of writing. I appreciate his sermons since Louie Giglio speaks from the heart as he is very transparent about his own life, the personal struggles he faced, and the steps he took to trust the Lord with his healing. In *Don't Give The Enemy A Seat At Your Table*; *It's Time To Win The Battle Of Your Mind* he discusses methods to overcome the negative thoughts which attempt to rule our minds. He also has a video series which complements the book which I thoroughly enjoyed, and I was greatly encouraged. The study guide is very insightful with thought-provoking questions and practical Biblical guidance for our lives. Giglio is the leader of *Passion City Church* in Atlanta, Georgia: (passioncitychurch.com/). He is also the founder of the *Passion Movement*: (passionconferences.com/) which focuses on college-age adults, and they hosts annual conferences. Louie Giglio is a pastor, author, and public speaker. Thank you Pastor Giglio for making the good news of Jesus so clear and relatable for all ages.

In Session Two of the *Don't Give The Enemy A Seat At Your Table* study guide there is a helpful chart which has two columns. One column includes a list of the lies the enemy will use in attempt to defeat us. The second column contains scripture verses from the Bible which defeat the lies. He believes it is important for us to be aware of the enemy and the tactics it uses against us. One way to face this battle is with the truth found in scripture. For example, if you believe the lie from the enemy that you are unlovable, the truth found in scripture is Jeremiah 31:3, God loves you with an everlasting love. The list mentions weakness, the past, worthless, rejection, peace, purpose: most things with which we struggle. Thank you Louie Giglio for this helpful chart!

I use this chart as a reminder to focus on God's Word and I refer to it often. As I glance at these verses sometimes, I also audibly say, *Get out satan in the name of Jesus Christ!* I command the enemy to flee my presence in the name of Jesus and the great thing is, he must obey because he must obey the Lord. I am able to speak these words aloud in the resurrected power of Jesus Christ. I hope you seek out the study guide and find this list helpful and that the verses encourage you as they encourage me. I hope you take time every day to review the list and be reminded that you are on the winning side of the battle when the Lord is on your side!

David Jeremiah has been in Christian ministry for over 60 years! Dr. Jeremiah is an author; he is the founder of *Turning Point Radio and Television Ministries*: (www.davidjeremiah.org/), and he is the senior pastor at *Shadow Mountain Community Church* in El Cajon, California: (shadowmountain.org/). I listened to *Turning Point* on the radio when I lived in Chicago, and today, it is wonderful to view his sermons online. He has wonderful, insightful, and helpful messages on fear and anxiety, along with the steps to take to find freedom. His book, *Overcomer; 8 Ways to Live a Life of Unstoppable Strength, Unmovable Faith, and Unbelievable Power* is so powerful. I read this book within a few days and it touched my heart. Not only is the book encouraging and interesting, it is very strategic. The author basically writes in the same calm and soothing, conversational manner in which he speaks and as I read the book, I could almost hear his unique, calm voice as if he were telling each story to me. Dr. Jeremiah shared stories of individuals who were in fearful situations, trusted in the Lord, and hung on for one more minute and acted in a courageous manner. What a great reminder that I am able to trust the Lord in every situation, and how at times the courage I exhibit is able to change a situation for the better.

His book provides practical, strategic ways to prepare for life and the challenges we face knowing that we can overcome our circumstances with prayer and scripture and not be defeated but live victoriously. *Overcomer* provides encouraging stories of various individuals who were overcomers regardless of their situations, along with additional scripture references throughout the book. I believe you will enjoy reading his book and watching the *Overcomer* sermon series online.

Thank you Dr. Jeremiah for standing firm in the faith and sharing your wealth of knowledge!

T. Rest

In Matthew 28: 11 Jesus tells us: *Come unto me, all ye that labour and are heavy laden, and* I *will give you rest.* The Lord makes Himself available to us and He understand that we are weighed down with life's burdens, and He is there to give us His peace and rest. It is so wonderful that I am able to take every care of this world to Him, and He provides rest for the weary body and the weary soul. Jesus understand the human condition and He invites us to give our heavy load of burdens to Him.

Sleep is a healthy, tangible thing to do when we are overwhelmed with the cares of this life, like worry, fear, and anxiety. Rest, down time, sleep...oh, some days those are much needed words and activities. Most days, I am awake before 7 a.m. and have a full day and ready to get some rest between 11 p.m. and midnight. Lights are low, the bedroom is quiet, the pets are settled for the night, and then I toss and turn. Some nights it can take over one hour for me to relax and be able to sleep. At times, the pets wake me and I must tend to their needs, and some nights I stay awake until 3 a.m. I can joke about it and tell people that I have not slept well in over forty years; however, lack of sleep is no joking matter.

There are days it seems difficult to stop thinking or overthinking life; this started years ago when I developed insomnia. It's interesting that sometimes in the wee hours of the morning, I get some unique ideas or think of things I want to do the next day or in the near future. I make notes or search something on my phone to have the page available the next day. This may sound interesting; however, it is not good. Sleep is something I desperately need and I wish sleep would come easy to me, and that I would be able to sleep through an entire night. I do take time to rest some days in the late afternoon, and I put up my feet and close my eyes. Most of the time, I able to rest and some days, surprisingly, I fall asleep and take a quick nap. I am self-aware of the cycle I live, and I know that there are herbal treatments and medications options available; however, I do struggles with taking pills, and of course, I refuse to take anything which may be habit forming. I started to think about the benefits of rest and sleep and found some helpful information which reinforced my need for sound sleep.

Summa Health has an article on the benefits of sleep: *7 Health Benefits to Getting a Good Night's Rest:* (rb.gy/cldm36). Getting sufficient sleep is good for our mood and for our health.

- *Heathier Heart*
- *Weight Control*
- *Improved Athletic Ability*
- *Sharper Brain Function*
- *Better Mood*
- *Balanced Blood Sugar*
- *Immune Boost*

U. Senses

As you start to feel anxious, try these sensory exercises to help you focus on something different and reset your thinking. You may start off by using the *Hand on Heart* technique. Place your hand over your heart and take several deep breaths. You may close your eyes and use your sense of touch to help yourself calm down and release anxious thoughts. Another sensory technique, the *5-4- 3- 2- 1 Coping Technique* involves the use of your senses: touch, sight, hearing, smell, and taste. Use your senses to focus on the present moment and not on the overwhelming, negative, compulsive, anxious thoughts. Take a deep breath. Find five things that you can touch, like the pen on your desk and a pad of paper or a stress ball. Find four things that you can smell like an apple, a cup of tea, or a flower. Find three things that you can hear like a bird singing or a song on the radio. Find two things you can you see like the light of day or a favorite picture. Find one thing you can taste like the cup of tea or a stick of gum. As you walk around your home or outside to find the objects, you will focus on the task of finding the sensory items, enjoy the process and reduce the anxious thoughts you experience. This is a simple technique and yet very helpful to be present in the moment and stop fixating on unpleasant thoughts. The University of Rochester Medical Center has some good information on these sensory techniques: (rb.gy/pxiarf).

V. Sound Therapy

Binaural beats have been used by medical practitioners for many years. I first learned of sound therapy while doing some research on cancer cells and found that some physicians successfully incorporate sound to treat their patients. My curiosity lead me to find that sound therapy is also being used to help patients who suffer from anxiety. Psychologist Hannah Chenoweth has an interesting article on this topic (rb.gy/uc6psz), *Binaural Beats Are Being Used as Sound Wave Therapy for Anxiety, but Does It Really Help?* After listening to binaural beats for the first time, some people notice reduced anxiety, and others may need to listen longer for an extended period of time, or may need to listen to different frequencies after a few weeks.

In one small study, people had a 26% drop in anxiety symptoms after listening to binaural beats for at least 20 minutes daily for two weeks in combination with therapy. Other studies show that binaural beats may benefit patients experiencing anxiety before surgery.

At night, I like to listen to music written in 528 Hertz frequency because it helps me to relax. I am able to focus on the music and stop thinking about other things which preoccupy my mind. Anecdotal evidence suggests that 528Hz frequencies can improve sleep quality, reduce stress and anxiety, increase energy levels, improve concentration and focus, improve digestion, and reduce pain and inflammation. The *Institute of Biochemistry and Biophysics* at the *University of Tehran,* conducted research on the frequency: (rb. gy/u1hohv). Their research shows that 528Hz frequency increases cell viability by 20%, and it has the ability to repair human deoxyribonucleic acid, DNA.

W. Support Groups

A kindred spirit…that is how I define support groups. I recall feeling so awful, so out of sorts after Jeremy died. I felt so alone in my situation; it seemed like I could not identify or relate with anyone. Most of the people I knew were single without children, married without children, or married with adult children. Sadly, even if I had the courage to talk about Jeremy with my friends, most of them would quickly change the subject and in the long run, most of them abandoned me. They wanted to give me space, which really meant, they left me alone to deal with my issues since it was uncomfortable for them. At the office, my colleagues withdrew and never asked me how I was doing either. One woman told me, *we did not worry about you because we knew your faith would carry you through this.* She was absolutely correct, my faith carried me through the difficult time; however, I missed my friends, their emotional support and presence in my life.

I do not recall who, perhaps it was someone at the doctor's office, who shared information about a support group for grieving parents which met at the hospital where Jeremy died. I decided to attend a meeting and I was very surprised to find the room filled with couples who recently had lost children. I actively listened as they shared their stories of their children and the illnesses which took their lives. We shared our stories, we cried, we laughed; it was so refreshing to be with people who understood everything I felt, thought, experienced without judging me or finding the need to say the right thing to me, since that does not exist. It was so good to be with these couples month after month, and although we were strangers in the beginning, we shared a kindred spirit because of our losses. The group facilitators provided books and other reading materials and I read everything they had available as part of my healing journey.

Years later, and after much prayer, and fear and trepidation, I started a support group when I lived in Illinois. My former pastor, the late, Pastor Wayne Lies, encouraged me to start the group and he prayed with me and for me. At that time, I was not confident to start a group; however, all I knew was I wanted to give other grieving parents a safe place to meet, share their stories of loss, and share the hope of Jesus with them. The *Mending Hearts* support group met monthly, and anyone could speak about their struggles, and about the things which were heavy on their hearts. I closed each meeting with an encouraging word, a hopeful story, Bible verses, an article or poem, and a prayer. It was amazing to see how month after month, the Lord worked in our lives. People came to the meetings feeling lost, overwhelmed, heartbroken, angry, and months later they each were confident that life had a purpose again. We gave our brokenness and anger to the Lord, and His Spirit moved in each of their lives. It was humbling to see how the Lord used me to share His peace, His hope, His love, His grace with the individuals in this group. It was incredible to see the transformation in the life of each person. It was powerful to be with kindred spirits, especially when Jesus became our focus. We had a renewed sense of living, even though our children were no longer with us. One thing I will say is, I do not take any credit for the work which was done in the lives of the members of this support group. The Lord is the one who provided the healing, I simply made myself available to walk the grief journey with the group.

When I moved to Arizona, I prayed about starting the support group again, and I waited on the Lord to answer that prayer and it never seemed like the right time. That prayer was clearly answered many years later. I met two pastors from *New Life Community Church,* at a book signing event, and they invited me to visit their church. I visited the church and after a few months, I decided to become a member. I was asked to speak one weekend with one of their former pastors, Pastor Patrick McCalla, when he preached a sermon on grieving. After praying about the next steps and details, I was able to start the support group. I was also asked to host an informational session on the grief process which was open to anyone. Facilitating the support group always came with a mixed blessing because I was sad to know that someone else lost a child, and blessed and honored that I was available to walk the journey with them. From that group and meeting, I met more people, and I started to meet with people in their homes to do one-on-one grief counseling. I created a plan to help individuals identify and work through the most challenging part of their journey.

Who would have ever thought that the loss of my son would allow and provide such a precious ministry? If after Jeremy's death, you told me that I would provide support to others through grief counseling, I probably would have said, *sure, right, probably not*! However, it is amazing how God works in our lives when we make ourselves available to His service. I am very blessed and honored to walk the personal healing journey with others. I know that when people host a party, their front door is wide open to let everyone inside; however, when we lose a loved one, the front door is barely cracked open, and only a few trusted individuals are allowed inside; I am very blessed.

One Bible verse which reminds me that God can create good out of any circumstance is Romans 8:28: *And we know that all things work together for good to them that love God, to them who are the called according to his purpose.* Keep in mind, this verse does not say that all things are good in life. This verse is a declaration that all things work together for good when the Lord is involved. Only the Lord can take a hopeless situation and bring something positive from it. Although I am no longer part of this church, I have fond memories of the individuals who trusted me with their hearts and stories of their precious children, and I know that I am blessed to have been part of their journey.

If you are in need of a support group to help you deal with anxiety, visit the *Recovery International* website and see what they may have available in your area: (recoveryinternational.org/). This is a safe place for you to listen and learn.

If you suffer from the trauma of the death of a loved one, there are two support groups which I am able to recommend to you: *The Compassionate Friends*: (www.compassionatefriends.org/) and *Grief Share*: (www.griefshare.org/). Search your local area for support groups and find a safe place to share your story surrounded by people who truly understand your grief.

Grief Share: https://www.griefshare.org/

❖

Recovery International: https://recoveryinternational.org/

❖

The Compassionate Friends: https://www.compassionatefriends.org/

❖

X. Tapping

Tapping is an *Emotional Freedom Technique, EFT*; it is a relaxation method, and when used correctly is an effective method to help deal with pain and anxiety. I use this method to cope with chronic pain and avoid pain medication. Many prescription pain killers are known to cause stomach and bowel problems and of course, many of them are habit forming; I tend to stay clear of them and find alternative ways to deal and cope with pain. Tapping is a wonderful, drug-free alternative and can be done anywhere. Tapping uses acupressure on the meridian points, pressure points the same way that acupuncture works, only without the needles! With tapping, I am able to tap on the pressure points on my head, my face, and the top of my chest, my hands, my back, and any pressure point on my body. I am able to breathe, and focus on counting the number of taps in each area. I also am able to tell my pain or anxiety that it will not get the best of me as I speak audibly which may sound silly; however, it helps with the process. If you are not familiar with tapping or pressure points, here is some medical research on the benefits of tapping.

Be Brain Fit, Better Mind, Better Life has a very detailed article online written by Deane Alban who explains tapping: the benefits, the research, and instructions on how to perform it: *11 Benefits of Tapping for Anxiety Relief:* (rb.gy/dcgj3l).

Tapping is a form of acupressure that uses fingertip taps in a particular sequence.

The theory behind tapping is that all negative emotions are caused by a disruption in the body's energy system and that tapping can restore balance to this system.

Tapping purportedly neutralizes any judgment you have about your anxiety and removes limiting beliefs you have developed that contribute to your anxiety.

There's evidence that these treatments may work by addressing imbalances of neurotransmitters and hormones, increasing blood flow, reducing muscle tension, and decreasing inflammation.

I highly recommend tapping since it is something simple, yet so healing and it costs nothing but time: time wisely spent to regain your mental and physical health! If you want to learn more about tapping and how to incorporate it in your life, you may want to visit *The Tapping Solution* and learn the technique from Nick Ortner, the author of the book: (www.thetappingsolution.com/).

Although I am familiar with tapping, after I visited their website I learned some new amazing facts:

- *You can reduce stress and anxiety by 41%.*
- *Reducing stress is vital on the journey to improving mental health, and the good news is: It's within reach.*
- *Research shows that tapping calms the amygdala in the brain, regulates our nervous system, and reduces stress and anxiety.*
- *Tapping regulates the nervous system, boosting the immune system.*
- *Tapping calms the brain and boost brainpower.*
- *Tapping eliminates stress and anxiety.*
- *EFT Tapping lowers the stress hormone cortisol by 43%.*
- *EFT Tapping is shown to be a fast, long-lasting treatment for anxiety.*
- *EFT Tapping treatment reduces PTSD symptoms by 52% in veterans.*

Y. Visualization

The *Visualization Relaxation Technique* is a common practice among professional athletes, actors, business professionals, as well as people who struggle with stress and fear. When we visualize being successful with the thing we fear, it may help us as we face and overcome the fear. For example, let's say that you have a fear of flying in an airplane. The therapist may recommend that you visualize yourself as you calmly walk into the airplane. Once settled in your seat, you focus on tasks such as on meditate, read a book, listen to an audio book or to music, or watch a movie during the flight. This will aid to ensure that you focus on the task and your breathing, and not focus on the fear of the takeoff and landing. Once you have visualized your success, then you will be prepared to walk into an airplane for your trip.

Another way to use visualization is to think of a pleasant scenario during an intense time. When you face an unpleasant situation and you start to feel anxious, rather than give into the anxiety and have an anxiety attack, think of something calm, pleasant, fun, enjoyable, something which brings joy to your life, and derail the anxiety. Sometimes when I feel stressed or anxious, I close my eyes and think of the beautiful beaches in Hawaii and take deep breaths. The helps reset my thinking and rather than focus on the thing or person causing stress in my life. I focus on a wonderful, calm setting for a few moments and allow those pleasant thoughts to wash over me. I recall a memory of being on a specific beach and I can visualize myself there as I walk along the shore. I also take a few moments to pray and take some deep breaths to help reset my thinking. Sometimes during stressful situations, I pace the floor and I sing as I visualize myself singing in front of others.

If you would like to learn more about visualization and put it into practice to cope with anxiety and fear, you may want to take a moment and read the practical steps outlined in *How to Overcome Your Fears Through Visualization* by Trudi Griffin, LPC, MS: (rb. gy/mqsx5u).

Z. Volunteer

When I spent time to prepare for the support group meetings, I found that the more I did to help the group, the less I focused on myself. Not that I was in denial, it was such a blessing to help the group with their journey, and in turn it helped me to travel my own grieving journey. When my focus is to help others, I think less of myself and my own problems. When I use my energy to help others I am able to focus less on the challenges I face. When I help others, it well worth my time. Although I am a busy person, I like to help others and I spend time as a mentor; I coach people and help them develop their skills. At times, I do pro bono work with resume writing especially when I know someone is in crisis and needs to get a job quickly.

When we help others we can focus on their needs, rather than waste energy on worry and fear. We can pour our energy into something positive, something which brings joy, and something in which we have passion. There are countless organizations which need volunteers. Use your passion to help others and in returned be blessed!

If you do not know where you can use your skills, here are a few types of organizations which may need your help! Check the listings in your local community for additional organizations which seek for volunteers. Some organizations will require that you pass a background check in order to help with children and senior citizens, and some organizations may require that you sign a confidentiality agreement and protect their client information. Check your local area for opportunities to invest time in the lives of others who could use your talents and your skills. It is so worth your time to help others and in turn be blessed.

- Advocacy and human rights groups
- Animal shelters
- Churches

- Community centers
- Crisis support
- Disability or special need groups
- Disaster Relief
- Foster care
- Homeless shelters
- Hospitals
- Immigrant and refugee centers
- Military and veteran groups
- Museums
- Nursing homes
- Police departments
- Political offices
- Senior centers
- Schools
- Soup kitchens
- Theaters
- Tutors
- Zoos

Move through it

So bottom line, if you want to ruin your physical and mental health, worry, live in fear and anxiety. However, I do not think I have ever met anyone who intentionally planned to sabotage their life or their well-being by living in constant or chronic fear. Literally, nothing good comes from living a life filled with fear, anxiety or depression. The good news is you do not have to live like this. There is hope in the Lord, and there are tangible things which you can do to help your situation. You do not have to live your life in bondage, you can find freedom from fear and anxiety. In summary, you have treatment options to help you reduce fear and anxiety: acupuncture, Bible reading, breathing exercises, community, counseling, exercise, gratitude, healthy eating, journaling, laughter, learn something new, light therapy, massage therapy, medications, meditation, music, positive verbal reinforcement, prayer, read, rest, sensory exercises, sound therapy, support groups, tapping, visualization, and volunteer work.

I have never appreciated the term *get over it*. After church one afternoon, a friend noticed I looked a bit sad. She asked me what happened, and I reminded her that I lost my son a few weeks prior to that day. Her response made me speechless when she asked, *Aren't you over that yet?* Clearly, she could never understand my situation since she had never lost a child.

We may never get over an event; however, I firmly believe that we are able to work through it and heal from it. Make a conscience choice to move through the challenges, and travel your journey, take steps to work through it. So let go of negative thoughts and feelings; choose to do something positive for yourself today. There is hope, there is always hope. We do not have to live in fear or anxiety; it makes no sense to literally hurt ourselves, hurt our minds, our bodies, because we choose to have negative, fearful, anxious thoughts. Be set free, give your thought life to God and let Him direct your ways. Seek professional help, talk to a counselor, a pastor. Move towards a better, healthier life style, release the fear and anxiety which keep you from enjoying your life. You only have one life, live it, enjoy it, and treat yourself with care; make the most of every day. Treat yourself with respect and dignity; do the healthy, tangible things to move to a better, healthier you.

FOUR

God's Love

Perspective

After *Go Forth and Get a Job!* was published, I was invited to host a book signing event at one of our local bookstores, and I invited some friends to the event. One of my friends, Alyssa pulled me aside, and asked me if the book was written from a Christian perspective. I laughed, and said *yes, since that is the only perspective I have*! So, with that in mind, I want to stop here and tell you about my Christian view.

I was raised in a home where Christianity and the Bible was talked about, and we attended church several times per week. I attended Sunday school, and I helped my parents with their inter-city mission projects. When I was in eighth grade, I attended a large gathering in downtown Chicago, which was hosted by Billy Graham, the evangelist. I heard him preach about knowing Jesus Christ, and the difference between knowing Him and knowing about Him. Mr. Graham typically ended his messages with a question which went something like this: *If you died tonight on the way home, would you see Jesus and be in Heaven?* That question caused me to stop and think about my spiritual condition. Although I had heard many gospel messages about Jesus, and knew who He was, I had never truly placed my faith in Him to know Him as my personal Savior. That night I decided to place my trust in Jesus Christ and believe on His name as the only name which offers salvation and eternal life, and I became a follower of Christ.

In high school, I shared many conversations about Jesus and the Bible with my classmates. During lunch, I read the Bible, and I had an opportunity to talk with several students about faith in the Lord. I found it easy to talk about my faith because I understood that it cost Jesus everything to offer salvation to me. I taught Sunday school to third grade boys, and I sang in the choir. I was not like most teenagers who focused on temporal things in life. I wanted my life to make a difference because of my faith.

I attended a Bible university in the south for the first year of college, and I also attended a Christian college when I returned to Illinois. When I entered the job market, I had many opportunities to share my faith with friends. I believe it is important to share my faith with others and from a young age, I learned that the Lord will honor those who honor Him, as we read in Matthew 10:32: *Whosoever therefore shall confess me before men, him will I confess also before my Father which is in heaven.*

I wish I could say I live a perfect life; however, that is not the case. I am a sinner who is saved by God's grace. I face struggles daily. Sadly, there were seasons in my life when I did not walk in faith, I made some terrible choices, and living a consistent life sadly was not a priority. When I was in my late twenty's, I made a decision to live a life which produced evidence of my faith. It is comforting to know that my life is not defined by all the mistakes I made; my life is defined in the righteousness of Jesus Christ. It is comforting to know that the Lord is a God of second chances.

The Gospel

You may not be a follower of Christ, or you may know about Him and have never trusted in Him. I want to take time to explain salvation to you as best as I can, and share the good news of the gospel of Jesus Christ. Jesus Christ was born of a virgin, Mary, and Joseph was Jesus's stepfather. Jesus humbled Himself and took on a human form, while He remained a perfect God. Although he was tempted like we are, Jesus Christ lived a perfect, sinless life, and thus was able to be the perfect sacrifice for the sin of the human race. He died on the cross, shed His precious blood to defeat sin, hell, and death. He was buried, and on the third day Jesus rose from the dead. Because of His sacrifice and resurrection, we celebrate Easter.

The Bible and several non-biblical historians such as Josephus, The Babylonian Talmud, Pliny the Younger, Mara bar-Serapion, and Tacitus, documented the life and ministry of Jesus Christ: (rb. gy/anpy10). During the time I wrote this book, I started to read the book of *Josephus*. It is so interesting to read many of the same stories which are contained in scripture, and how Flavius Josephus was careful to document history. The book of Josephus is a large, detailed historical account with hundreds of pages. This is a history book which I will study and I plan to take time to read it and have made notes along the way.

Jesus paid the penalty of my sin, your sin, and the sin of the entire human race. Whether you believe that Jesus is real or not, He is real. He does not need my or your validation: He is real! In Ephesians 2:8, 9 we are told, *For by grace are ye saved through faith; and that not of yourselves: it is the gift of God: not of works, lest any man should boast.* Salvation is a gift from God, and there is nothing I can ever do to earn it or to lose it; nothing! In John 3:16, we read, *For God so loved the world that He gave His only begotten Son that whoever believeth in Him shall not perish but have everlasting life.*

In John 14: 6 we have the words of Christ as he describes who He is: *I am the way, the truth, and the life: no man cometh unto the Father, but by me.* In Mark chapter 8, Jesus shares more insight regarding salvation: the term man is interpreted as people or the human race.

For whosoever will save his life shall lose it; but whosoever shall lose his life for my sake and the gospel's, the same shall save it. For what shall it profit a man, if he shall gain the whole world, and lose his own soul? Or what shall a man give in exchange for his soul? Whosoever therefore shall be ashamed of me and of my words in this adulterous and sinful generation; of him also shall the Son of man be ashamed, when he cometh in the glory of his Father with the holy angels.

When we believe in Jesus, and surrender our lives to Jesus Christ, He brings newness to our lives as we read in II Corinthians 5:17: *Therefore if any man be in Christ, he is a* new *creature: old things are passed away; behold, all things are become new.*

I am not perfect, and I never can be perfect. I am a sinner saved by God's grace. This is not a blanket statement or approval for believers to sin more, there is an expectation that we would want to sin less and focus more on living for Christ. I believe the Bible. The Bible teaches that Jesus is God, He lived a perfect, sinless life, died, rose from the grave, and today sits on the right hand of the throne of God, The Father. His love, grace, and salvation reached out to me, a sinner, and I recognize Him for who He is, He is my Redeemer, my Savior. He grants eternal life and is the coming King; I trust Him, believe in Him, love Him, and I surrender my life to Him. Jesus Christ is Lord, regardless of my opinion or my feelings. I have salvation through Jesus and that is something that no one can ever take from me, and there is nothing I can ever do to lose it. It is truly an amazing gift. Have you accepted this precious gift?

I want to make space to share several verses about salvation; all verses are from the King James Version. You may not be familiar with the Bible and seek for the truth about Jesus. I pray that you take time to read these verses; I pray that you place your trust in Jesus Christ. He is waiting for you with open arms. If you make a decision to become a follower of Jesus, let us know, and we will pray for you.

II Samuel 22:47: *The LORD liveth; and blessed be my rock; And exalted be the God of the rock of my salvation.*

Isaiah 5:22: *Look unto me, and be ye saved, all the ends of the earth: for I am God, and there is none else.*

Jonah 2:9: *But I will sacrifice unto thee with the voice of thanksgiving; I will pay that that I have vowed. Salvation is of the LORD.*

Matthew 1:21: *And she shall bring forth a son, and thou shalt call his name JESUS: for he shall save his people from their sins.*

Matthew 18:11: *For the Son of man is come to save that which was lost.*

Matthew 26:28: *…for this is my blood of the new testament, which is shed for many for the remission of sins.*

John 3:16: *For God so loved the world, that he gave his only begotten Son, that whosoever believeth in him should not perish, but have everlasting life.*

John 3:17: *For God sent not his Son into the world to condemn the world; but that the world through him might be saved.*

John 5:24: *Verily, verily, I say unto you, He that heareth my word, and believeth on him that sent me, hath everlasting life, and shall not come into condemnation; but is passed from death unto life.*

Acts 2:21: *And it shall come to pass, that whosoever shall call on the name of the Lord shall be saved.*

Acts 4:12: *Neither is there salvation in any other: for there is none other name under heaven given among men, whereby we must be saved.*

Acts 15:11 *But we believe that through the grace of the Lord Jesus Christ we shall be saved, even as they.*

Acts 16:31: *And they said, Believe on the Lord Jesus Christ, and thou shalt be saved...*

Romans 1:6: *For I am not ashamed of the gospel of Christ: for it is the power of God unto salvation to every one that believeth; to the Jew first, and also to the Greek.*

Romans 3:23...*for all have sinned, and come short of the glory of God;*

Romans 5:8 *But God commendeth his love toward us, in that, while we were yet sinners, Christ died for us.*

Romans 5:10: *For if, when we were enemies, we were reconciled to God by the death of his Son, much more, being reconciled, we shall be saved by his life.*

Romans 6:23: *For the wages of sin is death; but the gift of God is eternal life through Jesus Christ our Lord.*

Romans 8:1: *There is therefore now no condemnation to them which are in Christ Jesus, who walk not after the flesh, but after the Spirit.*

Romans 10:9: *...if thou shalt confess with thy mouth the Lord Jesus, and shalt believe in thine heart that God hath raised him from the dead, thou shalt be saved.*

Romans 10:13: *For whosoever shall call upon the name of the Lord shall be saved.*

I Corinthians 15:57: *But thanks be to God, which giveth us the victory through our Lord Jesus Christ.*

Ephesians 2:8: *For by grace are ye saved through faith; and that not of yourselves: it is the gift of God:*

Hebrews 5:9: *...and being made perfect, he became the author of eternal salvation unto all them that obey him;*

Hebrews 9:12: *...neither by the blood of goats and calves, but by his own blood he entered in once into the holy place, having obtained eternal redemption for us.*

Hebrews 9:22: *And almost all things are by the law purged with blood; and without shedding of blood is no remission.*

I John 1:9: *If we confess our sins, he is faithful and just to forgive us our sins, and to cleanse us from all unrighteousness.*

I John 2:2... *and he is the propitiation for our sins: and not for our's only, but also for the sins of the whole world.*

I John 4:10: *Herein is love, not that we loved God, but that he loved us, and sent his Son to be the propitiation for our sins.*

Nick at Night

Nicodemus, was a Pharisee who lived during the time of Jesus Christ, and he approached Jesus one night to ask questions about the miracles He performed. In the book of John, chapter three, we have the account of their conversation. Nicodemus raised some good questions, and Jesus explains the way of salvation to Nicodemus. Although everything Nicodemus heard may have not made sense to him or was different from what he anticipated hearing that night, Jesus carefully took time to be as clear as He could with His responses. It is amazing to know that Jesus presented the way of salvation first hand to Nicodemus, and many years later, we benefit from their conversation as we have a front row seat to their dialogue in the scriptures.

There was a man of the Pharisees, named Nicodemus, a ruler of the Jews: the same came to Jesus by night, and said unto him, Rabbi, we know that thou art a teacher come from God: for no man can do these miracles that thou doest, except God be with him.

Jesus answered and said unto him, Verily, verily, I say unto thee, Except a man be born again, he cannot see the kingdom of God.

Nicodemus saith unto him, How can a man be born when he is old? Can he enter the second time into his mother's womb, and be born?

Jesus answered, Verily, verily, I say unto thee, Except a man be born of water and of the Spirit, he cannot enter into the kingdom of God. That which is born of the flesh is flesh; and that which is born of the Spirit is spirit. Marvel not that I said unto thee, Ye must be born again. The wind bloweth where it listeth, and thou hearest the sound thereof, but canst not tell whence it cometh, and whither it goeth: so is every one that is born of the Spirit.

Nicodemus answered and said unto him, How can these things be? Jesus answered and said unto him, Art thou a master of Israel, and knowest not these things? Verily, verily, I say unto thee, We speak that we do know, and testify that we have seen; and ye receive not our witness. If I have told you earthly things, and ye believe not, how shall ye believe, if I tell you of heavenly things? And no man hath ascended up to heaven, but he that came down from heaven, even the Son of man which is in heaven. And as Moses lifted up the serpent in the wilderness, even so must the Son of man be lifted up: that whosoever believeth in him should not perish, but have eternal life. For God so loved the world, that he gave his only begotten Son, that whosoever believeth in him should not perish, but have everlasting life. For God sent not his Son into the world to condemn the world; but that the world through him might be saved. He that believeth on him is not condemned: but he that believeth not is condemned already, because he hath not believed in the name of the only begotten Son of God. And this is the condemnation, that light is come into the world, and men loved darkness rather than light, because their deeds were evil. For every one that doeth evil hateth the light, neither cometh to the light, lest his deeds should be reproved. But he that doeth truth cometh to the light, that his deeds may be made manifest, that they are wrought in God.

In the Midnight Hour

When the missionaries, Paul of Tarsus and his companion Silas, a fellow Roman citizen and a Hellenistic Jew were imprisoned in the city of Macedonia, a miracle happened. They healed a woman when they cast out the demon who possessed her; however, her employers were not happy about losing their source of income since they used her ability for fortune telling. Paul and Silas were beaten and arrested. The prisoners were under the watch of the guards, and if any of the prisoners were to escape, the guards were customary killed. Let's pick up the missionaries' story in the book of Acts, chapter 16.

And at midnight Paul and Silas prayed, and sang praises unto God: and the prisoners heard them. And suddenly there was a great earthquake, so that the foundations of the prison were shaken: and immediately all the doors were opened, and every one's bands were loosed. And the keeper of the prison awaking out of his sleep, and seeing the prison doors open, he drew out his sword, and would have killed himself, supposing that the prisoners had been fled. But Paul cried with a loud voice, saying, Do thyself no harm: for we are all here. Then he called for a light, and sprang in, and came trembling, and fell down before Paul and Silas, and brought them out, and said, Sirs, what must I do to be saved? And they said, Believe on the Lord Jesus Christ, and thou shalt be saved, and thy house. And they spake unto him the word of the Lord, and to all that were in his house.

Did you catch that? The two missionary prisoners were singing even though they had been badly beaten; amazing! Then the earthquake hit, and the bands which held them came loose and they could have run away. Paul was a Roman citizen and was familiar with their practices and knew that the guard would be executed for allowing the prisoners to escape. Paul knew the jailer would attempt to take his life assuming the prisoners had fled. Paul called out to him to not harm himself and told him all the prisoners were still there. The jailor asked them how to be saved and they gave a simple, clear, concise response, *believe on the Lord Jesus Christ*. Salvation is not complicated.

Salvation in No other name but Jesus

I believe in Jesus and I have faith in Him, and I know He is my Savior; I have eternal life through Him. The faith I have in Jesus Christ is a gift and I cannot boast in doing anything to earn it. There is nothing I can do to earn salvation: nothing. There are no good works or deeds I can do or any amount of money that I give away which will get me to Heaven; in my sinful condition, I am not good enough, I need Him. Once I surrender my life to Christ, then I stand in His righteousness, then He is enough. This of course is contrary to what the world teaches since we are to believe the, *I am good enough philosophy*, when in fact, I am not. Christ alone is enough and with His strength, I am able to do the things He calls me to do in this life.

The grace of God is available to each of us and Jesus died to defeat sin, death, and hell for all of us. He rose from the grave for all of us. That is the Good News...Jesus bridged the gap between humankind and God: Jesus is the Way to the Father. That is the Great News! Since I am a believer, a follower of Jesus, I want to live my life in the power of the resurrected Christ. Because of faith, I want to help others, it is a privilege to spread the gospel, and share the good news of His salvation. I can never earn my way to Heaven; however, I can accept the amazing free gift of salvation which cost Jesus everything when He died on the cross.

Let me share a basic example with you. I love the Hawaiian Islands. Before I visited there the first time, I read much about the islands, the people and their culture. If you would have asked me, I would have told you I know Hawaii; however, the reality of it is, I knew nothing until I was there in person. Once there, I experienced the culture, the food, the people, the public transportation, and the beautiful beaches. After several visits to different islands, I learned more about the people, the mountains, the vegetation, the customs, and the volcanos. I ate where the natives eat, shopped where the locals shop, I attended church, I took excursions around the islands, and I hiked many paths, now I am able to say, I know Hawaii! It is the same with people, I can tell you lots about some of the famous people I have read about in books or magazines; however, I do not know them simply by reading an article about them. Once I met them in person, then I am able to say that I know them. Knowing Jesus is the same, I can know about Him or I can know Him. Knowing about Him will only fill my mind with historical facts; knowing Him allows me to have a personal relationship with Him. Reading His Word allows me to know Him even more clearly and in a better way, a more personal way, and when I pray to Him, it is like speaking with a friend. I can either know about Him or I can know Him, believe in Him and trust Him for my salvation. Salvation, His gift, which allows me to pass from this life and be with Him in the next. I cannot do anything to earn my salvation: nothing, not one thing.

What about you? Do you believe in Jesus? Do you know Jesus? All it takes is the faith of the size of a tiny mustard seed to believe. If you have never trusted in Jesus, do it now, do it before it is too late. We never know when we will take our last breath, so trust in Him today. He died for you and rose from the grave for you. Jesus is not seeking for the perfect, the educated, the good looking, the tall, the thin, the smart, the beautiful; He seeks for sinful, broken people like you and like me. Pause here and tell Jesus that you believe He is God and you want to surrender your heart and life to Him. Believe in the name of the Lord Jesus Christ and you will be saved! If you believe, if you surrendered your heart and life to Him, be sure and let us know, and we will pray for you.

Only One Way?

You may be thinking, *wow, that is a really narrow view you have about Jesus. You really believe he is the only way to reach God and Heaven?* My response is *yes, absolutely!* You may be wondering, *don't all religions lead us to heaven?* The answer is *no.* Religion does not provide salvation, salvation is available only through Jesus Christ. Jesus came to earth to save us, and He did not come to earth to establish religion. James 4:7 defines religion for us, *Pure religion and undefiled before God and* the *Father is this, To visit* the *fatherless and* widows *in their affliction, and to keep himself unspotted from* the *world.*

Here's the thing, Jesus preached about God the Father, and that He is the only way of salvation. If you want to be angry about or disagree with His message, so be it; however, keep in mind, I am the messenger. I know this may sound counterintuitive to what the world teaches, they want us to believe that all roads lead us to heaven, that all gods lead to heaven, and I must tell you, that is simply not true. The world teaches that us that all we have to do is be a good person, and do good deeds and we will go to heaven. Sadly, without knowing Jesus, there will be many good-intended, kind-hearted people in eternal separation from God, in hell because they never trusted in Jesus Christ, and never placed their faith in His salvation. The Bible teaches us that there is only one way.

Keep in mind, many wide roads may lead to destruction and hell; however, the narrow road leads us to salvation in Jesus Christ because He is the Way, He is the Truth, and He is the Life. Jesus is the bridge which leads us to God. In Matthew 7, Jesus provides a warning to us:

Enter ye in at the strait gate: for wide is the gate, and broad is the way, that leadeth to destruction, and many there be which go in thereat: because strait is the gate, and narrow is the way, which leadeth unto life, and few there be that find it.

Let me share a simple example with you. I enjoy the theatre and I like to watch a good stage play. Let's say that on one occasion, I invite you to join me, and while we are intently watching the drama unfold on stage, we smell smoke, and the fire alarm sounds loudly, and the overhead sprinklers stream water. Although the sprinklers are on, we rush to the exit doors on the right side, only to find them unreachable due to the smoke and heat of the fire. We rush to the exit doors on the left side, and find the same danger. I rush down a side hallway next to the stage, and I see a window. I look around and find a heavy item backstage, and use blunt force to break open the window. I clear the glass and use the narrow window as a means to escape to safety. Several others escape too. I see you, and call out to you and ask you, I beg you to follow me and escape out the narrow window with me. You decide that since there are many exit doors in the theatre, you will find one or many of those doors available to you to exit to safety. You insult me, you curse at me, and tell me I have narrow-minded thinking! You ask me, *who are you to think you have the only way to a safe exit?* You tell me that all the exits will lead you to safety. As you rush out the back door into the lobby you realize that all the exits are covered in smoke and fire and you will never be able to get out to safety. You rush through the smoke and heat of the flames back to the hallway where I was and call out to me; however, I am no longer there since I was able to escape the fire through the narrow, safe window. Now the path to the window is covered in flames and you may have one last chance to exit. Yes, the theatre has many exit doors which may lead outside; however, the only safe passage was the narrow window. You have a decision to make, escape through the narrow window now or perish in the flames.

It is the same with our lives, we can think that many roads, many gods, little g…may lead us to heaven and God; however, that is not the reality. Regardless of my opinion, regardless of my feelings of the narrow way, only Jesus provides the means to reach God and Heaven. He is the Way, because of His perfect, sacrificial death on the cross, the shedding of His perfect, sinless blood, and His resurrection from death to life. He is the Way to salvation. This is a great reminder that regardless of my opinion, regardless of what I think and regardless of what I feel, the truth still stands: Jesus is the Way, the Truth and the Life. Because of Him, I have eternal life. You too can trust Jesus Christ for your salvation. Do it today: *Now is the accepted time; behold, now is the day of salvation*: II Corinthians 6:2.

The Life Which Pleases The Lord

Faith in Christ comes to us as a gift as we read in Ephesians 2:8, 9: *For by grace are ye saved through faith; and that not of yourselves: it is the gift of God: not of works, lest any man should boast.* And Romans teaches us that anyone who believes in and calls on the name of the Lord will be saved. Salvation is not complicated. Once we believe in Jesus Christ and call on His name, we are believers in Him. See, salvation in Jesus is about what He did on the cross. He lived a perfect, spotless life, died, and rose from the grave and sits on the right hand of God, the Father. He did the work on our behalf, and all we need to do is trust Him. Wow, what a wonderful, precious gift we truly have in Christ.

The scriptures encourage us, the believers, the followers of Jesus Christ, to live a godly life. What does that look like? This is no way means that once we are saved, we become perfect, far from that; however, once saved, we are open to His Spirit leading in our lives, and we desire to live a life which pleases and honors God. Honoring

God means that we love Him with our soul and our mind. Life in Christ does not come with a strict list of rules of dos and don'ts; remember, this is not religion, this is a personal relationship with Jesus. When we love the Lord, His Spirit drives an increased desire in us to live for Him, while having a decreased desire to live in sin. As John put it in chapter three: *He must increase and I must decrease* and continues with, *He that believeth on the Son hath everlasting life.* I know I mentioned earlier, the book of John is my favorite book in the Bible, because this book so clearly teaches us so much about Jesus, the purpose of His ministry, and the way of salvation.

When I think about the love I have for people, like my family and dear friends, I would never want to do anything to hurt them or dishonor them. When I think about the love I have for the Lord, it is very similar because I would never want to do anything which would dishonor or bring shame to His name. I know I am not perfect; however, with God's Spirit leading in my life, I want to bring glory to His name by loving Him and the people in my life. To honor the Lord, I want to have a posture of respect, self-control, and allow His Spirit to dictate my actions so in turn, I live a life which pleases the Lord. The scriptures encourage me to honor Him with my thoughts, words and actions, my work, my relationships, my values, my ethics, and my every day decisions. When He is the focus of my life, it is easy to go to Him with my thoughts, my questions, to ask guidance for decisions, and know that He would never ask me to do anything which contradicts His teachings.

I had the opportunity to hear a sermon by Pastor Wade Myers, the Lead Pastor at *Faith Bible Church*: (www.fbcaz.org/). Pastor Wade spoke about living a godly life and what that looks like for us. A life which pleases the Lord, is Christ-centric, empowered by His Spirit, an encouragement to others, and walk daily in the fear of the Lord. With his gracious permission, I share his key points and provide the scripture he shared. Thank you Pastor Myers! Take a moment and use your Bible to find the verses and read them and be encouraged to live a life which honors the Lord.

- *Christ-centered: Acts 9:19b-21: Then was Saul certain days with the disciples which were at Damascus. And straightway he preached Christ in the synagogues, that he is the Son of God. But all that heard him were amazed, and said; Is not this he that destroyed them which called on this name in Jerusalem, and came hither for that intent, that he might bring them bound unto the chief priests?*

- *Spirit empowered: Acts 9:22: But Saul increased the more in strength, and confounded the Jews which dwelt at Damascus, proving that this is very Christ.*

- *Encourage one another: Acts 9:26-27: And when Saul was come to Jerusalem, he assayed to join himself to the disciples: but they were all afraid of him, and believed not that he was a disciple. But Barnabas took him, and brought him to the apostles, and declared unto them how he had seen the Lord in the way, and that he had spoken to him, and how he had preached boldly at Damascus in the name of Jesus.*

- *Live in the fear of the Lord: Acts 9:31: Then had the churches rest throughout all Judea and Galilee and Samaria, and were edified; and walking in the fear of the Lord, and in the comfort of the Holy Ghost, were multiplied.*

Chip Ingram has a video Bible study called *The Book of Titus* which I enjoyed watching on *Right Now Media*. Chip Ingram is the Teaching Pastor and CEO of *Living on the Edge,* an international teaching and discipleship ministry: (livingontheedge.org/). The book of Titus is a three-chapter book in the New Testament which was written by the apostle Paul to Titus, his apprentice; the letter is considered an epistle, a letter for didactic or academic purpose. Paul's letter was to encourage Titus on how to live in the faith and how to select the leadership of the church. Today, this epistle encourages us in our faith walk with the Lord. Ingram calls chapter two, *the theology of grace* as we learn how the grace of God appears to us and leads us.

Three main takeaways from his teaching are how God' grace reveals:

1. *His presence in our lives.*
2. *His priority in our lives.*
3. *His purpose in our lives.*

In Titus 2:11-15 we read, *For the grace of God that bringeth salvation hath appeared to all men, teaching us that, denying ungodliness and worldly lusts, we should live soberly, righteously, and godly, in this present world; looking for that blessed hope, and the glorious appearing of the great God and our Saviour Jesus Christ; who gave himself for us, that he might redeem us from all iniquity, and purify unto himself a peculiar people, zealous of good works. These things speak, and exhort, and rebuke with all authority. Let no man despise thee.* Titus 2: 11-15

Chip Ingram tells us that doing good deeds does not help us to get right with God or be in a good position with God. When we are right with God, we want to do good deeds. We cannot do good deeds to earn God's love, but because we have God's love, we do good deeds. In Matthew chapter five, we read the words of Jesus and how he exhorts us to live.

Ye are the salt of the earth: but if the salt have lost his savour, wherewith shall it be salted? it is thenceforth good for nothing, but to be cast out, and to be trodden under foot of men. Ye are the light of the world. A city that is set on an hill cannot be hid. Neither do men light a candle, and put it under a bushel, but on a candlestick; and it giveth light unto all that are in the house. Let your light so shine before men, that they may see your good works, and glorify your Father which is in heaven.

When our purpose in life is to please and honor the Lord, we follow the prompting of the Holy Spirit to direct our steps. If you are wondering, *can I…* or *should I…* with activities in your life, then I recommend and urge you to follow the guidance of scripture and the Holy Spirit. As a life coach and mentor, I encourage people to live in the power of the resurrected Christ, and then they have the answer on the dos and don'ts in life. I can guide people to the Word of God; however, I am not the Holy Spirit who touches the hearts and minds of people. If what you plan to do can be supported by scripture, then pray about your choice and let the Lord lead you in your journey; however, keep in mind, scripture does not ever support doing anything contrary to teachings of the Lord. We cannot justify sinning in order to do something good, as truly, the ends does not justify the means. For example, the Lord is probably not very pleased if we decide to steal money to give an offering at church: that is counterintuitive, and goes against the teachings of the Lord since He tells us not to steal. If your choices in life are directed by you, the gospel written by_____, your name, then most likely, your actions are not spirit led.

I like the quote by Ralph Waldo Emerson, *Your actions speak so loudly, I can not hear what you are saying.* I also like the quote which may or may not have been said by St. Francis of Assisi, *Preach the gospel at all times. And if necessary, use words.* So, yes, our lives reflect our devotion to the Lord and follow the leading of the Spirit and the Word. When we are followers of Christ, people watch our lives, whether we are aware of it or not. When we want to live for the Lord, for the audience of one, then our actions align with His Word and teachings.

I believe Romans 12 summarizes it really well:

I beseech you therefore, brethren, by the mercies of God, that ye present your bodies a living sacrifice, holy, acceptable unto God, which is your reasonable service. And be not conformed to this world: but be ye transformed by the renewing of your mind, that ye may prove what is that good, and acceptable, and perfect, will of God. For I say, through the grace given unto me, to every man that is among you, not to think of himself more highly than he ought to think; but to think soberly, according as God hath dealt to every man the measure of faith.

You may be thinking, *hey, I know some Christians and they are hypocrites, and do not walk the talk of their faith.* To that, I say, *yes, me too.* All I can do for us is pray that God touches our hearts and rebukes our choices and behavior; however, I am not the judge and jury. I will say though, when I know a friend is not living according to scripture, then I will ask to meet with them privately, and ask if I can pray with them. I am not there to judge them, I simply want to make them aware that I aware of their actions. As a true friend, I want the best for them, and encourage them to walk on the Lord's path. I would want a true friend to this for me.

Oh, and by the way, I know someone who is a believer in Christ, and needs lots of prayer daily. She struggles with things in her life and sometimes needs to remember that she is a daughter of the King. She forgets too easily sometimes, that in His eyes she is beautiful and loved. She feels alone in this life, and needs to take her personal struggles to the Lord, so that her life does not get in the way of the grace of God, and she can share the good news with others. At times she fails at living a consistent, faithful life. Sometimes, she can be critical, opinionated, stubborn, and a bit of a control freak. So, when I wake up in the morning, I look in the bathroom mirror and say a loud, *Drop dead!* I do not want my life or my sin to get in the way of others hearing the message of salvation. I want my sinful ways to die, so I can live in the freedom of the grace of God, live a consistent faithful life, and be able to share His message with others. See, once a believer in Christ, I did not become perfect. I am a child of the King, saved by grace, and open to the leading of His Spirit in my life. It is through prayer and Bible reading that I am encouraged to live a life which pleases the Lord; it is completely impossible to do this in my own strength.

Your actions speak so loudly, I can not hear what you are saying.

Preach the gospel at all times. And if necessary, use words.

The Enemy

I know that when I start to doubt, worry about life or fear comes to my mind, that fear does not come from God, the fear comes from the enemy, satan, the devil. Whether you believe that the devil is real or not, is irrelevant; he is real. His existence is not dependent of my opinion or what I think of him. From reading and understanding scripture, I know that the devil is not equal to Jesus, the devil was an angel, a fallen angel. I do not like the devil and he is my enemy. I do not like to talk about him or say his name. Although his name is a proper noun, I chose not to capitalize it; I simply call him the enemy. I know it is the enemy who brings doubtful thoughts to my mind. The enemy attempts to strike fear into my mind and heart because his goal is to keep me from focusing on Jesus.

The enemy seeks to kill and destroy and when I see him for who he is, he is horrid. He is a murderer, a destroyer, and he seeks to destroy my relationship with Jesus and the people in my life. The enemy is an accuser, he is an instigator, a liar, a thief, and I need to think of him as a serial killer. He is my adversary. Scripture calls him *the father of lies*. So, in that context, why would I ever want to listen to his lies? We would never open our doors to a serial killer holding a knife, a gun, or a bottle of poison, and invite them to sit at our table and share a meal. No, that would not make any sense. We would not invite a serial killer to have access to our children, would we? No, absolutely not! Why would we ever allow ourselves to be under a serial killer's influence? When I feel afraid, that is the enemy who plants those untruthful seeds in my mind; I must remember daily that I have the power of Jesus, His Spirit, and His Word and with that, I am able to refute the enemy. *Get out satan, in the name of Jesus Christ* are words I say aloud when the enemy attempts a stronghold in my life. I command him to flee my home in the name of Christ because I can trust in the resurrected power of Jesus Christ.

Here are some insightful Bible verses regarding the enemy:

John 8:44: *Ye are of your father the devil, and the lusts of your father ye will do. He was a murderer from the beginning, and abode not in the truth, because there is no truth in him. When he speaketh a lie, he speaketh of his own: for he is a liar, and the father of it.*

Ephesians 4:27: *Never give place to the devil.*

James 4:7: *Submit yourselves therefore to God. Resist the devil, and he will flee from you.*

I Peter 5:8: *Be sober, be vigilant; because your adversary the devil, as a roaring lion, walketh about, seeking whom he may devour:*

Ephesians 6:10-17 provides the secret to prepare for combat and be protected from the enemy. Actually, it is a powerful, strategic way to be victorious, and it is not a secret, it is available to all of us!

Finally, my brethren, be strong in the Lord, and in the power of his might. Put on the whole armour of God, that you may be able to stand against the wiles of the devil. For we wrestle not against flesh and blood, but against principalities, against powers, against the ruler of the darkness of this world, against spiritual wickedness in high places. Wherefore take unto you the whole armour of God, that ye may be able to withstand in the evil day, and having done all, to stand. Stand therefore, having your loins girt about with truth, and having on the breastplate of righteousness; and your feet shod with the preparation of the gospel of peace; above all, taking the shield of faith, wherewith ye shall be able to quench all the fiery darts of the wicked. And take the helmet of salvation, and the sword of the Spirit, which is the word of God.

FIVE

Real Life Struggles

Rationale or Not?

Some of the fears we face may be considered rationale, and some, not so much. I always say, *the mind is a terrible thing...period.* Our minds can lead us into dark areas where we were never intended to enter. You may have heard the saying, whether you think you can or can't, you are correct. The mind tends to move us into action, and that is why it is vital that we think rationally, realistically, and not allow our thoughts to trail off in a terrible negative direction.

Let's look at some examples of fear. I live in the desert, and there are lots of different snakes in the area. When I hike in the mountains, I am careful to watch the path to ensure I do not accidently enter an area which is rattle snake infested. There have been several times that I encountered rattle snakes while hiking, and I am very glad that they made noise before my dog or I spotted them. In hearing them, I know to walk a different way during my hike and I warn other hikers coming in their direction.

Now, if I told you that I were afraid of being bit by a rattle snake, you would most likely tell me to not go near them, right? Of course you would. If after hearing or seeing a rattle snake during my hike, I go home, and then I become afraid of being bitten by a rattle snake, you would tell me there was nothing to worry about since there are no snakes in my yard or in my home. If I decided I could no longer exit my home in case a rattle snake were waiting to bite me, you would tell me that my thinking and fear make no sense, correct? Well, at least I would hope that you would! You would be correct in telling me that now my fears are not rationale. There has never been a rattle snake in my yard, and chances are, there will never be a rattle snake in my yard since I live too far from the mountain and the open desert area. You would tell me it was alright to exit my house, and would want me to join you for coffee, a movie, or dinner. You would worry about me and my irrational thinking if I decided to decline your invitation, and I were to lock myself inside my home, never to exit again. My irrational fear is a nice way to say that I have developed a phobia, which is a polite way of saying that I have a mental health issue. Hopefully, you would advise me to get professional help.

Now, what if we were hiking and I were bit by a rattle snake? You would make the emergency call and get help for me, right? Yes, of course you would. If after receiving treatment, I told you that I would need to take a break from hiking because I were afraid to see another snake and get bit again, you would understand since my fear would be rationale. The fear would be rational and based on an actual previous event.

What if you had a friend or a relative who lived with someone who drank too much alcohol or took drugs and were violent? Let's say that she regularly yelled at her partner and struck him or threw objects at him? One evening while waiting for her to return home, he began to wonder if she would were to repeat her behavior and he were to become fearful. That type of fear would be rationale and there were be a strong probability that the negative behavior would continue without intervention. The fear of repeated violence may be rationale; however, staying in a relationship filled with domestic violence does not make sense. Hopefully, you would advise him to call the police, leave that person and step away from the relationship, and seek professional help.

If you or someone you know lives with domestic violence, be sure to contact the National Domestic Violence Hotline: (www. thehotline.org/). Their website offers several ways to contact them. You may reach them by phone: **800. 799.7233**, via live chat, or via text message: text the word, **Start** to **88788**.

National Domestic Violence Hotline: <ins>https://www.thehotline.org/</ins>.
Their website offers several ways to contact them.
You may reach them by phone: **800.
799.7233**, via chat live chat,
or via text message: text the word, *Start* to **88788**.

All these fears!

A phobia is an anxiety disorder with an extreme or irrational fear of an object or a situation, like acrophobia, the fear of heights. Phobias are considered one of the most common mental health illnesses. Most people with extreme fears may not realize there are treatments available to them to help them overcome their fears. The *American Psychiatric Association, APA,* has three categories for phobias: social phobias, agoraphobia, and specific phobias. The specific phobias focus on four general areas: natural environment, animals, medical treatment, and situations. Kendra Cherry has an insightful article and short video on phobias on the *Very well mind* website: (rb.gy/atgzfn). You will find she has a long list of many of the different types of phobias.

Some phobias are more common, while others are often quite rare. A few of the most common phobias include arachnophobia (the fear of spiders), ophidiophobia (the fear of snakes), and glossophobia (the fear of public speaking).

The fear of public speaking is so common that some researchers have estimated that as much as 77% of people have some level of this fear.

Rare phobias may be novel terms coined to identify a single, unique case. A few of the more uncommon specific phobias include spectrophobia (the fear of mirrors), chiclephobia (the fear of chewing gum), and hippopotomonstrosesquipedaliophobia (the fear of long words).

After reviewing the long list of phobias I will confess, some of the things on this list made me giggle, not out of disrespect to anyone who suffers from these fears, but merely because I had never thought that anyone would fear some of the things. Then I saw coulrophobia on the list, okay, now I am not laughing! Perhaps I have read too many books and find that I can feel uneasy at times when I am exposed to people with lots of facial makeup and red rubber noses. Good thing, I am not regularly in situations where I would see a clown. One out of ten people experience coulrophobia, so be mindful of that if you decide to send a clown to a party or to an ill child. You may want to cheer them and instead upset them.

Get Help!

If you took time to view the long list of phobias listed in Cherry's article and the things on that list made you feel uneasy or made your skin crawl just thinking about the fears, then you may want to consider getting professional help. If you read that list and were able to identify the fear or fears which keep you up at night, is a good thing because being self-aware is such a healthy thing and the first step to healing. Now, take your list of fears and visit a therapist who will be able to help you work through those fears, and find a safe way to confront them and be free from the hold they have on your mind and your life. Seek freedom from the bondage of the chains of fear and be good to yourself and take good care of your mental health.

Other Fears

Let's take a moment to discuss other, different fears which may cause anxiety in our lives, and most people do not like to discuss these fears. Many times we try to hide behind the fear, the sorrow, and the heartaches because it is difficult to be open and honest with ourselves and others. We may have difficulty being vulnerable, open, and afraid of being hurt again, which is perfectly understandable. Many times we fall for the lie that no one will care or understand us and our situations, and of course, the other lie, what will people think of us? Will they leave us, will they hate us, and will they judge us? My response to all of that is, *who cares*! Seriously, who cares? I cannot live my life constantly worrying about the opinion of others, which takes too much energy and too much time. This does not mean that I will not be polite, respectful, kind, and sincere with people, it means that others are free to think whatever they chose, and they will. Sure, it is really nice when I meet someone who likes me; however, I can never, ever please every person I meet. I am not on this plant to ensure that everyone likes me or understands me or to worry about who judges me. I am not here solely on this planet for the approval of others; I am on this planet to honor God and bring glory to His name. I like to think about my life as living it for the approval of one: the Lord. When I make mistakes, when I am not in a good place, I seek His care, His love, and I am accepted by Him just as I am; however, God loves me so much that He wants to transform me and bring newness to my life. I cannot allow the opinion of others to hold me back from doing the right thing in my life. The way I see it, if my friends know the truth about my life and they are not able to deal with it or handle it and they leave me, then so be it, because obviously, they were not real or genuine friends. A true friend, a loving, genuine friend will accept me, will care about me, they will have lively, crucial conversations with me, pray with me, pray for me, and be supportive to me in my time of need.

Forgiveness

When someone wrongs us, it is very easy to allow our minds to travel down a dark road and think of all the ways we can get even, retaliate against the person who has done us wrong, as they say, teach them a lesson. However, this is not our place in life; we are not to take matters into our own hands and retaliate against the person who has wronged us and become vigilantes. Jesus taught His disciples to love their enemies and to pray for those who wrongfully use us, which of course is very counterintuitive to what the world wants us to think. *Bless them that curse you, and pray for them which despitefully use you*, Luke 6: 28. *See that none render evil for evil unto any man; but ever follow that which is good, both among yourselves, and to all men,* I Thessalonians 5:15. Romans 12:21 is also a good reminder, *Be not overcome of evil, but overcome evil with good.*

With God's help, I am able to pray for the person who wronged me, and there have been times when I had to pray many times about an individual or a situation. By praying for the other person, it helps to remind me that I am not perfect, and never will be, and perhaps I have wronged someone without even being aware that I hurt them. When I pray for the other person, I am reminded that when I confess my sins to Jesus, He is able to forgive my sins, so then, how can I ever withhold forgiveness from anyone else?

Once there was one person in my life, Patricia, who truly hurt me, she was not very kind to me even though I helped her many times. For over one year, I prayed for her and for myself. I asked the Lord for the ability to forgive her and move through the situation. I knew she would never come to me and ask for forgiveness, and sadly, she never did; however, I had no expectation about it, so therefore, I did not allow room for disappointment. After all that time and energy I poured into prayer, I was finally able to forgive her. Today, I can able to speak of her without any ill will, animosity, or hurt feelings. The Lord helped me to release my anger, my pain, and be able to move past the entire situation. I am glad that I was able to forgive her and when Patricia died, I was sad to hear that she had passed. I was very grateful that with God' help, I had a clear conscience knowing that I no longer resented her or had any lingering feelings of animosity, unforgiveness or ill will towards her. Unforgiveness only pollutes the spirit, the body, and the mind, and forgiveness brings freedom, release, and relief. I thank the Lord that with His help, I was able to forgive and learn from this experience.

Sometimes, forgiveness comes with forgetting; however, not in every situation. I am able to forgive a person, and going forward, I may still have memories of the situation; however, the memories are no longer painful. If I were to still have interactions with the person, sadly, I may never completely trust that individual again. I would need to set healthy boundaries within the relationship. There must be a reason to trust people and if they continue to exhibit the same negative behavior, I am able to make a healthy choice about the relationship. See, forgiveness is never really about the person who hurt me; forgiveness is about me and the ability to release the bitterness, the anger, the hurt, even when the other person never asks me to forgive them. I once heard someone say, when they withhold forgiveness from another person, it is like having a glass of poison and drinking it, meaning that the only person I hurt is myself when I do not allow myself to forgive the person who wronged me. Forgiveness is like a scar, the pain may be gone; however, I may never forget how the scar got there. I do not have to forget the transgression the other person committed towards me; however, with the help of the Lord, I am able to release the pain, sorrow, and heartache they caused so that I am able to forgive the other person, and be free of any resentment or bitterness towards them.

You may be thinking, *but, you don't know what they did to me!* That is true, I do not know, and frankly, it is not important that I do know; however, that may be a private discussion to hold with a pastor, a therapist or a counselor and allow them to help you bring closure to the event. I am sorry that someone hurt you; I am sorry that you experienced something negative. The one thing I do know, is that the ground at the foot of the cross is level, which means that my sin is not greater or less than anyone else's. We are all sinners, and when I stand or knee at the cross, sin is sin; there is no little or big sin, it is all sin. When I confess my sin to the Lord, He forgives me, so then, why would I ever withhold forgiveness to anyone else? I have no power or control over anyone else, and I am not able to force someone to ask me for forgiveness; that is counterintuitive. So instead, I choose to forgive people and this way, once again, I am able to focus on what I can control. This may not be easy, it is challenging to forgive another person when they do not ever acknowledge the pain which they caused, when they do not have or take responsibility, ownership or accountability for their actions. It is very challenging when they do not take responsibility for their negative behavior or make an attempt to change it. I find that it takes so much energy to be angry, bitter, resentful, and unforgiving. I rather spend my life in being free and focus my energy and time in something much more positive.

In Matthew, chapter 18, we read about the conversation that Peter and Jesus had when Peter asked the Lord if he should forgive someone seven times, and Jesus replied: *I say not unto thee, Until seven times: but, Until seventy times seven.* I would venture to think that Peter may have felt really good about himself or proud of himself thinking that he would be able to forgive someone seven times. Jesus wants us to gain a clear understanding of forgiveness by expanding the number of times we can forgive others. Keep in mind, this is not a lesson in math, it is a lesson in forgiveness. Jesus did not mean that we must forgive others 490 times, and not 491 times. He wants us to understand that His forgiveness is available to us for more times than we deserve; therefore, we can forgive others many times even though they do not deserve it. As I mentioned, forgiveness is never truly about the other person. It is about the ability to forgive others and move forward in life, and not be bogged down with anger, bitterness, resentment, and unforgiveness in our hearts.

Dawson McAllister, wrote an article about forgiveness titled, *6 Myths About Forgiveness,* which is on *The Hope Line* website: (rb. gy/mdoqqq). McAllister breaks down the information with what forgiveness is and what forgiveness is not.

So to summarize, forgiving is not forgetting, avoiding, or excusing what has happened to you. You don't have to feel forgiving to forgive someone. And just because you forgive someone, it doesn't mean you won't ever get upset and have to make the choice to forgive them again. It also doesn't mean your relationship must go back the way it was before the offense.

What happens when the person we need to forgive is ourselves? We probably have all been in this spot where we know we said the wrong thing, did the wrong thing, and hurt someone else. This may be a lonely and uncomfortable place to be because we have to go through several steps of reconciliation first with God and then ourselves, before we can ever approach the person we hurt and ask them for their forgiveness. In these situations, I need to pray for myself, and ask God to forgive me, then I need to pray for the person whom I have hurt, for their brokenness and their ability to forgive me. Then I am able to humbly approach the other person, ask for their forgiveness, and attempt to restore the relationship. Keep in mind, it is my responsibility to ask for forgiveness, and I am not responsible for their response or decision to my request.

Charlotte Phillips is a contributing author with the *Becky Eldredge Ignatian Ministries,* and she wrote an insightful article on forgiveness based on her own experience: *Praying When It's Hard: Praying When Trying to Forgive Myself:* (rb.gy/clv0d0). She shares six practical steps about prayer and working through the process of self-forgiveness.

1. *Keep showing up.*
2. *Name what you are feeling.*
3. *Ask God for forgiveness first.*
4. *Pray for the person you hurt.*
5. *Ask God for the grace to do better in the future.*
6. *Remember that God loves and forgives you.*

Guilt and Shame

Today some people, many people do whatever they want whenever they want to do it without much thought or concern about their behavior. They take no thought about consequences, social rules or the law, and if or when they experience shame, it is usually something they do not like to discuss with others. I do not watch the news on television; however, once or twice per week, I glance at the news headlines online. I see headlines of people being shamed online or they admit they are ashamed with their behavior and the ill-choices they have made in life, and the damage a person did or caused to someone else. Although we may not like to admit it, we may all experience guilt and shame during our lives, we are human. We can wrestle with the emotions of being rejected, being excluded, or when we have unreal expectations and we fail. It may be the spouse who broke their marriage vows, and cheated on their partner or did something to hurt the other person. Shame may come when we make a mistake or when we fail. Think about the student who cheated on an assignment or exam, or the student who failed a class; the person who made a costly error at work, the person who lost control and said or did something hurtful to someone else, the driver who got on the highway and headed in the wrong direction and killed someone; the driver who drove too fast in the residential area and hit a child or killed a child who ran into the street to retrieve their ball; the driver who is angry at life and acts on their anger in road rage; the drunk driver who injured or killed another driver. These people have one thing in common, they made mistakes, and perhaps they may all experience guilt and shame, openly or subconsciously. The best way to deal with shame, is to discuss it openly and honestly with a professional therapist or an understanding friend. When shame is not dealt with in a correct healthy manner, it may cause fear and anxiety, and may lead to more negative behavior.

Scientific American has a helpful article by Annette Kämmerer: *The Scientific Underpinnings and Impacts of Shame*; *People who feel shame readily are at risk for depression and anxiety disorders*: (rb.gy/nhyjcs). Here is a brief summary of her findings:

We feel shame when we violate the social norms we believe in. At such moments we feel humiliated, exposed and small and are unable to look another person straight in the eye. We want to sink into the ground and disappear.

Shame makes us direct our focus inward and view our entire self in a negative light. Feelings of guilt, in contrast, result from a concrete action for which we accept responsibility. Guilt causes us to focus our attention on the feelings of others.

Women are quicker to feel humiliated than men, and adolescents feel shame more intensely than adults do. As a result, women and adolescents are more susceptible to the negative effects of shame, such as low self-esteem and depression.

Keep in mind, yes, you could have done something terrible, horrible, unimaginable, and unlawful; however, there is nothing that you can confess to the Lord which He is not willing to forgive. He wants you to admit your shame and guilt to Him, He loves you. He wants you to ask for forgiveness, and He wants you to repent of your actions. Repent means making a conscience decision to never to repeat the same actions. Repent means making a conscience choice to do the complete opposite, like making a 180 degree turn on the road. You know you are heading in the wrong direction and you turn around.

If you are experiencing guilt and shame, please talk to someone who will listen to you and who will provide the encouragement and support that you need to work through the shame. Pray about your situation and know that there is nothing you can do in this life which will separate you from the love of God. God is omnipresent and He see everything we do, so whatever shameful thing you have done, He is already aware of it; there are no secrets or surprises. Give your shame to Him, ask Him for guidance, ask Him for forgiveness, and ask Him to give you the strength and courage you need to work through your situation. When we repent, the Lord will never withhold forgiveness from us. Seek professional help, call a pastor, a counselor, an understanding friend; do not suffer in silence and please do not suffer alone.

Honesty

Some people have a problem with being honest because they are afraid of hurting others by speaking the truth. This is counterintuitive since the truth brings freedom. If you cannot be honest with the people you care about, then with whom could you be honest? Tell the truth, it will set you free. It may be uncomfortable to be open and honest; however, it is the best way to live. Lies only cover a situation for a short time, and more lies make the situation much worse. Did you lie to someone, deceive them, did you withhold vital information from them? Is there is something which you need to disclose, confess to another person? Set aside time to speak with them. I believe it is important to treat the other person the same way you would want to be treated, especially in sensitive situations like this one. I typically make an attempt to tell the truth in love, and I would want others to treat me the same when they are honest with me.

Is there conflict you want to resolve? Then be sure to keep your emotions out of the conversation, be calm, and focus on the details of what needs to be discussed and resolved. Do not overthink the conversation. Do not overthink what you will say or anticipate and assume what they will say, and how you will respond. We can assume and overthink ourselves into analysis paralysis. At times, many times, we can make more of a situation in our minds by overthinking or assuming how the conversation will go for us, when in reality, that is further from actually happens. Pray about the situation, ask God to give you courage, then meet with the individual and tell them the truth in love. Be honest, be respectful, be considerate, and be mindful of the words you choose; be calm, be rational, and speak the truth: tell the truth in love.

Be mindful to stay clear from using inflammatory words such as always, never, all the time, name calling and off-colored language. These types of words or phrases only create distance between people and do not aid in conflict resolution. So basically, do not say things which are harmful; I believe Ephesians 4:29 summarizes this well for us: *Let no corrupt communication proceed out of your mouth, but that which is good to the use of edifying, that it may minister grace unto the hearers.*

How would you want someone to approach you? The truth is not meant to be hurtful and words are not meant to be used as weapons. Apologize to the other person, ask for forgiveness, and give them time to accept and process the information. Allow them to take the time they need, do not rush them to provide a response to you. You are responsible to tell the truth, you are not responsible for the other person's response or reaction to the truth. Be mindful and if you believe the other person may act out in an irrational or violent manner after hearing the truth, then take another person along with you to be there in case you need help or meet in a public place where you can reach out to others for help if needed.

Live

When suicide ideology fills the mind, it may be difficult to rid these thoughts without help, without intervention. Sadly, some people respond to suicide ideology by pretending they are not experiencing these thoughts. I have read of people who acted extremely happy with their friends while on the telephone or at a party, and afterwards, they went home and killed themselves. Sometimes people decide to take their lives because they feel rejected, they have been abused, or they may have abused someone, or they have done something which they deem terrible and unforgivable. Sadly, they believe the lie that they are worthless, that they are a failure, that they will never amount to anything, that no one will ever love them, that they are unforgivable, and they fear and doubt that anyone will understand them or ever truly care about them. They hit bottom and think there is no way out of their situation. Sadly, they are blinded by their situation and hurt, and not able to see the options available to them to continue in life. Perhaps they lost their job, have ten dollars left in their pocket, and have bills to pay and a family to support, and they are deceived in believing everyone would be better off without them, when in reality, they leave their family in the mess of life and the trauma of their loss. Their sorrow blinds them and they fail to realize that their decision is not selfless; they have options with social and community programs, food pantries, friends and family who can help them. They come to the pinnacle of thought: everyone else will be better off without them; how sad, how untrue. Sometimes people think, what will other people say when they find out who I really am? What will people say when they find out what I have done? The fear is overwhelming and they believe there is only one way out, and sadly, that is one of the biggest lies the enemy presents. The enemy never wants us to see that there is always hope, and that we can trust in the Lord and have options to work through our situations.

The harsh reality of life is that yes, people can and will reject us; however, we are not on this planet to please everyone and be accepted by everyone. That is an impossible task: we cannot please everyone, so please stop trying. Sadly, yes, sometimes the people we trust the most in this life may hurt us the most as they verbally abuse us, physically abuse us, and sexually abuse us. Yes, people may tell us that we are worthless and treat us in that manner; however, no one is worthless, everyone, every person has value, including you. The enemy will have us believe his lies; do not be fooled, remember the enemy is a liar who seeks to destroy. I Peter 5:8 reminds us to be aware, to be vigilant of the attacker. *Be sober, be vigilant; because your adversary the devil, as a roaring lion, walketh about, seeking whom he may devour.* James 4:7 is another great reminder: *Submit yourselves therefore to God. Resist the devil, and he will flee from you.* Do not allow the enemy to have a foothold on your thoughts, your mind, your feelings, your life, and your actions. Call out to the Lord and

He will listen to you, He will be there for you. He loves you, and He loves you more than anyone in this life, and His love is pure, it is perfect; He will never reject you. He will never abandon you.

One thing to consider about your past: it is in the past and the past is gone. Whatever has happened to you or whatever you have done, is gone. You have today, and God willing, you may have tomorrow. You are on a journey in this life so see what is in front of you and not behind you. Think about driving a car, the windshield is in front of you so that you have wide visibility of the road ahead of you, and the rear view mirror is small, so that you are able to see what is behind you. The further you get down the road, the object which was directly in front of you, gets smaller and then is gone from your view. Life is similar, we have today, and the view of today, and yesterday, is in the rear view mirror. We do not drive a car and only look in the rear view mirror – it would be unwise for us to do so. Nor do we drive a car in reverse all the time and only look through the narrow rearview mirror. That would not make sense. We keep our eyes on the road directly in front of us and we continue to view the road and our surroundings through the windshield. So, please, stop looking in the rear view mirror of your life and focus on the journey which is in directly in front of you. Your life is valuable; regardless of your feelings and your own opinion or the opinion of others. God loves you more than any one in your life is able to love you. Take a moment right now and call out to Him and let Him know how you feel, what you think, and trust Him for the rest of your journey.

Let me take a moment to talk about feelings. Many times, I do not trust my feelings because my feelings may not be rational or reliable. I do not want my feelings to dictate the way I think or act since many times my feelings are not rational, and my feelings may change from morning to mid-day. Today, I may feel sad about past events in my life; however, I do not have to act on my feelings since those events are in the past and are not able to harm me any longer. I may feel like a person who is worthless, sure; however, those feelings do not validate my worth to the Lord. I need to take a step back and see myself through God's eyes. Many times I am not able to trust my feelings and I need to evaluate my feelings, assess them, or determine their value, judge them, use my critical thinking skills and determine if I should follow my feelings or not. Put it this way, just because I feel something does not make it correct, accurate, or worth acting on it.

If I feel like I want to eat three large pizzas for lunch that does not mean that is a wise choice. Acting on those feelings will cause terrible consequences and the physical aftermath would be painful. If I feel like I want to drink an entire 32 ounce bottle of vodka for lunch that does not mean that is a wise choice either. Acting on those feelings is not wise, and the health consequences are not worth it, in addition I could make another unwise choice of driving my car. So, today, I may feel like a cat, I can dress like a cat, I can look like a cat; however, I am not a cat regardless of my feelings. I can feel like a banana; I can sit on the table, in a yellow outfit; however, I am not a banana. I must not allow my clouded feelings to dictate my behavior. If I were to choose to live out my days based on my feelings rather than rational thinking that would not make sense. Sure, I can feel like I want to dress like a cat; however, that does not make me a cat. If I choose to live my life as a cat rather than a human, I rob myself of the wonder and experiences of life which the Lord intended for me, just the way I am. Scripture teaches us in Psalm 139: 14, that we are *fearfully* and *wonderfully* made: so regardless of my feelings, God did not err when He created me as a human and not a cat.

The School of Life: (www.theschooloflife.com/) offers psychotherapy online services, and they have a helpful video on *YouTube* which describes how our feelings can be distorted and it is not wise to use our feelings as a gauge for decision making. *Why You Shouldn't Trust Your Feelings* is worth watching: (rb.gy/1npfkt). They explain that we are human and our feelings give us a distorted view of life, as if looking through a dirty window. Our negative feelings most likely exist when we are tired, and since we have human, flawed minds, feelings may mislead us to a tendency to error.

Have you ever heard the phrase, follow your heart? I have and sadly, oh goodness, I have used this phrase in the past, and it is total non-sense! When I follow my heart or in other words, my feelings, I am heading down the wrong path. If I ever told you to do in the past, goodness, seriously, forgive me. Follow my heart or my feelings? That is one of the worst mistakes I can make in life. Why would I ever want to follow my dark, selfish, sinful, egotistical, conceited, prideful, unwise heart to make decisions? My feelings may arise from fear or the misinterpretation of a person or situation. I must acknowledge my feelings, ask myself where the feelings originate, and realize that they may tainted by negativity or previous behavior. I am not always right, and I need to get my ego out of the way, and check the reality of those feelings. Most of us do not take the time and the appropriate steps to evaluate our feelings and sadly we act on those misguided feelings. Following my heart will only lead me to more problems. Jeremiah 17:9 teaches us: *The heart is deceitful above all things, and desperately wicked: who can know it?*

The *Christian Today* website has an article by JB Cachila entitled, *One Big Reason Why We Should Not Trust in Our Feelings* which encourages us not to trust or follow our hearts and feelings: (rb.gy/7isxnx).

Many of us claim to understand our hearts better than any other; many of us believe that we know our hearts very well. If we're honest enough, we know that our hearts cannot be relied on as a guide or a compass. We cannot let our feelings dictate what we do.

Are you looking at your life through a flawed, dirty pane of glass by trusting your feelings? Have you taken the time to evaluate the reality of your feelings? Where did those feelings originate? Are your feelings tainted by negativity or previous behavior, your's or someone else's? Have you misinterpreted a person or a situation? Can you trust any of it, is it reality? Probably not, and how sad if you do not allow yourself the time and opportunity to examine, assess or evaluate those feelings before it is too late. Today, you may feel like you need to kill yourself; however, can you accurately trust those feelings enough to act on them? I sincerely and certainly hope not. If you responded yes to that question, then know that your thinking is clouded by distorted feelings, so please do not act on those feelings.

What if the overwhelming suicidal thoughts you are experiencing are because of an undetected physical, medical condition? You may be experiencing suicide ideology because of the medication you are taking or a chemical imbalance in your body. You may be hearing voices telling you to take your life and these voices are not allowing you to think clearly. You may be dealing with the self-imposed judge and jury ideals of your thoughts and life, and have not contacted anyone for help. There is no shame in getting the help you need. Please understand that you are one phone call away from getting the medical attention you need. Pick up the phone and call emergency services, call 911, and let them know that you need help. You may have a doctor's appointment scheduled for days or weeks from today; however, the overwhelming thoughts and voices need to be stopped immediately, and you need to call for help right now. Do not delay.

Step away from the thoughts of self-harm; please, put away whatever you plan to use. Today, you may feel unloved; however, you are not. You may feel alone; however, you are not. You may feel worthless; however, you are not. You may feel like no one understands you; however, that is not true. Please understand, it does not matter what you have done: seriously. God knows every detail about you and your life. You are valuable, you are worthy of God's love. The opinion of others does not change your value. Let me put it this way: if I have a one hundred dollar bill in my pocket, and I spill water on myself, the money is still worth the same. If I drop the money in the mud, the value of the money is the same. If I wash the mud off and the money is all wrinkled, it is still worth the same value. Do not think for one moment that you are worth less because of your situation. God knows your name, He loves you and your life matters to Him.

Do you need forgiveness? Ask for God's forgiveness, forgive yourself, and forgive others. Ask God to give you the courage to live in freedom from the fear and anxiety caused by others' actions or words or your own unwise decisions. Jesus is waiting for you with open arms; cry out to Him. Talk to Him, tell Him all the reasons why you think your situation is hopeless, and tell Him why you believe it is necessary to take your life. Ask Him to fill your mind and spirit with His love, His peace, and the clarity of mind, the clarity of thought you need to step out of the darkness and the fog and step into His Light. Jesus came to earth to save sinners, like me and like you. He came for the broken people, like you and like me. He loves you and He will never reject you, ever. He is never too busy to hear your cry for help. He is right there waiting for you to call out His name. Give your life, your heart, and your entire situation to Him, and He will fill your heart with His love, peace, grace, and His mercy, His forgiveness. The Lord will accept you, forgive you, love you, and comfort you. Give your life to Him and He will give you His peace. He will accept you just like you are, you are His child, He cares for you and loves you so much and more, and better than anyone you know. If Jesus did not think you are worthy of His love, please realize, He would have never shed His precious blood for you or died on the cross for you. Trust Him and break free of the fear to live, and live every day in His power, His strength and His joy. My prayer for you is that you would go to Him, and surrender to Him, and find the courage to live in His strength and His peace.

At times people say things like, if you only knew what people think about me. Let me assure you, people probably do not think about you as often as you think they do, so, why focus on what others may or may not think about you or their opinion. Focus on the opinion of the one person whose opinion actually matters: Jesus. He loves you, He cares about you and He has a plan for your life. In the book of Jeremiah, chapter 29 we read the great reminder about the plans God has for the people who trust in Him today the same way people trusted Him years ago.

For I know the thoughts that I think toward you, saith the LORD, thoughts of peace, and not of evil, to give you an expected end. Then shall ye call upon me, and ye shall go and pray unto me, and I will harken unto you. And ye shall seek me, and find me, when ye shall search for me with all your heart.

Other translations put it this way: *I know the plans I have for you, to give you a hope and a future.* God has a plan and purpose for each one of His children, for those who place their faith and trust in Him. If you believe in the name of the Lord Jesus Christ, that means you, God has a plan and a purpose for you. Why not take a moment right now to speak with Him and surrender everything to Him so in turn, He is able to work in your life and reveal His plan and purpose to you. You have nothing to lose and everything to gain. I know someone reading this book, this section is in desperate need of help. Just know, through tears, as I wrote these words, I prayed for you. I am sincerely passionate about people finding hope in Jesus, and I asked the Lord that anyone reading this right now who has suicidal thoughts, that the hope and light of Jesus will break through and give you clarity of thought. Say a prayer, get your phone and make the call; get help now. Please.

If you have thoughts of self-harm, please, contact the *National Suicide Prevention Lifeline* at 988. They abbreviated their phone number from 800.233.8255 to 988, so that you can have convenient access to them. You will be able to speak with someone about your situation and what you are experiencing: (rb.gy/2tgsji). Please, make the call. Please do not hesitate, call them now.

You may also contact the *Crisis Hotline*: (rb.gy/q7ehfr); text the word, Home to 741741 to reach a volunteer crisis counselor. You may call them, send a text message or a message through *WhatsApp,* the private message application: (www.whatsapp.com/). If you decide to contact them and move forward with your life, please let us know. We will pray for you and ask the Lord to give you His courage, His strength, His peace.

Help is available to you: call or send a text message.

Crisis Hotline	Text *Home to 741741*

National Suicide Prevention Lifeline	Call *988*

Trauma

Trauma is a person' emotional response to a terrible, sudden, unpredictable, uncontrollable event such as an accident, death, military combat, physical attack, sexual assault, or a threat to life. The brain, the amygdala, sends a warning signal to the central nervous system which stimulates the stress hormones to prepare the body for a response such as fight or flight or a freeze response. This bodily response occurs when we are in the heat of the moment of the stressful situation and also the body may respond in the same manner even after the threat has passed. Many people relive the situation and have difficulty getting past the traumatic experience. We see this with individuals who suffer from post-traumatic stress syndrome or PTSD.

Sadly, I am no stranger to trauma and PTSD. There have been several events in my life which were very traumatic, and some events where I felt as if I were right back at the original event after the experience. I humbly share a few of the very traumatic situations I have experienced, and worked through by the grace of God.

When I was in my early twenties, I stood at the side of my father's hospital bed as he slept. As I stood next to him, I decided to read a passage from my Bible. My father opened his eyes and asked where my mother was, and I told him she was in the chapel downstairs. He closed his eyes and took his last breath. I was speechless as the alarm sounded on the medical equipment, and the first-response team came into the room with the crash cart, and someone ushered me out of the room. I quickly ran down to the chapel and told my mother what happened and she rushed out the chapel door. My family gathered in a nearby waiting room and within minutes, the doctor came to see us to let us know that my father was gone. That was a very traumatic situation. At my father's funeral, I lay my hand on his chest, and was startled by his body temperature since I had not anticipated he would be so cold. After my father's death, I had trouble dealing with death and attending funerals and seeing dead people in coffins. I recall one day while attending a wake, a viewing time, it took a minute for me to realize that everyone had stepped out of the chapel room and they were chatting in the breakroom and the hallway. I looked around the room and saw it was empty and I looked at the open coffin; I got out of that room as quickly as I could. The trauma was very difficult for me to handle.

The day Jeremy died, I was holding him, and I heard him take a very deep breath. Little did I know at the time that would be his last breath. I performed cardiopulmonary resuscitation, CPR on Jeremy and I was so hopeful, so optimistic that he would be alright. We were taken to the hospital by ambulance, and there he was pronounced dead. My head was spinning and I felt so helpless and confused.

Within months of my son, Jeremy' death, a friend, Frank, passed. He was a sweet man and had a great family. One day, he was at home in the kitchen with his children, he looked at them, said the words I love you, and he fell to the floor and died. I was so heartbroken, and I started to feel very anxious. The day of his funeral, I wept and wept, uncontrollably, and it took several minutes before I could calm myself. I was very sad that my friend died and I realized later the impact of another sudden death, basically took me back to the day of Jeremy's funeral.

Years later, my step-son, Joel died suddenly in his apartment. The landlord found him a few days later. We made the long trip back to Chicago and visited the city morgue to identify his body. We were ushered into a room with a television monitor and shown a very unclear picture of a person. I went back to the front desk and let the receptionist know that from that picture we saw, we could not clearly identify him, and we did not feel right about signing the release documents. A medical tech walked us down the hall and around the corner was a body on gurney. It was absolutely startling. The examiner had completed the autopsy and the person' chest was cut open, a black bag which contained his organs, rested on top of him. I looked at the medical tech and told him that it would have been nice of him to warn us, give us a heads up about what we were about to see. I walked around the gurney and looked closely at the body, the hair line, and saw the tattoo on his leg, and I knew this was Joel. My heart sank and my stomach was not doing well. After a minute, I ran down the hall to the lady' room, where I splashed cold water on my face. There have been many times when I have relived this day – so many times I wish it had been different, that somehow it was all a mistake. This was such a traumatic experience and I do not wish this on any parent.

There are specific triggers which can cause me to relive an experience. Triggers, a confluence of stimuli which cause painful memories to resurface, such as a date, a scent, a sound, a song, a location. Triggers may cause us to experience flashbacks, focus on the sad or painful memories of the traumatic event or relive those events; our bodies and minds respond the same way we did when the event occurred. One theory of why this occurs is the lack of community or social support, and I am able to understand and relate to this notion. When I lost my father, I focused on my mother and I helped her with contacting all of my father's friends, and I did not stop to focus on my grief. While I attended college, I had a part-time and I quit the job and school to get a full-time job to care for my mother. I ensured we paid off the balance of her mortgage and kept up with the taxes and her monthly bills. I did the bulk of the grocery shopping, took care of her banking, took her to the hair salon, and would take her to her doctor and dentist appointments and ensured she took her medications. I visited the local Internal Revenue Service office to ensure that I completed my father's income tax forms correctly. I worked full-time, paid the bills, took my mom shopping whenever she felt like going, and we visited the cemetery. I shoveled the driveway in the winter, and did the lawn work in the spring and summer. I stayed busy, and I felt isolated, and I did not have anyone to talk to about what was going on with my life.

After Joel passed, several people said that they could no longer be friends with our family or pray for our family because Joel's death was drug related, and they assumed it was not an accidental overdose. Once again community failed me and that too was a trigger which brought back memories of losing Jeremy and the loneliness I experienced without the emotional support I needed.

Recently, there was an accident very near to my home, it was car verses motorcycles. Around midnight, sadly, the driver in the car was intoxicated and as she made a left-hand turn, she plowed into a group of young adults who were on motorcycles. She was injured and one person was killed and others injured. The accident happened just after midnight, I was not aware of it since I do not watch the news. On Sunday afternoon as I returned home from church, there was a candle vigil on the corner near the intersection where the accident occurred. As I stopped for the red light, I could see people crying, the cross, and the candles. This was a trigger for me. The sight was heartbreaking and I was so sad for these people, these total strangers; I cried. A few days later, I went online and read about the accident, and I saw a picture of the handsome young man who died, and for several days, I cried. I was so sad for his family and friends, and for the woman who caused the accident. I prayed for all of them and I asked God to help these individuals forgive the woman, for her to be able to forgive herself, and to bring comfort to all of them. I cried for several days because the reality of their pain stirred the emotion of sudden loss within me. I wish I could say, I could control this; however, triggers are so overwhelming. I did pray, a lot, which helped me cope. Occasionally, I still see individuals sit in the vigil area, and now my mind is able to accept the reality without the sudden, uncontrollable emotion, and I continue to pray for the family and friends who were impacted by this accident and sudden loss of someone important in their lives.

A Guide to PTSD Triggers (and How to Cope) is a resourceful article written by, Kara-Marie Hall, BSN, RN, CCRN. Hall shares some coping skill ideas to help deal with the triggers. I appreciate the information because she focuses on using mediation, music, dance, comedy, and the use of a journal! The article is a good read, informative and it is available on the *GoodRx* website: (rb.gy/9my1eg).

- *Perform relaxation techniques, such as breathing exercises, meditation, muscle relaxation exercises, listening to soothing music, or getting in touch with nature.*
- *Think about something positive such as the smile on a loved one's face, a pretty flower, or the sun setting.*
- *Get moving. Activities like going for a walk, dancing around your bedroom, playing ping-pong, or any other form of physical movement will help you stay present.*

In order to help myself through traumatic situations, I have done the following tangible things to work through the issues in life.

1. I call the trauma what is it, trauma. I never label it or myself by calling it my trauma. I am not defined in life by the traumatic events which occurred in my life.
2. Prayer: I take my thoughts and emotions to the Lord in prayer and ask Him for help to calm my heart and mind and ask for clarity of thought.
3. Breathing exercise 5. 6. 7: I inhale and take a deep breath for five seconds. I hold my breath for six seconds, and I slowly exhale within seven seconds. This helps me to reset my breathing and thinking.
4. Support groups: Over the years I have attended various support groups so that I can meet with others who will listen to me and be supportive of my situation. I also had the privilege of facilitating a support group which allowed me to be available to others.
5. Professional therapy: At various times in my life, I have visited with a professional therapist and talked about my experiences.
6. Journal: I write about my feelings, my thoughts, and experiences in my personal journal.
7. List: A few years ago, I decided to make a list of all the difficult things and trauma I have experienced. I made sure

to include everything I could remember from childhood to adulthood. I never want to use this list as a means to stop myself from being healed, move forward or be used for God. I never want to play the victim card in life. I prayed and I burned the list.

8. Move: I take time to be outdoors and I garden, I take walks, and spend time on the tree swing in my yard. I listen to music, exercise, and sing and dance.

9. Take time to be grateful to the Lord.

Psychology Today has an informative article, titled *Trauma* which I found very helpful: (rb.gy/dhyli7). They focus on the different types of trauma we can experience, and the effects of trauma in our lives and in our bodies, the treatment options for trauma, and the controversies about trauma which I found interesting. This is one section of the article I appreciated because it talks about the reality of hope:

Another common misconception about trauma is that it will destroy your life forever. Some people who experience trauma assume the identity of a victim, expecting the world to harm them and seeing slights where they don't exist; this tendency has helped to create a culture of victimhood that does more harm than good by ignoring people's capacity for growth through challenge. Letting go of the victim label can enable people to see themselves instead as survivors, allowing them to grow and feel optimistic about the future.

Here are some resources to help with PTSD:

- *Health Resources & Services Administration*: rb.gy/xukx69
- *National Alliance on Mental Illness*: rb.gy/9rlxp2
- *National Institute of Mental Health*: rb.gy/bzhz4b
- *US Department of Veterans Affairs*: rb.gy/7mxano

If you are experiencing trauma, please get professional help. Do not live with the negative emotions of your experience. There is hope, there is always hope, and you do not have to be stuck or stay stuck in the never-ending circle of trauma. Please call a professional therapist and get the help you need, the help you deserve. If you serviced in the military, first, thank you very much for your unselfish service; second, if you suffer from combat-related PTSD be sure to let the therapist know so that they can build an appropriate therapy plan for you and help you break the cycle.

Resources to help with PTSD:

- *Health Resources & Services Administration*: www.hrsa.gov/
- *National Alliance on Mental Illness*: www.nami.org/
- *National Institute of Mental Health*: www.nimh.nih.gov/
- *US Department of Veterans Affairs*: www.ptsd.va.gov/

SIX

Courageous

I hope that you found the information about fear, the mind, and the body helpful. I hope you found hope in Jesus Christ and have dedicated your life to Him, and gave your fear, worry, anxiety, and depression to Him. My hope for you is that you have the courage to contact a pastor, professional therapist, and counselor and make time to speak to someone about your situation and find release from fear, anxiety, and depression.

Courage

Let's continue in our journey as we talk about courage in the midst of a fearful situation. I think we all have a preconceived notion about what courage is when we think of individuals who have been heroes while in critical situations. We all have heard stories about a person who rushed at another individual who was holding a gun and took them down as they were able to take possession of the weapon and got others to safety. There are stories of individuals who attempted to stop a robbery, an abduction; we hear about that person who rescued a child from a burning building. Let me tell you what each of those heroes have in common: fear. Each one of looked fear in the face and hung on for one more minute and used courage or clear headiness, to overcome the fearful situation or person in front of them. Sometimes we have the notion that the person acted in courageous way because they were not afraid; however, I believe the complete opposite. The situation is fearful, and the heroes step up in spite of their fear and act in a courageous manner.

Right Now Media is a streaming library which contains thousands of Bible messages, sermons, and Bible studies. Many churches offer this service to their congregations and I am very blessed to have this amazing library available any time, day or night that I want to learn about a specific topic. Call the church office where you attend, and find out if they have this service available for your congregation. If they do not offer it, then be sure to recommend it to them. This is a valuable resource.

I had the opportunity to view Dr. J.D. Greear' study on the book of *Judges* on *Right Now Media*. J. D. Greear is a pastor, author, and theologian: (jdgreear.com/). Greear is the pastor of *The Summit Church* in Raleigh, North Carolina: (summitchurch.com/). He hosts a television program and the *Ask Me Anything* podcast. I actively listened as he spoke about how God uses fearful situations and gives courage when needed and I took some notes. If you are not familiar with the book of *Judges*, I recommend reading it – spoiler alert, the book of *Judges* is not for the faint-hearted as some of the stories do not end well. I want to share some of the things I gleamed from viewing and listening to the Bible study.

- God saves through our weakness; we will want to lean into God's grace.
- Being available is more important than our abilities. It's not about what God can do for us, it's about what God can do through us.
- God does not call the brave to a task; He makes brave those He calls to the task.
- God calls us by the name of what He will make us.

- Courage is not the absence of fear in a situation; courage is when we follow God in the midst of the fear.
- The antidote to fear is not courage, it is our ability to trust and our willingness to take the final step of obedience.
- Where trust exists in our lives, fear subsides.

As I took notes during the sermons, I kept saying audibly, Yes, Amen! I appreciate the point J.D. Greear made when he said, *God does not call the brave. He makes brave those He calls. Courage is not the absence of fear; courage is following God in the midst of the fear.* So true! God may not change my circumstance; however, God can change my mind, my attitude, my heart, my spirit throughout the circumstance and provide the courage I need to face my giants; all I have to do is trust Him. What a wonderful reminder that I may be fearful; however, I do not have to live in fear. I may be anxious; however, I do not have to give into the anxiety.

God does not call the brave to a task;
He makes brave those He calls to the task.

Courage is not the absence of fear in a situation;
courage is when we follow God in the midst of the fear.

Goliath: Take One

Scripture teaches us the story of David, the Shepheard boy who when he delivered supplies to his brothers at the battle front lines, he saw Goliath, the Philistine who mocked the Israelites. David wondered why no solider had stepped up to fight against the very tall, large, built, giant of a man, Goliath. In the story we read that David picked up five smooth stones and headed off to face, Goliath, the giant. David called on the name of the Lord and with one rock in his sling, he was able to defeat the giant.

I faced a Goliath once, so, no, not a very tall, large, giant of a man, but a giant corporation. My youngest son and I had the amazing opportunity to travel to Alaska. It was during the fall and prior to the trip, it was fun to find winter clothes in the clearance section of my favorite store, and be ready for the cold weather. We stayed in a lovely, cozy, little cottage, which had everything we needed: two rooms to sleep, a tiny kitchen, and a small bathroom, and it was minutes from downtown Anchorage. Upon arrival at the airport, we rented a car from a large car rental company. We had a comfortable vehicle for our land trip and we spent a wonderful time driving to our day trip destinations. As a photographer, this was such a wonderful trip and I have the thousand pictures to prove it!

After our week of exploration was over, we headed to the airport for our return flight. When we arrived at the rental car return garage, there was no attendant on duty and no signage visible as to what to do next. Since both my son and I have traveled for business, we were used to leaving the car keys in a secure location or safely in the vehicle in the line of other returned cars.

About one week after we were home, I received a phone call from the car rental company, they asked when I planned to return their vehicle. I was extremely surprised to get their call. Of course, my sense of humor kicked in, and I gave them a silly response: *Well, it was a nice car; however, since it would not fit in the overhead compartment, I decided to leave the car in Alaska!*

I let the agent know the date and time, I returned the vehicle and I asked them to check their surveillance video. The next day, the rental company called again and let me know that they found the video and saw me leave their car: nice. Then they proceeded to tell me that shortly after I left the vehicle, they see another person in the video who entered the vehicle and drove away with their car. So, of course, the question begged: how is this my problem? Along with, you have insurance, file a claim! The caller proceeded to explain to me that since I was the last person to have possession of their vehicle, I was financially responsible for their vehicle. Which I countered with, as per your video, you were the last people to have possession of your vehicle, and therefore you are responsible. This went on for several minutes and sadly they kept calling me. They also sent invoices to me via the mail and somehow they assumed I would pay for their vehicle.

For a moment I wondered, can they do this? Can they expect me to pay for their car? Part of me was a bit concerned, and the other part of me, would not stand for this! Being a collaborative person, I called the Anchorage, Alaska police department and explained the situation, and they too were a bit confused as to why I would notify them of the theft. However, in attempts to be a good citizen, I went ahead and filed the police report and I shared the number with the car rental company expecting this would be the end of this ordeal.

Nope. One week later, the police found the vehicle and now the car rental company sent an invoice expecting me to cover the cost of the damage done to the car along with the cost to tow the car from Fairbanks to Anchorage to get the car back to them. I wanted to scream, go away; however, I remained calm as I spoke to the several people at this agency. I did my best to reiterate the process they needed to take and asked them to stop contacting me. Which they did not. I was afraid that this large, beast of an organization would find a way to mess with my credit or sue me. So in the face of fear of going against one of the largest car rental companies in the nation, I prayed. I prayed very specifically about this situation.

I had to courage to contact them again. I did some research and found the names of their leaders. I sent an email to the company chief executive officer, and sent another email to their chief financial officer explaining the situation and asked them to close the invoices their organization sent to me and stop bothering me with their issues; I waited.

I received yet another phone call from the rental company to remind me to pay the invoices. I let them know that I contacted their corporate office and asked them to take this issue and their invoices to the top leaders in their organization. Again I waited. Within weeks of that conversation, I received yet another phone call, letting me know that they changed their mind, and now I was not financially responsible for the invoices! Yay! Weeks later I received a letter in the mail along with an email from this beast of a company letting me know that once again, I am a customer in good standing and they are eager to assist me to rent a car from them whenever I am ready!

Overall, that was one wild situation – the people at this this large organization assumed that since it was me against them that they would win. However, what they did not know, it was me and God against them. Once I had the clarity of mind to contact their top leaders, I knew their fight was over; I just needed the clarity of mind for this battle. That is what courage really is, it is the clarity of mind to stand in a fearful situation and move forward in the battle. I am very happy that this ordeal ended with a positive resolution in my favor, and I am grateful to the Lord for the outcome. I am also grateful to the Lord that I did not have to take this battle into a courtroom and fight against this large company in a costly hearing. To date, I have not rented a vehicle from this organization and wonder if I ever will. I imagine that when I walk up to their service counter and tell them my name and when they type it into the computer, lights will flash, bells and whistles will sound!

Goliath: Take Two

I once worked at an organization where healthy boundaries, respect, and professionalism were not the standard, routine way of how the employees were treated. The managers did not see any problem with their raised voices, insults, profanity, their condescending manner of addressing our sales team, nor did they see any issue with sexually harassing employees. I suppose they figured that the louder they became or the harder they came down on us, sales would increase. It reminded me of the saying, *the beatings will continue until morale increases*. I was promised a promotion, and had the salary discussion with the director, and after a few months of following up with him on the timing of the change, he let me know that he changed his mind and I no longer had the career opportunity. The dysfunctional behavior continued and sadly, day by day, the toxic environment became more and more challenging to handle. A few people walked out on their jobs because they no longer could take the harassment. In spite of looking for a new opportunity elsewhere, no doors had opened for me, and I knew I had to wait on the Lord.

I discussed the issue with the director and I let him that I did not appreciate his behavior and that I would appreciate it if he would treat me and my colleagues with respect. He barely listened to me as I spoke with him, he did not take ownership for his behavior or the managers who reported to him; sadly, it continued to be a very sad environment. I believe in following the chain of command, and I went to him first, and then I spoke with the human resources department.

I sat in a room alone and waited to be called into a meeting to discuss my concerns. I knew something had to change for me and for my colleagues, and I took a stand. Although I had prayed every day leading up to the day of this meeting, including that morning, suddenly, I became nervous. I knew the meeting would be rough, and they would do their best to smash me like a bug. Once again, I was going against a giant. However, I had confidence that whether they admitted their guilt or not, I had the Lord on my side regardless of the outcome. While I waited, I prayed; I prayed silently and I prayed aloud.

I remembered the song, *I Raise a Hallelujah* and I started to sing: *I raise a hallelujah in the presence of my enemies; I raise a hallelujah louder than the unbelief; I raise a hallelujah, my weapon is a melody; I raise a hallelujah; Heaven comes to fight for me; I'm gonna sing in the middle of the storm; Louder and louder, you're gonna hear my praises roar; Up from the ashes, hope will arise; Death is defeated, the King is alive.*

After I prayed and after I sang, I knew that no matter the outcome of that meeting, the Lord was with me in the battle, and I could praise Him. No matter the outcome, I knew He was with me in the presence of the enemies, and I was confident that the battle was His and no longer mine. Praise God, the outcome was positive. I sang praise to the Lord for the victory. I was confident that going forward life would be different and better for me and for my colleagues.

Past to Future

Future behavior is based on past behavior. We base, evaluate individuals on their historical behavior. I will tell you that after dealing with the major rental car company, I walked away from that situation feeling very confident that I can always place my trust in the Lord. There were several situations which I encountered after that event, where I was the little gal who faced the giants in the scenarios. I prayed specifically about each situation, and although I could have remained in the fear, instead I chose to trust the Lord and went against the Goliaths I faced. It was a wonderful feeling and knowing that in every battle, God was on my side regardless of the outcome. It was one of those moments in life when I could say, *I'm with Him.* I know that sometimes God calms the storms in life and sometimes He calms my heart in the middle of the storm.

None of us know what the future holds for any of us. Jesus told us in His Word that we will have trials, we will have troubles. I know that times can be uncertain, un-nerving, and the things which happen in our lives sometimes are down-right frightening. The only constant, the only thing I know is that in every trial, in every ounce of trouble, in every frightening situation, I can trust in the Lord. I like the phrase by Ralph Abernathy: *I don't know what the future may hold, but I know who holds the future:* (rb.gy/ogwfw5). Abernathy was a minister, a civil rights activist; he earned a bachelor and master degree, and he was a mentor to Martin Luther King, Jr. Although he believed in peaceful demonstrations, he experienced some horrible things, like being beaten and left for dead, arrested many times, and yet, Ralph Abernathy knew he could trust the Lord.

This gives hope to me because I know that no matter what... no matter what, I can trust the Lord to be with me. This does not mean I get to win every battle in life, far from it; this simply means that God goes before me, walks with me, and behind me in each battle, and all He asks of me is to trust Him. Some days, yes, easier said than done because the trial or the issue or the events seem overwhelming and like that giant Goliath. However, I know that the Lord is always with me, in the good, the bad, the small and the huge situations in this life. I am very blessed to know Him and live my life dependent on Him.

Giants

We all face giants in our lives and I like to hear stories about individuals who faced their giants and were able to walk away victoriously. The Kendrick Brothers, Alex, Stephen, Shannon, write, direct, and produce some amazing films about courageous individuals who take a step of faith in the midst of their storms and fears: (kendrickbrothers.com/). If you are not familiar with their work, I highly recommend that you take the time to watch their films. The titles and stories are powerful and the characters in each film are relatable because they are just you and me, real, fearful, and yet so dependent on the Lord. I have seen their movies several times, the stories and characters are relatable, and the message of hope in the Lord is powerful. Watching a movie about individuals who faced and conquered their fears is encouraging, similar to reading a book about an overcomer. Their films are *Fly Wheel, Facing The Giants, Fire Proof, Courageous, War Room, Overcomer, Show Me the Father,* and *Lifemark.*

Glory to God

When the fog of grief lifted from me, I re-read the story in scripture about Jesus' disciples who came across a blind man. The disciples asked Jesus about the man' situation. We find the story in John 9:1-7. Let me share it with you:

And as Jesus passed by, he saw a man which was blind from his birth. And his disciples asked him, saying, Master, who did sin, this man, or his parents, that he was born blind?

Jesus answered, Neither hath this man sinned, nor his parents: but that the works of God should be made manifest in him. I must work the works of him that sent me, while it is day: the night cometh, when no man can work. As long as I am in the world, I am the light of the world.

When he had thus spoken, he spat on the ground, and made clay of the spittle, and he anointed the eyes of the blind man with the clay, and said unto him, Go, wash in the pool of Siloam, (which is by interpretation, Sent.) He went his way therefore, and washed, and came seeing.

This story blessed me and it also took my breath away, thinking that the Lord allowed the death of my son and other life-altering events in my life so that He could get the glory. That was a wow moment in life for me because I realized, yes, we have hardships in life, and yet, God can still be praised, and what we decide to do with the hardship can bring glory to Him. The reason the disciples were able to witness the healing of the blind man was so that God could get the glory. What they witnessed increased their faith in Jesus. I realized that I have a tall order in life when hardships and fearful situations hit me. I can allow God to work in each event and I can praise Him regardless of the situation or I can sit paralyzed by the fear and the anxiety.

After Jeremy' death, someone told me, that God would not have allowed this in my life unless He trusted me with it. At the time, I thought, *sure, right, funny.* However, later knowing and understanding what God did in my life, and how He was with me in my grieving journey, and brought healing to my heart; then to be able to help others with their journeys, yes, I am able to say, to God be the glory! I am able to say that his thoughts are not my thoughts and yes, He is a good God, a loving God, and a merciful God. I recall someone mentioned to me that when I get to heaven and see Jesus, He will provide an explanation to me as to exactly why Jeremy died to which I replied, *are you kidding me?* Jesus died to pay the penalty for my sin and if I am able to trust Him for my salvation, that is all He needs to do for me. Jesus is Lord, He is Sovereign, and He in no way owes me an explanation for anything which happens in my life. There is no deli counter in heaven where I can pull a service ticket and wait in line for God to explain Himself. He is God, He created me, and He does not owe me any explanations. I know I am able to freely trust Him with my life.

While grieving, I came face to face with some realities. I did an evaluation of sorts to help me cope. Fist, God is perfect. Yes, regardless of my opinion, regardless of my feelings. God is perfect. Second, God does not lie. He is truth; I can trust Him and His Word completely. Third, since God is perfect, God does not make mistakes. Yes, regardless of my opinion, regardless of my feelings, He does not make mistakes. So, if God is perfect, and He does not lie to me, and He does not make mistakes, then who am I to tell Him that He is wrong or makes mistakes? I have to evaluate everything in life through God's filter, I want to see my life through heaven's eyes and know that there is a purpose to everything, everything in my life, the good, the difficult, the sad, and the sorrowful, just like the happy, the good times, the laughter, and the joy.

Many years ago, I remember Chuck Swindoll saying something so profound about the events which happen in our lives: *Life is 10% what happens to you and 90% how you react to it.*

I try to remember this and some days I am good about keeping a balanced perspective on life and many days it is more challenging. I know you can relate because you face challenges daily with work, or lack of work or the struggles in finding work, your family, dysfunctional relationships, finances, the news, world events, pandemics, and the fear of what tomorrow may bring into your life. Go online and read Chuck R. Swindoll's quote. You can find it on *Brainy Quote:* (rb.gy/fk1saa). I recommend that you print it and hang it where you will see it on a daily basis and read it aloud to yourself. Perhaps use it as one of your daily affirmations!

Chuck Swindoll is the founder and Senior Pastor of *Stonebriar Community Church* in Fresno, Texas. He is also the founder and speaker of the radio broadcast, *Insight for Living:* (www.insight.org/). I have listened to his sermons and radio broadcasts over the years and can recommend him to you. He has been in ministry for over 50 years, and he has written numerous books. Dr. Swindoll is a veteran who served in the Marines. Thank you Dr. Swindoll for your service to our country and your life-long ministry service to the Lord.

I enjoy visits to resale shops and on one trip to make a donation, I decided to walk around the bookstore. Well, this shops is more than a bookstore since they sell music, instruments, home décor, board games, and much more. I took my time and walked around the large store, and I came across a print, a wall art with a thoughtful quote and I decided to purchase the item. It hung in my home for several years, until the day I moved when I down-sized, and today, the print hangs in my son's home.

> *The will of God will never take you, where the*
> *grace of God will not protect you.*

This is such a wonderful reminder that nothing touches my life without God being aware of it and protecting me through it. I think the person who originally penned those words may have been thinking about Psalm 91.

Decades ago, Billy Graham said something very similar, you can view this quote online along with some of his other quotes on *Good Reads*: (rb.gy/hqdlsv). *The will of God will not take us where the grace of God cannot sustain us.*

Both of these statements remind me of the quote, *Has it ever dawned on you, that nothing dawns on God?* I do not know who originally penned those words; if you do, then be sure and let us know. I like this quote because God is aware of every detail of my life, nothing comes as a surprise to Him! I do not need to ask Him, *did you see that?* The Lord is completely aware of my name, and my thoughts and the details of my life.

*I don't know what the future may hold, but
I know who holds the future.*

Life is 10% what happens to you and 90% how you react to it.

*The will of God will never take you, where the
grace of God will not protect you.*

*The will of God will not take us where the
grace of God cannot sustain us.*

The Bible

Fear is such an interesting topic and some time ago, while I read my Bible, I kept track of the scripture verses which contain the words fear, afraid, dismayed. While my list was not comprehensive, I learned about individuals who faced fear due to their nature, their behavior, and their decisions. When I realized the scope of finding every verse in scripture which contains the word fear, I knew that project would take much time to complete and then I wondered if I would actually find every verse! I heard that there are 366 verses with do not fear, and I sought out to find out if this were true. As I read the Bible in my personal study time, I created a spreadsheet and tracked verses by Old and New Testament. One day, I remembered that Bible students and pastors use a concordance to locate detailed information on words in Bible verses, and I purchased a *Strong's Concordance*. Over a century ago, Dr. James Strong, did some incredible research and cataloged every word in the Bible and created an index of the location of each word. This amazing resource contains the list of all the Bible verses which contain the word fear. I was very excited when I opened the concordance and found the letter f, and then word fear and I was even more excited when I saw the long list of scripture references, and when I compared my list to the list in the concordance, I was pleasantly surprised to know that I had found many of the verses!

I grew up reading the Bible, I learned Bible stories in Sunday school, and from the pastor's sermons, and our church used the King James Bible. After all these years, I still read the King James Version and prefer this version, because I love the old English and the poetic style of writing and because it is an accurate translation. The King James Version, KJV or King James Bible, KJB is the authorized version of scripture and is considered one of the most accurate English translations, and it is probably the most widely known Bible translation. It was originally published in 1611 under the sponsorship of King James I, King of England. However, if old English is not for you, you have many options because there are many translations written in common, every day, relatable English and they are available in digital and in print form.

As you seek for an easy to read version of scripture, be sure that the translation you select follows the original scripture and is not written or translated by one person. Biblical scholars use the Hebrew, Aramaic, and Greek writings as well as the Dead Sea Scrolls to accurately translate scripture. To avoid confusion, do not use a translation which is not a literal translation of the original scripture. I do not recommend versions which are watered-down to make them easier to comprehend and do not contain the truth or use the original writings as their foundation.

Here are some credible options on Bible versions to consider reading which provide an accurate translation:

- *Christian Standard Bible, CSB*
- *English Standard Version, ESV*
- *New American Standard Bible, NASB*
- *New English Translation, NET*
- *New King James Version, NKJV*
- *New Living Translation, NLT*

Feel free to do your own research and do a comparison of each version so that you are able to trust the translation you read. I believe *YouVersion* has over 50 Bible translations to choose from in their digital library, and that is just in English! They also have the Bible available in over 1000 languages. I like to read the Bible in both a digital format and physical book versions. If you enjoy reading electronic books then I recommend *YouVersion:* (www.bible.com/). I use *YouVersion* and bible.com almost daily. You can search verses online and you can also download the *YouVersion* application to your smartphone. If you prefer having a hard copy of the Bible, then visit your local or online book store and purchase the Bible translation of your choice. So whether you download the Bible or have a hard copy of scripture, be sure to read it! Fall in love with God's Word.

In case you do not have a book store near you or not sure where to purchase a Bible, here is a resource list for you.

Barnes & Noble: www.barnesandnoble.com/
Bible Bookstore: biblestore.com/
Bibles: bibles.com/
Bibles At Cost: www.biblesatcost.com/
Christian Book Distributors: www.christianbook.com/
Discount Bible Book and Music Store:
www.discountbibleonline.com/
Lifeway: www.lifeway.com/
Shop The Word: www.shoptheword.com/

SEVEN

Do Not Fear!

When I was in the early stages of this writing project, I decided to raise a question on social media: *Facebook and LinkedIn.* I asked: *What is your favorite scripture verse from either the Old or New Testament on fear and why?* I was curious what scripture verses other people cling to when they are afraid. Here are some responses I received:

Aida: 2 Timothy 1:7 For God has not given us the spirit of fear, but of power and of love and of a sound mind. This verse reminds me that God has given me the tools to trust and to lean on Him.

Anthony: Psalm 118:6 – The Lord is on my side; I will not fear. What can man do to me? This scripture speaks boldly to me regarding fear because it gives me the bold assurance and conviction that God is with me. It does not matter how big the giant is, it cannot do anything to me. So I rest in the comfort of the Almighty God to handle all of my giants, big and small.

Julia: 2 Timothy 1:7: For God hath not given us the spirit of fear; but of power, and of love, and of a sound mind. If God doesn't give us fear, then it's the enemy that does. That fear causes us to lose our power, love and our mental acuity. But God gives us power, love and a sound mind. This is fundamental to a healthy life, physically, emotionally and mentally.

Linda: Matthew 6:25-34 – I come from a family of worriers and glass half empty types. I think this verse helps me to see what a waste of time worrying is because when push comes to shove, I am not in control.

Miriam: PS 42:5 doesn't use the word fear but it was when I was going through difficult pregnancies. Why art thou cast down, O my soul? And why art thou disquieted in me? hope thou in God: for I shall yet praise him for the help of his countenance.

Sandra: Isiah 41:10 So do not fear, for I am with you; do not be dismayed, for I am your God. I will strengthen you and help you; I will uphold you with my righteous right hand. (Helps me remember that he is greater and will always be there for me, no matter what.)

The List!

I am very excited to share the scripture verses on afraid and fear! This project was time consuming and I am thrilled that I am able to share these verses with you to help you in your faith walk. All scripture is from the King James Bible. Here you will see the scripture location or reference, and the verse text written for your convenience. These verses will make more sense to you as you read the entire chapter where each verse is located. It is helpful to understand the setting, the people in the stories, and the events in their lives. This list is not meant for you to simply gloss over or to read without knowing the entire story or situation each person encountered. I encourage you to discover how the Lord worked in their lives. It is very helpful to know the details of who, the what, the why, and the where of the story.

Use this as a personal Bible study or with a group and ask your family or friends to join you. All of us face fear in our lives and this is a way to help others and encourage them. Take your time, seek the scriptures and to gain a better, a clearer understanding of the fear each person faced, and how the Lord worked in their situation and lives. Ask the Lord to help you overcome fear since He is able and loves you. The list is separated by the Old Testament, and the New Testament. Happy reading!

Old Testament Verses: Afraid

1. *Genesis 3:10: And he said, I heard thy voice in the garden, and I was afraid, because I was naked; and I hid myself.*
2. *Genesis 18:15: Then Sarah denied, saying, I laughed not; for she was afraid. And he said, Nay; but thou didst laugh.*
3. *Genesis 20:8: Therefore Abimelech rose early in the morning, and called all his servants, and told all these things in their ears: and the men were sore afraid.*
4. *Genesis 28:17: And he was afraid, and said, How dreadful is this place! this is none other but the house of God, and this is the gate of heaven.*
5. *Genesis 31:31: And Jacob answered and said to Laban, Because I was afraid: for I said, Peradventure thou wouldest take by force thy daughters from me.*
6. *Genesis 32:7: Then Jacob was greatly afraid and distressed: and he divided the people that was with him, and the flocks, and herds, and the camels, into two bands;*
7. *Genesis 42:28: And he said unto his brethren, My money is restored; and, lo, it is even in my sack: and their heart failed them, and they were afraid, saying one to another, What is this that God hath done unto us?*
8. *Genesis 42:35: And it came to pass as they emptied their sacks, that, behold, every man's bundle of money was in his sack: and when both they and their father saw the bundles of money, they were afraid.*

9. *Genesis 43:18: And Joseph said unto them, What deed is this that ye have done? wot ye not that such a man as I can certainly divine?*

10. *Exodus 3:6: Moreover he said, I am the God of thy father, the God of Abraham, the God of Isaac, and the God of Jacob. And Moses hid his face; for he was afraid to look upon God.*

11. *Exodus 14:10: And when Pharaoh drew nigh, the children of Israel lifted up their eyes, and, behold, the Egyptians marched after them; and they were sore afraid: and the children of Israel cried out unto the LORD.*

12. *Exodus 15:14: The people shall hear, and be afraid: Sorrow shall take hold on the inhabitants of Palestina.*

13. *Exodus 34:30: And when Aaron and all the children of Israel saw Moses, behold, the skin of his face shone; and they were afraid to come nigh him.*

14. *Leviticus 26:6 And I will give peace in the land, and ye shall lie down, and none shall make you afraid: and I will rid evil beasts out of the land, neither shall the sword go through your land.*

15. *Numbers 12:8: With him will I speak mouth to mouth, even apparently, and not in dark speeches; and the similitude of the LORD shall he behold: wherefore then were ye not afraid to speak against my servant Moses?*

16. *Numbers 22:3: And Moab was sore afraid of the people, because they were many: and Moab was distressed because of the children of Israel.*

17. *Deuteronomy 1:17: Ye shall not respect persons in judgment; but ye shall hear the small as well as the great; ye shall not be afraid of the face of man; for the judgment is God's: and the cause that is too hard for you, bring it unto me, and I will hear it.*

18. *Deuteronomy 1:29: Then I said unto you, Dread not, neither be afraid of them.*

19. *Deuteronomy 2:4: And command thou the people, saying, Ye are to pass through the coast of your brethren the children of Esau, which dwell in Seir; and they shall be afraid of you: take ye good heed unto yourselves therefore:*

20. *Deuteronomy 5:5: (I stood between the LORD and you at that time, to shew you the word of the LORD: for ye were afraid by reason of the fire, and went not up into the mount;)*

21. *Deuteronomy 7:18: Thou shalt not be afraid of them: but shalt well remember what the LORD thy God did unto Pharaoh, and unto all Egypt;*

22. *Deuteronomy 7:19: the great temptations which thine eyes saw, and the signs, and the wonders, and the mighty hand, and the stretched out arm, whereby the LORD thy God brought thee out: so shall the LORD thy God do unto all the people of whom thou art afraid.*

23. *Deuteronomy 9:19: For I was afraid of the anger and hot displeasure, wherewith the LORD was wroth against you to destroy you. But the LORD hearkened unto me at that time also.*

24. *Deuteronomy 18:22: When a prophet speaketh in the name of the LORD, if the thing follow not, nor come to pass, that is the thing which the LORD hath not spoken, but the prophet hath spoken it presumptuously: thou shalt not be afraid of him.*

25. *Deuteronomy 20:1: When thou goest out to battle against thine enemies, and seest horses, and chariots, and a people more than thou, be not afraid of them: for the LORD thy God is with thee, which brought thee up out of the land of Egypt.*

26. *Deuteronomy 28:10: And all people of the earth shall see that thou art called by the name of the LORD; and they shall be afraid of thee.*

27. *Deuteronomy 28:60: Moreover he will bring upon thee all the diseases of Egypt, which thou wast afraid of; and they shall cleave unto thee.*

28. *Deuteronomy 31:6: Be strong and of a good courage, fear not, nor be afraid of them: for the LORD thy God, he it is that doth go with thee; he will not fail thee, nor forsake thee.*

29. *Joshua 1:9: Have not I commanded thee? Be strong and of a good courage; be not afraid, neither be thou dismayed: for the LORD thy God is with thee whithersoever thou goest.*

30. *Joshua 9:24: And they answered Joshua, and said, Because it was certainly told thy servants, how that the LORD thy God commanded his servant Moses to give you all the land, and to destroy all the inhabitants of the land from before you, therefore we were sore afraid of our lives because of you, and have done this thing.*

31. *Joshua 11:6: And the LORD said unto Joshua, Be not afraid because of them: for to morrow about this time will I deliver them up all slain before Israel: thou shalt hough their horses, and burn their chariots with fire.*

32. *Judges 7:3: Now therefore go to, proclaim in the ears of the people, saying, Whosoever is fearful and afraid, let him return and depart early from mount Gilead. And there returned of the people twenty and two thousand; and there remained ten thousand.*

33. *Ruth 3:8: And it came to pass at midnight, that the man was afraid, and turned himself: and, behold, a woman lay at his feet.*

34. *I Samuel 4:7: And the Philistines were afraid, for they said, God is come into the camp. And they said, Woe unto us! for there hath not been such a thing heretofore.*

35. *I Samuel 7:7: And when the Philistines heard that the children of Israel were gathered together to Mizpeh, the lords of the Philistines went up against Israel. And when the children of Israel heard it, they were afraid of the Philistines.*

36. *I Samuel 17:11: When Saul and all Israel heard those words of the Philistine, they were dismayed, and greatly afraid.*

37. *I Samuel 17:24: And all the men of Israel, when they saw the man, fled from him, and were sore afraid.*

38. *I Samuel 18:12: And Saul was afraid of David, because the LORD was with him, and was departed from Saul.*

39. *I Samuel 18:15: Wherefore when Saul saw that he behaved himself very wisely, he was afraid of him.*

40. *I Samuel 18:29: And Saul was yet the more afraid of David; and Saul became David's enemy continually.*

41. *I Samuel 21:1: Then came David to Nob to Ahimelech the priest: and Ahimelech was afraid at the meeting of David, and said unto him, Why art thou alone, and no man with thee?*

42. *I Samuel 21:12: And David laid up these words in his heart, and was sore afraid of Achish the king of Gath.*

43. *I Samuel 23:3: And David's men said unto him, Behold, we be afraid here in Judah: how much more then if we come to Keilah against the armies of the Philistines?*

44. *I Samuel 28:5: And when Saul saw the host of the Philistines, he was afraid, and his heart greatly trembled.*

45. *I Samuel 28:13: And the king said unto her, Be not afraid: for what sawest thou? And the woman said unto Saul, I saw gods ascending out of the earth.*

46. *I Samuel 28:20: Then Saul fell straightway all along on the earth, and was sore afraid, because of the words of Samuel: and there was no strength in him; for he had eaten no bread all the day, nor all the night.*

47. *I Samuel 31:4: Then said Saul unto his armourbearer, Draw thy sword, and thrust me through therewith; lest these uncircumcised come and thrust me through, and abuse me. But his armourbearer would not; for he was sore afraid. Therefore Saul took a sword, and fell upon it.*

48. *II Samuel 1:14: And David said unto him, How wast thou not afraid to stretch forth thine hand to destroy the LORD's anointed?*

49. *II Samuel 6:9: And David was afraid of the LORD that day, and said, How shall the ark of the LORD come to me?*

50. *II Samuel 14:15: Now therefore that I am come to speak of this thing unto my lord the king, it is because the people have made me afraid: and thy handmaid said, I will now speak unto the king; it may be that the king will perform the request of his handmaid.*

51. *II Samuel 17:2: and I will come upon him while he is weary and weak handed, and will make him afraid: and all the people that are with him shall flee; and I will smite the king only:*

52. *II Samuel 22:5: When the waves of death compassed me, The floods of ungodly men made me afraid;*

53. *II Samuel 22:46: Strangers shall fade away, And they shall be afraid out of their close places.*

54. *I Kings 1:49: And all the guests that were with Adonijah were afraid, and rose up, and went every man his way.*

55. *II Kings 1:15: And the angel of the LORD said unto Elijah, Go down with him: be not afraid of him. And he arose, and went down with him unto the king.*

56. *II Kings 10:4: But they were exceedingly afraid, and said, Behold, two kings stood not before him: how then shall we stand?*

57. *II Kings 19:6: And Isaiah said unto them, Thus shall ye say to your master, Thus saith the LORD, Be not afraid of the words which thou hast heard, with which the servants of the king of Assyria have blasphemed me.*

58. *II Kings 25:26: And all the people, both small and great, and the captains of the armies, arose, and came to Egypt: for they were afraid of the Chaldees.*

59. *I Chronicles 10:4: Then said Saul to his armourbearer, Draw thy sword, and thrust me through therewith; lest these uncircumcised come and abuse me. But his armourbearer*

would not; for he was sore afraid. So Saul took a sword, and fell upon it.

60. *I Chronicles 13:12: And David was afraid of God that day, saying, How shall I bring the ark of God home to me?*

61. *I Chronicles 21:30: But David could not go before it to enquire of God: for he was afraid because of the sword of the angel of the LORD.*

62. *II Chronicles 20:15: and he said, Hearken ye, all Judah, and ye inhabitants of Jerusalem, and thou king Jehoshaphat, Thus saith the LORD unto you, Be not afraid nor dismayed by reason of this great multitude; for the battle is not your's, but God's.*

63. *II Chronicles 32:7: Be strong and courageous, be not afraid nor dismayed for the king of Assyria, nor for all the multitude that is with him: for there be more with us than with him:*

64. *Nehemiah 2:2: Wherefore the king said unto me, Why is thy countenance sad, seeing thou art not sick? this is nothing else but sorrow of heart. Then I was very sore afraid,*

65. *Nehemiah 4:14: And I looked, and rose up, and said unto the nobles, and to the rulers, and to the rest of the people, Be not ye afraid of them: remember the Lord, which is great and terrible, and fight for your brethren, your sons, and your daughters, your wives, and your houses.*

66. *Nehemiah 6:9: For they all made us afraid, saying, Their hands shall be weakened from the work, that it be not done. Now therefore, O God, strengthen my hands.*

67. *Nehemiah 6:13: Therefore was he hired, that I should be afraid, and do so, and sin, and that they might have matter for an evil report, that they might reproach me.*

68. *Esther 7:6: And Esther said, The adversary and enemy is this wicked Haman. Then Haman was afraid before the king and the queen.*

69. *Job 3:25: For the thing I greatly feared is come upon me, And that which I was afraid of is come unto me.*

70. *Job 5:21: Thou shalt be hid from the scourge of the tongue: Neither shalt thou be afraid of destruction when it cometh.*

71. *Job 5:22: At destruction and famine thou shalt laugh: Neither shalt thou be afraid of the beasts of the earth.*

72. Job 6:21*: For now ye are nothing; Ye see my casting down, and are afraid.*

73. *Job 9:28: I am afraid of all my sorrows, I know that thou wilt not hold me innocent.*

74. *Job 11:19: Also thou shalt lie down, and none shall make thee afraid; Yea, many shall make suit unto thee.*

75. *Job 13:11: Shall not his excellency make you afraid? And his dread fall upon you?*

76. *Job 13:21: Withdraw thine hand far from me: And let not thy dread make me afraid.*

77. *Job 15:24: Trouble and anguish shall make him afraid; They shall prevail against him, as a king ready to the battle.*

78. *Job 18:11: Terrors shall make him afraid on every side, And shall drive him to his feet.*

79. *Job 19:29: Be ye afraid of the sword: For wrath bringeth the punishments of the sword, That ye may know there is a judgment.*

80. *Job 21:6: Even when I remember I am afraid, And trembling taketh hold on my flesh.*

81. *Job 23:15: Therefore am I troubled at his presence: When I consider, I am afraid of him.*

82. *Job 32:6: And Elihu the son of Barachel the Buzite answered and said, I am young, and ye are very old; Wherefore I was afraid, and durst not shew you mine opinion.*

83. *Job 33:7: Behold, my terror shall not make thee afraid, Neither shall my hand be heavy upon thee.*

84. *Job 39:20: Canst thou make him afraid as a grasshopper? The glory of his nostrils is terrible.*

85. *Job 41:25: When he raiseth up himself, the mighty are afraid: By reason of breakings they purify themselves.*

86. *Psalm 3:6: I will not be afraid of ten thousands of people, That have set themselves against me round about.*
87. *Psalm 18:4: The sorrows of death compassed me, And the floods of ungodly men made me afraid.*
88. *Psalm 18:45: The strangers shall fade away, And be afraid out of their close places.*
89. *Psalm 27:1: The LORD is my light and my salvation; whom shall I fear? The LORD is the strength of my life; of whom shall I be afraid?*
90. *Psalm 49:16: Be not thou afraid when one is made rich, When the glory of his house is increased;*
91. *Psalm 56:3: What time I am afraid, I will trust in thee.*
92. *Psalm 56:11: In God have I put my trust: I will not be afraid what man can do unto me.*
93. *Psalm 65:8: They also that dwell in the uttermost parts are afraid at thy tokens: Thou makest the outgoings of the morning and evening to rejoice.*
94. *Psalm 77:16: Vow, and pay unto the LORD your God: Let all that be round about him Bring presents unto him that ought to be feared.*
95. *Psalm 83:15: So persecute them with thy tempest, And make them afraid with thy storm.*
96. *Psalm 91:5: Thou shalt not be afraid for the terror by night; Nor for the arrow that flieth by day;*
97. *Psalm 112:7: He shall not be afraid of evil tidings: His heart is fixed, trusting in the LORD.*
98. *Psalm 112:8: His heart is established, he shall not be afraid, Until he see his desire upon his enemies.*
99. *Psalm 119:120: My flesh trembleth for fear of thee; And I am afraid of thy judgments.*
100. *Proverbs 3:24: When thou liest down, thou shalt not be afraid: Yea, thou shalt lie down, and they sleep shall be sweet.*
101. *Proverbs 3:25: Be not afraid of sudden fear, Neither of the desolation of the wicked, when it cometh.*

102. *Proverbs 31:21: She is not afraid of the snow for her household: For all her household are clothed with scarlet.*

103. *Ecclesiastes 12:5: also when they shall be afraid of that which is high, and fears shall be in the way, and the almond tree shall flourish, and the grasshopper shall be a burden, and desire shall fail: because man goeth to his long home, and the mourners go about the streets:*

104. *Isaiah 8:12: Say ye not, A confederacy, to all them to whom this people shall say, A confederacy; neither fear ye their fear, nor be afraid.*

105. *Isaiah 10:24: Therefore thus saith the Lord GOD of hosts, O my people that dwellest in Zion, be not afraid of the Assyrian: he shall smite thee with a rod, and shall lift up his staff against thee, after the manner of Egypt.*

106. *Isaiah 10:29: they are gone over the passage: they have taken up their lodging at Geba; Ramah is afraid; Gibeah of Saul is fled.*

107. *Isaiah 12:2: Behold, God is my salvation; I will trust, and not be afraid: for the LORD JEHOVAH is my strength and my song; he also is become my salvation.*

108. *Isaiah 13:8: and they shall be afraid: pangs and sorrows shall take hold of them; they shall be in pain as a woman that travaileth: they shall be amazed one at another; their faces shall be as flames.*

109. *Isaiah 17:2: The cities of Aroer are forsaken: they shall be for flocks, which shall lie down, and none shall make them afraid.*

110. *Isaiah 19:16: In that day shall Egypt be like unto women: and it shall be afraid and fear because of the shaking of the hand of the LORD of hosts, which he shaketh over it.*

111. *Isaiah 19:17: And the land of Judah shall be a terror unto Egypt, every one that maketh mention thereof shall be afraid in himself, because of the counsel of the LORD of hosts, which he hath determined against it.*

112. *Isaiah 20:5: And they shall be afraid and ashamed of Ethiopia their expectation, and of Egypt their glory.*

113. *Isaiah 31:4: For thus hath the LORD spoken unto me, Like as the lion and the young lion roaring on his prey, when a multitude of shepherds is called forth against him, he will not be afraid of their voice, nor abase himself for the noise of them: so shall the LORD of hosts come down to fight for mount Zion, and for the hill thereof.*

114. *Isaiah 31:9: And he shall pass over to his strong hold for fear, and his princes shall be afraid of the ensign, saith the LORD, whose fire is in Zion, and his furnace in Jerusalem.*

115. *Isaiah 33:14: The sinners in Zion are afraid; fearfulness hath surprised the hypocrites. Who among us shall dwell with the devouring fire? who among us shall dwell with everlasting burnings?*

116. *Isaiah 37:6: And Isaiah said unto them, Thus shall ye say unto your master, Thus saith the LORD, Be not afraid of the words that thou hast heard, wherewith the servants of the king of Assyria have blasphemed me.*

117. *Isaiah 40:9: O Zion, that bringest good tidings, get thee up into the high mountain; O Jerusalem, that bringest good tidings, lift up thy voice with strength; lift it up, be not afraid; say unto the cities of Judah, Behold your God!*

118. *Isaiah 41:5: The isles saw it, and feared; the ends of the earth were afraid, drew near, and came.*

119. *Isaiah 44:8: Fear ye not, neither be afraid: have not I told thee from that time, and have declared it? ye are even my witnesses. Is there a God beside me? yea, there is no God; I know not any.*

120. *Isaiah 51:7: Hearken unto me, ye that know righteousness, the people in whose heart is my law; fear ye not the reproach of men, neither be ye afraid of their revilings.*

121. *Isaiah 51:12: I, even I, am he that comforteth you: who art thou, that thou shouldest be afraid of a man that shall die, and of the son of man which shall be made as grass;*

122. *Isaiah 57:11: And of whom hast thou been afraid or feared, that thou hast lied, and hast not remembered me, nor laid it to thy heart? have not I held my peace even of old, and thou fearest me not?*

123. *Jeremiah 1:8: Be not afraid of their faces: for I am with thee to deliver thee, saith the LORD.*

124. *Jeremiah 2:12: Be astonished, O ye heavens, at this, and be horribly afraid, be ye very desolate, saith the LORD.*

125. *Jeremiah 10:5: They are upright as the palm tree, but speak not: they must needs be borne, because they cannot go. Be not afraid of them; for they cannot do evil, neither also is it in them to do good.*

126. *Jeremiah 26:21: and when Jehoiakim the king, with all his mighty men, and all the princes, heard his words, the king sought to put him to death: but when Urijah heard it, he was afraid, and fled, and went into Egypt;*

127. *Jeremiah 30:10: Therefore fear thou not, O my servant Jacob, saith the LORD; neither be dismayed, O Israel: for, lo, I will save thee from afar, and thy seed from the land of their captivity; and Jacob shall return, and shall be in rest, and be quiet, and none shall make him afraid.*

128. *Jeremiah 36:16: Now it came to pass, when they had heard all the words, they were afraid both one and other, and said unto Baruch, We will surely tell the king of all these words.*

129. *Jeremiah 36:24: Yet they were not afraid, nor rent their garments, neither the king, nor any of his servants that heard all these words.*

130. *Jeremiah 38:19: And Zedekiah the king said unto Jeremiah, I am afraid of the Jews that are fallen to the Chaldeans, lest they deliver me into their hand, and they mock me.*

131. *Jeremiah 39:17: But I will deliver thee in that day, saith the LORD: and thou shalt not be given into the hand of the men of whom thou art afraid.*

132. *Jeremiah 41:18: because of the Chaldeans: for they were afraid of them, because Ishmael the son of Nethaniah had slain Gedaliah the son of Ahikam, who the king of Babylon made governor in the land.*

133. *Jeremiah 42:11: Be not afraid of the king of Babylon, of whom ye are afraid; be not afraid of him, saith the LORD: for I am with you to save you, and to deliver you from his hand.*

134. *Jeremiah 42:16: then it shall come to pass, that the sword, which ye feared, shall overtake you there in the land of Egypt, and the famine, whereof ye were afraid, shall follow close after you there in Egypt, and there ye shall die.*

135. *Jeremiah 46:27: But fear not thou, O my servant Jacob, and be not dismayed, O Israel: for, behold, I will save thee from afar off, and thy seed from the land of their captivity; and Jacob shall return, and be in rest and at ease, and none shall make him afraid.*

136. *Ezekiel 2:6: And thou, son of man, be not afraid of them, neither be afraid of their words, though briers and thorns be with thee, and thou dost dwell among scorpions: be not afraid of their words, nor be dismayed at their looks, though they be a rebellious house.*

137. *Ezekiel 27:35: All the inhabitants of the isles shall be astonished at thee, and their kings shall be sore afraid, they shall be troubled in their countenance.*

138. *Ezekiel 30:9: In that day shall messengers go forth from me in ships to make the careless Ethiopians afraid, and great pain shall come upon them, as in the day of Egypt: for, lo, it cometh.*

139. *Ezekiel 32:10: Yea, I will make many people amazed at thee, and their kings shall be horribly afraid for thee, when I shall brandish my sword before them; and they shall tremble at every moment, every man for his own life, in the day of thy fall.*

140. *Ezekiel 34:28: And they shall no more be a prey to the heathen, neither shall the beast of the land devour them; but they shall dwell safely, and none shall make them afraid.*

141. *Ezekiel 39:26: after that they have borne their shame, and all their trespasses whereby they have trespassed against me, when they dwelt safely in their land, and none made them afraid.*

142. *Daniel 4:5: I saw a dream which made me afraid, and the thoughts upon my bed and the visions of my head troubled me.*

143. *Daniel 8:17: So he came near where I stood: and when he came, I was afraid, and fell upon my face: but he said unto me, Understand, O son of man: for at the time of the end shall be the vision.*

144. *Joel 2:22: Be not afraid, ye beasts of the field: for the pastures of the wilderness do spring, for the tree beareth her fruit, the fig tree and the vine do yield their strength.*

145. *Amos 3:6: shall a trumpet be blown in the city, and the people not be afraid? shall there be evil in a city, and the LORD hath not done it?*

146. *Jonah 1:5: Then the mariners were afraid, and cried every man unto his god, and cast forth the wares that were in the ship into the sea, to lighten it of them.*

147. *Jonah 1:10: Then were the men exceedingly afraid, and said unto him, Why hast thou done this? For the men knew that he fled from the presence of the LORD, because he had told them.*

148. *Micah 4:4: But they shall sit every man under his vine and under his fig tree; and none shall make them afraid: for the mouth of the LORD of hosts hath spoken it.*

149. *Micah 7:17: They shall lick the dust like a serpent, they shall move out of their holes like worms of the earth: they shall be afraid of the LORD our God, and shall fear because of thee.*

150. *Nahum 2:11: Where is the dwelling of the lions, and the feedingplace of the young lions, where the lion, even the old lion, walked, and the lion's whelp, and none made them afraid?*

151. *Habakkuk: 2:17: For the violence of Lebanon shall cover thee, and the spoil of beasts, which made them afraid, because of*

men's blood, and for the violence of the land, of the city, and of all that dwell therein.

152. *Habakkuk: 3:2: O LORD, I have heard thy speech, and was afraid: O LORD, revive thy work in the midst of the years, In the midst of the years make known; In wrath remember mercy.*

153. *Zephaniah 3:13: The remnant of Israel shall not do iniquity, nor speak lies; neither shall a deceitful tongue be found in their mouth: for they shall feed and lie down, and none shall make them afraid.*

154. *Malachi 2:5: My covenant was with him of life and peace; and I gave them to him for the fear wherewith he feared me, and was afraid before my name.*

New Testament Verses: Afraid

155. *Matthew 2:22: But when he heard that Archelaus did reign in Judea in the room of his father Herod, he was afraid to go thither: notwithstanding, being warned of God in a dream, he turned aside into the parts of Galilee:*

156. *Matthew 14:27: But straightway Jesus spake unto them, saying, Be of good cheer; it is I; be not afraid.*

157. *Matthew 14:30: But when he saw the wind boisterous, he was afraid; and beginning to sink, he cried, saying, Lord, save me.*

158. *Matthew 17:6: And when the disciples heard it, they fell on their face, and were sore afraid.*

159. *Matthew 17:7: And Jesus came and touched them, and said, Arise, and be not afraid.*

160. *Matthew 25:25: and I was afraid, and went and hid thy talent in the earth: lo, there thou hast that is thine.*

161. *Matthew 28:10: Then said Jesus unto them, Be not afraid: go tell my brethren that they go into Galilee, and there shall they see me.*

162. *Mark 5:15: And they come to Jesus, and see him that was possessed with the devil, and had the legion, sitting, and clothed, and in his right mind: and they were afraid.*

163. *Mark 5:36: As soon as Jesus heard the word that was spoken, he saith unto the ruler of the synagogue, Be not afraid, only believe.*

164. *Mark 6:50: for they all saw him, and were troubled. And immediately he talked with them, and saith unto them, Be of good cheer: it is I; be not afraid.*

165. *Mark 9:6: For he wist not what to say; for they were sore afraid.*

166. *Mark 9:32: But they understood not that saying, and were afraid to ask him.*

167. *Mark 10:32: And they were in the way going up to Jerusalem; and Jesus went before them: and they were amazed; and as they followed, they were afraid. And he took again the twelve, and began to tell them what things should happen unto him.*

168. *Mark 16:8: And they went out quickly, and fled from the sepulchre; for they trembled and were amazed: neither said they any thing to any man; for they were afraid.*

169. *Luke 2:9: And, lo, the angel of the Lord came upon them, and the glory of the Lord shone round about them: and they were sore afraid.*

170. *Luke 8:25: And he said unto them, Where is your faith? And they being afraid wondered, saying one to another, What manner of man is this! for he commandeth even the winds and water, and they obey him.*

171. *Luke 8:35: Then they went out to see what was done; and came to Jesus, and found the man, out of whom the devils were departed, sitting at the feet of Jesus, clothed, and in his right mind: and they were afraid.*

172. *Luke 12:4: And I say unto you my friends, Be not afraid of them that kill the body, and after that have no more that they can do.*

173. *Luke 24:5: and as they were afraid, and bowed down their faces to the earth, they said unto them, Why seek ye the living among the dead?*

174. *John 6:19: So when they had rowed about five and twenty or thirty furlongs, they see Jesus walking on the sea, and drawing nigh unto the ship: and they were afraid.*

175. *John 6:20: But he saith unto them, It is I; be not afraid.*

176. *John 14:27: Peace I leave with you, my peace I give unto you: not as the world giveth, give I unto you. Let not your heart be troubled, neither let it be afraid.*

177. *John 19:8: When Pilate therefore heard that saying, he was the more afraid;*

178. *Acts 9:26: And when Saul was come to Jerusalem, he assayed to join himself to the disciples: but they were all afraid of him, and believed not that he was a disciple.*

179. *Acts 10:4: And when he looked on him, he was afraid, and said, What is it, Lord? And he said unto him, Thy prayers and thine alms are come up for a memorial before God.*

180. *Acts 18:9: Then spake the Lord to Paul in the night by a vision, Be not afraid, but speak, and hold not thy peace:*

181. *Acts 22:9: And they that were with me saw indeed the light, and were afraid; but they heard not the voice of him that spake to me.*

182. *Acts 22:29: Then straightway they departed from him which should have examined him: and the chief captain also was afraid, after he knew that he was a Roman, and because he had bound him.*

183. *Romans 13:3: For rulers are not a terror to good works, but to the evil. Wilt thou then not be afraid of the power? do that which is good, and thou shalt have praise of the same:*

184. *Romans 13:4: for he is the minister of God to thee for good. But if thou do that which is evil, be afraid; for he beareth not the sword in vain: for he is the minister of God, a revenger to execute wrath upon him that doeth evil.*

185. *Galatians 4:11: I am afraid of you, lest I have bestowed upon you labour in vain.*

186. *Hebrews 11:23: By faith Moses, when he was born, was hid three months of his parents, because they saw he was a proper child; and they were not afraid of the king's commandment.*

187. *I Peter 3:6: even as Sara obeyed Abraham, calling him lord: whose daughters ye are, as long as ye do well, and are not afraid with any amazement.*

188. *I Peter 3:14: But and if ye suffer for righteousness' sake, happy are ye: and be not afraid of their terror, neither be troubled;*

189. *II Peter 2:10: but chiefly them that walk after the flesh in the lust of uncleanness, and despise government. Presumptuous are they, selfwilled, they are not afraid to speak evil of dignities.*

Old Testament Verses: Fear

1. *Genesis 9:2: And the fear of you and the dread of you shall be upon every beast of the earth, and upon every fowl of the air, upon all that moveth upon the earth, and upon all the fishes of the sea; into your hand are they delivered.*

2. *Genesis 15:1: After these things the word of the LORD came unto Abram in a vision, saying, Fear not, Abram: I am thy shield, and thy exceeding great reward.*

3. *Genesis 20:11: And Abraham said, Because I thought, Surely the fear of God is not in this place; and they will slay me for my wife's sake.*

4. *Genesis 21:17: And God heard the voice of the lad; and the angel of God called to Hagar out of heaven, and said unto her, What aileth thee, Hagar? fear not; for God hath heard the voice of the lad where he is.*

5. *Genesis 26:24: And the LORD appeared unto him the same night, and said, I am the God of Abraham thy father: fear*

not, for I am with thee, and will bless thee, and multiply thy seed for my servant Abraham's sake.

6. *Genesis 31:42: Except the God of my father, the God of Abraham, and the fear of Isaac, had been with me, surely thou hadst sent me away now empty. God hath seen mine affliction and the labour of my hands, and rebuked thee yesternight.*

7. *Genesis 31:53: The God of Abraham, and the God of Nahor, the God of their father, judge betwixt us. And Jacob sware by the fear of his father Isaac.*

8. *Genesis 32:11: Deliver me, I pray thee, from the hand of my brother, from the hand of Esau: for I fear him, lest he will come and smite me, and the mother with the children.*

9. *Genesis 35:17: And it came to pass, when she was in hard labour, that the midwife said unto her, Fear not; thou shalt have this son also.*

10. *Genesis 42:18: And Joseph said unto them the third day, This do, and live; for I fear God:*

11. *Genesis 43:23: And he said, Peace be to you, fear not: your God, and the God of your father, hath given you treasure in your sacks: I had your money. And he brought Simeon out unto them.*

12. *Genesis 46:3: And he said, I am God, the God of thy father: fear not to go down into Egypt; for I will there make of thee a great nation:*

13. *Genesis 50:19: And Joseph said unto them, Fear not: for am I in the place of God?*

14. *Genesis 50:21: Now therefore fear ye not: I will nourish you, and your little ones. And he comforted them, and spake kindly unto them.*

15. *Exodus 9:30: But as for thee and thy servants, I know that ye will not yet fear the LORD God.*

16. *Exodus 14:13: And Moses said unto the people, Fear ye not, stand still, and see the salvation of the LORD, which he will*

shew to you to day: for the Egyptians whom ye have seen to day, ye shall see them again no more for ever.

17. *Exodus 15:16: Fear and dread shall fall upon them; by the greatness of thine arm they shall be as still as a stone; till thy people pass over, O LORD, till the people pass over, which thou hast purchased.*

18. *Exodus 18:21: Moreover thou shalt provide out of all the people able men, such as fear God, men of truth, hating covetousness; and place such over them, to be rulers of thousands, and rulers of hundreds, rulers of fifties, and rulers of tens:*

19. *Exodus 20:20: And Moses said unto the people, Fear not: for God is come to prove you, and that his fear may be before your faces, that ye sin not.*

20. *Exodus 23:27: I will send my fear before thee, and will destroy all the people to whom thou shalt come, and I will make all thine enemies turn their backs unto thee.*

21. *Leviticus 19:3: Ye shall fear every man his mother, and his father, and keep my sabbaths: I am the LORD your God.*

22. *Leviticus 19:14: Thou shalt not curse the deaf, nor put a stumbling block before the blind, but shalt fear thy God: I am the LORD.*

23. *Leviticus 19:32: Thou shalt rise up before the hoary head, and honour the face of the old man, and fear thy God: I am the LORD.*

24. *Leviticus 25:17: Ye shall not therefore oppress one another; but thou shalt fear thy God: for I am the LORD your God.*

25. *Leviticus 25:36: Take thou no usury of him, or increase: but fear thy God; that thy brother may live with thee.*

26. *Leviticus 25:43: Thou shalt not rule over him with rigour; but shalt fear thy God.*

27. *Numbers 14:9: Only rebel not ye against the LORD, neither fear ye the people of the land; for they are bread for us: their defence is departed from them, and the LORD is with us: fear them not.*

28. *Numbers 21:34: And the LORD said unto Moses, Fear him not: for I have delivered him into thy hand, and all his people, and his land; and thou shalt do to him as thou didst unto Sihon king of the Amorites, which dwelt at Heshbon.*

29. *Deuteronomy 1:21: Behold, the LORD thy God hath set the land before thee: go up and possess it, as the LORD God of thy fathers hath said unto thee; fear not, neither be discouraged.*

30. *Deuteronomy 2:25: This day will I begin to put the dread of thee and the fear of thee upon the nations that are under the whole heaven, who shall hear report of thee, and shall tremble, and be in anguish because of thee.*

31. *Deuteronomy 3:2: And the LORD said unto me, Fear him not: for I will deliver him, and all his people, and his land, into thy hand; and thou shalt do unto him as thou didst unto Sihon king of the Amorites, which dwelt at Heshbon.*

32. *Deuteronomy 3:22: Ye shall not fear them: for the LORD your God he shall fight for you.*

33. *Deuteronomy 4:10: Specially the day that thou stoodest before the LORD thy God in Horeb, when the LORD said unto me, Gather me the people together, and I will make them hear my words, that they may learn to fear me all the days that they shall live upon the earth, and that they may teach their children.*

34. *Deuteronomy 5:29: O that there were such an heart in them, that they would fear me, and keep all my commandments always, that it might be well with them, and with their children for ever!*

35. *Deuteronomy 6:2: That thou mightest fear the LORD thy God, to keep all his statutes and his commandments, which I command thee, thou, and thy son, and thy son's son, all the days of thy life; and that thy days may be prolonged.*

36. *Deuteronomy 6:13: Thou shalt fear the LORD thy God, and serve him, and shalt swear by his name.*

37. *Deuteronomy 6:24: And the LORD commanded us to do all these statutes, to fear the LORD our God, for our good always, that he might preserve us alive, as it is at this day.*

38. *Deuteronomy 8:6: Therefore thou shalt keep the commandments of the LORD thy God, to walk in his ways, and to fear him.*

39. *Deuteronomy 10:12: And now, Israel, what doth the LORD thy God require of thee, but to fear the LORD thy God, to walk in all his ways, and to love him, and to serve the LORD thy God with all thy heart and with all thy soul.*

40. *Deuteronomy 10:20: Thou shalt fear the LORD thy God; him shalt thou serve, and to him shalt thou cleave, and swear by his name.*

41. *Deuteronomy 11:25: There shall no man be able to stand before you: for the LORD your God shall lay the fear of you and the dread of you upon all the land that ye shall tread upon, as he hath said unto you.*

42. *Deuteronomy 13:4: Ye shall walk after the LORD your God, and fear him, and keep his commandments, and obey his voice, and ye shall serve him, and cleave unto him.*

43. *Deuteronomy 13:11: And all Israel shall hear, and fear, and shall do no more any such wickedness as this is among you.*

44. *Deuteronomy 14:23: And thou shalt eat before the LORD thy God, in the place which he shall choose to place his name there, the tithe of thy corn, of thy wine, and of thine oil, and the firstlings of thy herds and of thy flocks; that thou mayest learn to fear the LORD thy God always.*

45. *Deuteronomy 17:13: And all the people shall hear, and fear, and do no more presumptuously.*

46. *Deuteronomy 17:19: And it shall be with him, and he shall read therein all the days of his life: that he may learn to fear the LORD his God, to keep all the words of this law and these statutes, to do them:*

47. *Deuteronomy 19:20: And those which remain shall hear, and fear, and shall henceforth commit no more any such evil among you.*

48. *Deuteronomy 20:3: And shall say unto them, Hear, O Israel, ye approach this day unto battle against your enemies: let not your hearts faint, fear not, and do not tremble, neither be ye terrified because of them;*

49. *Deuteronomy 21:21: And all the men of his city shall stone him with stones, that he die: so shalt thou put evil away from among you; and all Israel shall hear, and fear.*

50. *Deuteronomy 28:58: If thou wilt not observe to do all the words of this law that are written in this book, that thou mayest fear this glorious and fearful name, THE LORD THY GOD;*

51. *Deuteronomy 28:66: And thy life shall hang in doubt before thee; and thou shalt fear day and night, and shalt have none assurance of thy life:*

52. *Deuteronomy 28:67: In the morning thou shalt say, Would God it were even! and at even thou shalt say, Would God it were morning! for the fear of thine heart wherewith thou shalt fear, and for the sight of thine eyes which thou shalt see.*

53. *Deuteronomy 31:6: Be strong and of a good courage, fear not, nor be afraid of them: for the LORD thy God, he it is that doth go with thee; he will not fail thee, nor forsake thee.*

54. *Deuteronomy 31:8: And the LORD, he it is that doth go before thee; he will be with thee, he will not fail thee, neither forsake thee: fear not, neither be dismayed.*

55. *Deuteronomy 31:12: Gather the people together, men, and women, and children, and thy stranger that is within thy gates, that they may hear, and that they may learn, and fear the LORD your God, and observe to do all the words of this law;*

56. *Deuteronomy 31:13: And that their children, which have not known any thing, may hear, and learn to fear the LORD your*

God, as long as ye live in the land whither ye go over Jordan to possess it.

57. *Joshua 4:24: That all the people of the earth might know the hand of the LORD, that it is mighty: that ye might fear the LORD your God for ever.*

58. *Joshua 8:1: And the LORD said unto Joshua, Fear not, neither be thou dismayed: take all the people of war with thee, and arise, go up to Ai: see, I have given into thy hand the king of Ai, and his people, and his city, and his land:*

59. *Joshua 10:8: And the LORD said unto Joshua, Fear them not: for I have delivered them into thine hand; there shall not a man of them stand before thee.*

60. *Joshua 10:25: And Joshua said unto them, Fear not, nor be dismayed, be strong and of good courage: for thus shall the LORD do to all your enemies against whom ye fight.*

61. *Joshua 22:24: And if we have not rather done it for fear of this thing, saying, In time to come your children might speak unto our children, saying, What have ye to do with the LORD God of Israel?*

62. *Joshua 24:14: Now therefore fear the LORD, and serve him in sincerity and in truth: and put away the gods which your fathers served on the other side of the flood, and in Egypt; and serve ye the LORD.*

63. *Judges 4:18: And Jael went out to meet Sisera, and said unto him, Turn in, my lord, turn in to me; fear not. And when he had turned in unto her into the tent, she covered him with a mantle.*

64. *Judges 6:10: And I said unto you, I am the LORD your God; fear not the gods of the Amorites, in whose land ye dwell: but ye have not obeyed my voice.*

65. *Judges 6:23: And the LORD said unto him, Peace be unto thee; fear not: thou shalt not die.*

66. *Judges 7:10: But if thou fear to go down, go thou with Phurah thy servant down to the host:*

67. *Judges 9:21: And Jotham ran away, and fled, and went to Beer, and dwelt there, for fear of Abimelech his brother.*

68. *Ruth 3:11: And now, my daughter, fear not; I will do to thee all that thou requirest: for all the city of my people doth know that thou art a virtuous woman.*

69. *I Samuel 4:20: And about the time of her death the women that stood by her said unto her, Fear not; for thou hast born a son. But she answered not, neither did she regard it.*

70. *I Samuel 11:7: And he took a yoke of oxen, and hewed them in pieces, and sent them throughout all the coasts of Israel by the hands of messengers, saying, Whosoever cometh not forth after Saul and after Samuel, so shall it be done unto his oxen. And the fear of the LORD fell on the people, and they came out with one consent.*

71. *I Samuel 12:14: If ye will fear the LORD, and serve him, and obey his voice, and not rebel against the commandment of the LORD, then shall both ye and also the king that reigneth over you continue following the LORD your God:*

72. *I Samuel 12:20: And Samuel said unto the people, Fear not: ye have done all this wickedness: yet turn not aside from following the LORD, but serve the LORD with all your heart;*

73. *I Samuel 12:24: Only fear the LORD, and serve him in truth with all your heart: for consider how great things he hath done for you.*

74. *I Samuel 21:10: And David arose, and fled that day for fear of Saul, and went to Achish the king of Gath.*

75. *I Samuel 22:23: Abide thou with me, fear not: for he that seeketh my life seeketh thy life: but with me thou shalt be in safeguard.*

76. *I Samuel 23:17: And he said unto him, Fear not: for the hand of Saul my father shall not find thee; and thou shalt be king over Israel, and I shall be next unto thee; and that also Saul my father knoweth.*

77. *I Samuel 23:26: And Saul went on this side of the mountain, and David and his men on that side of the mountain: and David made haste to get away for fear of Saul; for Saul and his men compassed David and his men round about to take them.*

78. *II Samuel 9:7: And David said unto him, Fear not: for I will surely shew thee kindness for Jonathan thy father's sake, and will restore thee all the land of Saul thy father; and thou shalt eat bread at my table continually.*

79. *II Samuel 13:28: Now Absalom had commanded his servants, saying, Mark ye now when Amnon's heart is merry with wine, and when I say unto you, Smite Amnon; then kill him, fear not: have not I commanded you? be courageous, and be valiant.*

80. *II Samuel 23:3: The God of Israel said, the Rock of Israel spake to me, He that ruleth over men must be just, ruling in the fear of God.*

81. *I Kings 8:40: That they may fear thee all the days that they live in the land which thou gavest unto our fathers.*

82. *I Kings 8:43: Hear thou in heaven thy dwelling place, and do according to all that the stranger calleth to thee for: that all people of the earth may know thy name, to fear thee, as do thy people Israel; and that they may know that this house, which I have builded, is called by thy name.*

83. *I Kings 17:13: And Elijah said unto her, Fear not; go and do as thou hast said: but make me thereof a little cake first, and bring it unto me, and after make for thee and for thy son.*

84. *I Kings 18:12: And it shall come to pass, as soon as I am gone from thee, that the Spirit of the LORD shall carry thee whither I know not; and so when I come and tell Ahab, and he cannot find thee, he shall slay me: but I thy servant fear the LORD from my youth.*

85. *II Kings 4:1: Now there cried a certain woman of the wives of the sons of the prophets unto Elisha, saying, Thy servant my husband is dead; and thou knowest that thy servant did fear*

the LORD: and the creditor is come to take unto him my two sons to be bondmen.

86. *II Kings 6:16: And he answered, Fear not: for they that be with us are more than they that be with them.*

87. *II Kings 17:28: Then one of the priests whom they had carried away from Samaria came and dwelt in Bethel, and taught them how they should fear the LORD.*

88. *II Kings 17:34: Unto this day they do after the former manners: they fear not the LORD, neither do they after their statutes, or after their ordinances, or after the law and commandment which the LORD commanded the children of Jacob, whom he named Israel;*

89. *II Kings 17:35: With whom the LORD had made a covenant, and charged them, saying, Ye shall not fear other gods, nor bow yourselves to them, nor serve them, nor sacrifice to them;*

90. *II Kings 17:36: But the LORD, who brought you up out of the land of Egypt with great power and a stretched out arm, him shall ye fear, and him shall ye worship, and to him shall ye do sacrifice.*

91. *II Kings 17:37: And the statutes, and the ordinances, and the law, and the commandment, which he wrote for you, ye shall observe to do for evermore; and ye shall not fear other gods.*

92. *II Kings 17:38: And the covenant that I have made with you ye shall not forget; neither shall ye fear other gods.*

93. *II Kings 17:39: But the LORD your God ye shall fear; and he shall deliver you out of the hand of all your enemies.*

94. *II Kings 25:24: And Gedaliah sware to them, and to their men, and said unto them, Fear not to be the servants of the Chaldees: dwell in the land, and serve the king of Babylon; and it shall be well with you.*

95. *I Chronicles 14:17: And the fame of David went out into all lands; and the LORD brought the fear of him upon all nations.*

96. *I Chronicles 16:30: Fear before him, all the earth: the world also shall be stable, that it be not moved.*

97. *I Chronicles 28:20: And David said to Solomon his son, Be strong and of good courage, and do it: fear not, nor be dismayed: for the LORD God, even my God, will be with thee; he will not fail thee, nor forsake thee, until thou hast finished all the work for the service of the house of the LORD.*

98. *II Chronicles 6:31: That they may fear thee, to walk in thy ways, so long as they live in the land which thou gavest unto our fathers.*

99. *II Chronicles 6:33: Then hear thou from the heavens, even from thy dwelling place, and do according to all that the stranger calleth to thee for; that all people of the earth may know thy name, and fear thee, as doth thy people Israel, and may know that this house which I have built is called by thy name.*

100. *II Chronicles 14:14: And they smote all the cities round about Gerar; for the fear of the LORD came upon them: and they spoiled all the cities; for there was exceeding much spoil in them.*

101. *II Chronicles 17:10: And the fear of the LORD fell upon all the kingdoms of the lands that were round about Judah, so that they made no war against Jehoshaphat.*

102. *II Chronicles 19:7: Wherefore now let the fear of the LORD be upon you; take heed and do it: for there is no iniquity with the LORD our God, nor respect of persons, nor taking of gifts.*

103. *II Chronicles 19:9: And he charged them, saying, Thus shall ye do in the fear of the LORD, faithfully, and with a perfect heart.*

104. *II Chronicles 20:17: Ye shall not need to fight in this battle: set yourselves, stand ye still, and see the salvation of the LORD with you, O Judah and Jerusalem: fear not, nor be dismayed; to morrow go out against them: for the LORD will be with you.*

105. *II Chronicles 20:29: And the fear of God was on all the kingdoms of those countries, when they had heard that the LORD fought against the enemies of Israel.*

106. *Ezra 3:3: And they set the altar upon his bases; for fear was upon them because of the people of those countries: and they offered burnt offerings thereon unto the LORD, even burnt offerings morning and evening.*

107. *Nehemiah 1:11: O Lord, I beseech thee, let now thine ear be attentive to the prayer of thy servant, and to the prayer of thy servants, who desire to fear thy name: and prosper, I pray thee, thy servant this day, and grant him mercy in the sight of this man. For I was the king's cupbearer.*

108. *Nehemiah 5:9: Also I said, It is not good that ye do: ought ye not to walk in the fear of our God because of the reproach of the heathen our enemies?*

109. *Nehemiah 5:15: But the former governors that had been before me were chargeable unto the people, and had taken of them bread and wine, beside forty shekels of silver; yea, even their servants bare rule over the people: but so did not I, because of the fear of God.*

110. *Nehemiah 6:14: My God, think thou upon Tobiah and Sanballat according to these their works, and on the prophetess Noadiah, and the rest of the prophets, that would have put me in fear.*

111. *Nehemiah 6:19: Also they reported his good deeds before me, and uttered my words to him. And Tobiah sent letters to put me in fear.*

112. *Esther 8:17: And in every province, and in every city, whithersoever the king's commandment and his decree came, the Jews had joy and gladness, a feast and a good day. And many of the people of the land became Jews; for the fear of the Jews fell upon them.*

113. *Esther 9:2: The Jews gathered themselves together in their cities throughout all the provinces of the king Ahasuerus, to*

lay hand on such as sought their hurt: and no man could withstand them; for the fear of them fell upon all people.

114. *Esther 9:3: And all the rulers of the provinces, and the lieutenants, and the deputies, and officers of the king, helped the Jews; because the fear of Mordecai fell upon them.*

115. *Job 1:9: Then Satan answered the LORD, and said, Doth Job fear God for nought?*

116. *Job 4:6: Is not this thy fear, thy confidence, thy hope, and the uprightness of thy ways?*

117. *Job 4:14: Fear came upon me, and trembling, which made all my bones to shake.*

118. *Job 6:14: To him that is afflicted pity should be shewed from his friend; but he forsaketh the fear of the Almighty.*

119. *Job 9:34: Let him take his rod away from me, and let not his fear terrify me.*

120. *Job 9:35: Then would I speak, and not fear him; but it is not so with me.*

121. *Job 11:15: For then shalt thou lift up thy face without spot; yea, thou shalt be stedfast, and shalt not fear.*

122. *Job 15:4: Yea, thou castest off fear, and restrainest prayer before God.*

123. *Job 21:9: Their houses are safe from fear, neither is the rod of God upon them.*

124. *Job 22:4: Will he reprove thee for fear of thee? will he enter with thee into judgment?*

125. *Job 22:10: Therefore snares are round about thee, and sudden fear troubleth thee;*

126. *Job 25:2: Dominion and fear are with him, he maketh peace in his high places.*

127. *Job 28:28: And unto man he said, Behold, the fear of the Lord, that is wisdom; and to depart from evil is understanding.*

128. *Job 31:34: Did I fear a great multitude, or did the contempt of families terrify me, that I kept silence, and went not out of the door?*

129. *Job 37:24: Men do therefore fear him: he respecteth not any that are wise of heart.*

130. *Job 39:16: She is hardened against her young ones, as though they were not hers: her labour is in vain without fear;*

131. *Job 39:22: He mocketh at fear, and is not affrighted; neither turneth he back from the sword.*

132. *Job 41:33: Upon earth there is not his like, who is made without fear.*

133. *Psalms 2:11: Serve the LORD with fear, and rejoice with trembling.*

134. *Psalms 5:7: But as for me, I will come into thy house in the multitude of thy mercy: and in thy fear will I worship toward thy holy temple.*

135. *Psalms 9:20: Put them in fear, O LORD: that the nations may know themselves to be but men. Selah.*

136. *Psalms 14:5: There were they in great fear: for God is in the generation of the righteous.*

137. *Psalms 15:4: In whose eyes a vile person is contemned; but he honoureth them that fear the LORD. He that sweareth to his own hurt, and changeth not.*

138. *Psalms 19:9: The fear of the LORD is clean, enduring for ever: the judgments of the LORD are true and righteous altogether.*

139. *Psalms 22:23: Ye that fear the LORD, praise him; all ye the seed of Jacob, glorify him; and fear him, all ye the seed of Israel.*

140. *Psalms 22:25: My praise shall be of thee in the great congregation: I will pay my vows before them that fear him.*

141. *Psalms 23:4: Yea, though I walk through the valley of the shadow of death, I will fear no evil: for thou art with me; thy rod and thy staff they comfort me.*

142. *Psalms 25:14: The secret of the LORD is with them that fear him; and he will shew them his covenant.*

143. *Psalms 27:1: The LORD is my light and my salvation; whom shall I fear? the LORD is the strength of my life; of whom shall I be afraid?*

144. *Psalms 27:3: Though an host should encamp against me, my heart shall not fear: though war should rise against me, in this will I be confident.*

145. *Psalms 31:11: I was a reproach among all mine enemies, but especially among my neighbours, and a fear to mine acquaintance: they that did see me without fled from me.*

146. *Psalms 31:13: For I have heard the slander of many: fear was on every side: while they took counsel together against me, they devised to take away my life.*

147. *Psalms 31:19: Oh how great is thy goodness, which thou hast laid up for them that fear thee; which thou hast wrought for them that trust in thee before the sons of men!*

148. *Psalms 33:8: Let all the earth fear the LORD: let all the inhabitants of the world stand in awe of him.*

149. *Psalms 33:18: Behold, the eye of the LORD is upon them that fear him, upon them that hope in his mercy;*

150. *Psalms 34:7: The angel of the LORD encampeth round about them that fear him, and delivereth them.*

151. *Psalms 34:9: O fear the LORD, ye his saints: for there is no want to them that fear him.*

152. *Psalms 34:11: Come, ye children, hearken unto me: I will teach you the fear of the LORD.*

153. *Psalms 36:1: The transgression of the wicked saith within my heart, that there is no fear of God before his eyes.*

154. *Psalms 40:3: And he hath put a new song in my mouth, even praise unto our God: Many shall see it, and fear, And shall trust in the LORD.*

155. *Psalms 46:2: Therefore will not we fear, though the earth be removed, and though the mountains be carried into the midst of the sea;*

156. *Psalms 48:6: Fear took hold upon them there, and pain, as of a woman in travail.*

157. *Psalms 49:5: Wherefore should I fear in the days of evil, when the iniquity of my heels shall compass me about?*

158. *Psalms 52:6: The righteous also shall see, and fear, and shall laugh at him:*

159. *Psalms 53:5: There were they in great fear, where no fear was: for God hath scattered the bones of him that encampeth against thee: thou hast put them to shame, because God hath despised them.*

160. *Psalms 55:19: God shall hear, and afflict them, even he that abideth of old. Selah. Because they have no changes, therefore they fear not God.*

161. *Psalms 56:4: In God I will praise his word, in God I have put my trust; I will not fear what flesh can do unto me.*

162. *Psalms 60:4: Thou hast given a banner to them that fear thee, that it may be displayed because of the truth. Selah.*

163. *Psalms 61:5: For thou, O God, hast heard my vows: thou hast given me the heritage of those that fear thy name.*

164. *Psalms 64:1: Hear my voice, O God, in my prayer: preserve my life from fear of the enemy.*

165. *Psalms 64:4: That they may shoot in secret at the perfect: suddenly do they shoot at him, and fear not.*

166. *Psalms 64:9: And all men shall fear, and shall declare the work of God; for they shall wisely consider of his doing.*

167. *Psalms 66:16: Come and hear, all ye that fear God, and I will declare what he hath done for my soul.*

168. *Psalms 67:7: God shall bless us; and all the ends of the earth shall fear him.*

169. *Psalms 72:5: They shall fear thee as long as the sun and moon endure, throughout all generations.*

170. *Psalms 85:9: Surely his salvation is nigh them that fear him; that glory may dwell in our land.*

171. *Psalms 86:11: Teach me thy way, O LORD; I will walk in thy truth: unite my heart to fear thy name.*
172. *Psalms 90:11: Who knoweth the power of thine anger? Even according to thy fear, so is thy wrath.*
173. *Psalms 96:9: O worship the LORD in the beauty of holiness: fear before him, all the earth.*
174. *Psalms 102:15: So the heathen shall fear the name of the LORD, and all the kings of the earth thy glory.*
175. *Psalms 103:11: For as the heaven is high above the earth, so great is his mercy toward them that fear him.*
176. *Psalms 103:13: Like as a father pitieth his children, so the LORD pitieth them that fear him.*
177. *Psalms 103:17: But the mercy of the LORD is from everlasting to everlasting upon them that fear him, and his righteousness unto children's children;*
178. *Psalms 105:38: Egypt was glad when they departed: for the fear of them fell upon them.*
179. *Psalms 111:5: He hath given meat unto them that fear him: he will ever be mindful of his covenant.*
180. *Psalms 111:10: The fear of the LORD is the beginning of wisdom: a good understanding have all they that do his commandments: his praise endureth for ever.*
181. *Psalms 115:11: Ye that fear the LORD, trust in the LORD: he is their help and their shield.*
182. *Psalms 115:13: He will bless them that fear the LORD, both small and great.*
183. *Psalms 118:4: Let them now that fear the LORD say, that his mercy endureth for ever.*
184. *Psalms 118:6: The LORD is on my side; I will not fear: what can man do unto me?*
185. *Psalms 119:38: Stablish thy word unto thy servant, who is devoted to thy fear.*
186. *Psalms 119:39: Turn away my reproach which I fear: for thy judgments are good.*

187. *Psalms 119:63: I am a companion of all them that fear thee, and of them that keep thy precepts.*

188. *Psalms 119:74: They that fear thee will be glad when they see me; because I have hoped in thy word.*

189. *Psalms 119:79: Let those that fear thee turn unto me, and those that have known thy testimonies.*

190. *Psalms 119:120: My flesh trembleth for fear of thee; and I am afraid of thy judgments.*

191. *Psalms 135:20: Bless the LORD, O house of Levi: ye that fear the LORD, bless the LORD.*

192. *Psalms 145:19: He will fulfil the desire of them that fear him: he also will hear their cry, and will save them.*

193. *Psalms 147:11: The LORD taketh pleasure in them that fear him, in those that hope in his mercy.*

194. *Proverbs 1:7: The fear of the LORD is the beginning of knowledge: but fools despise wisdom and instruction.*

195. *Proverbs 1:26: I also will laugh at your calamity; I will mock when your fear cometh;*

196. *Proverbs 1:27: When your fear cometh as desolation, and your destruction cometh as a whirlwind; when distress and anguish cometh upon you.*

197. *Proverbs 1:29: For that they hated knowledge, and did not choose the fear of the LORD:*

198. *Proverbs 1:33: But whoso hearkeneth unto me shall dwell safely, and shall be quiet from fear of evil.*

199. *Proverbs 2:5: Then shalt thou understand the fear of the LORD, and find the knowledge of God.*

200. *Proverbs 3:7: Be not wise in thine own eyes: fear the LORD, and depart from evil.*

201. *Proverbs 3:25: Be not afraid of sudden fear, neither of the desolation of the wicked, when it cometh.*

202. *Proverbs 8:13: The fear of the LORD is to hate evil: pride, and arrogancy, and the evil way, and the froward mouth, do I hate.*

203. *Proverbs 9:10: The fear of the LORD is the beginning of wisdom: and the knowledge of the holy is understanding.*

204. *Proverbs 10:24: The fear of the wicked, it shall come upon him: but the desire of the righteous shall be granted.*

205. *Proverbs 10:27: The fear of the LORD prolongeth days: but the years of the wicked shall be shortened.*

206. *Proverbs 14:26: In the fear of the LORD is strong confidence: and his children shall have a place of refuge.*

207. *Proverbs 14:27: The fear of the LORD is a fountain of life, to depart from the snares of death.*

208. *Proverbs 15:16: Better is little with the fear of the LORD than great treasure and trouble therewith.*

209. *Proverbs 15:33: The fear of the LORD is the instruction of wisdom; and before honour is humility.*

210. *Proverbs 16:6: By mercy and truth iniquity is purged: and by the fear of the LORD men depart from evil.*

211. *Proverbs 19:23: The fear of the LORD tendeth to life: and he that hath it shall abide satisfied; he shall not be visited with evil.*

212. *Proverbs 20:2: The fear of a king is as the roaring of a lion: whoso provoketh him to anger sinneth against his own soul.*

213. *Proverbs 22:4: By humility and the fear of the LORD are riches, and honour, and life.*

214. *Proverbs 23:17: Let not thine heart envy sinners: but be thou in the fear of the LORD all the day long.*

215. *Proverbs 24:21: My son, fear thou the LORD and the king: and meddle not with them that are given to change:*

216. *Proverbs 29:25: The fear of man bringeth a snare: But whoso putteth his trust in the LORD shall be safe.*

217. *Ecclesiastes 3:14: I know that, whatsoever God doeth, it shall be for ever: nothing can be put to it, nor any thing taken from it: and God doeth it, that men should fear before him.*

218. *Ecclesiastes 5:7: For in the multitude of dreams and many words there are also divers vanities: but fear thou God.*

219. *Ecclesiastes 8:12: Though a sinner do evil an hundred times, and his days be prolonged, yet surely I know that it shall be well with them that fear God, which fear before him:*

220. *Ecclesiastes 12:13: Let us hear the conclusion of the whole matter: Fear God, and keep his commandments: for this is the whole duty of man.*

221. *Song of Solomon 3:8: They all hold swords, being expert in war: every man hath his sword upon his thigh because of fear in the night.*

222. *Isaiah 2:10: Enter into the rock, and hide thee in the dust, for fear of the LORD, and for the glory of his majesty.*

223. *Isaiah 2:19: And they shall go into the holes of the rocks, and into the caves of the earth, for fear of the LORD, and for the glory of his majesty, when he ariseth to shake terribly the earth.*

224. *Isaiah 2:21: To go into the clefts of the rocks, and into the tops of the ragged rocks, for fear of the LORD, and for the glory of his majesty, when he ariseth to shake terribly the earth.*

225. *Isaiah 7:4: And say unto him, Take heed, and be quiet; fear not, neither be fainthearted for the two tails of these smoking firebrands, for the fierce anger of Rezin with Syria, and of the son of Remaliah.*

226. *Isaiah 7:25: And on all hills that shall be digged with the mattock, there shall not come thither the fear of briers and thorns: but it shall be for the sending forth of oxen, and for the treading of lesser cattle.*

227. *Isaiah 8:12: Say ye not, A confederacy, to all them to whom this people shall say, A confederacy; neither fear ye their fear, nor be afraid.*

228. *Isaiah 8:13: Sanctify the LORD of hosts himself; and let him be your fear, and let him be your dread.*

229. *Isaiah 11:2: And the spirit of the LORD shall rest upon him, the spirit of wisdom and understanding, the spirit of counsel and might, the spirit of knowledge and of the fear of the LORD;*

230. *Isaiah 11:3: And shall make him of quick understanding in the fear of the LORD: and he shall not judge after the sight of his eyes, neither reprove after the hearing of his ears:*

231. *Isaiah 14:3: And it shall come to pass in the day that the LORD shall give thee rest from thy sorrow, and from thy fear, and from the hard bondage wherein thou wast made to serve,*

232. *Isaiah 19:16: In that day shall Egypt be like unto women: and it shall be afraid and fear because of the shaking of the hand of the LORD of hosts, which he shaketh over it.*

233. *Isaiah 21:4: My heart panted, fearfulness affrighted me: the night of my pleasure hath he turned into fear unto me.*

234. *Isaiah 24:17: Fear, and the pit, and the snare, are upon thee, O inhabitant of the earth.*

235. *Isaiah 24:18: And it shall come to pass, that he who fleeth from the noise of the fear shall fall into the pit; and he that cometh up out of the midst of the pit shall be taken in the snare: for the windows from on high are open, and the foundations of the earth do shake.*

236. *Isaiah 25:3: Therefore shall the strong people glorify thee, the city of the terrible nations shall fear thee.*

237. *Isaiah 29:13: Wherefore the Lord said, Forasmuch as this people draw near me with their mouth, and with their lips do honour me, but have removed their heart far from me, and their fear toward me is taught by the precept of men:*

238. *Isaiah 29:23: But when he seeth his children, the work of mine hands, in the midst of him, they shall sanctify my name, and sanctify the Holy One of Jacob, and shall fear the God of Israel.*

239. *Isaiah 31:9: And he shall pass over to his strong hold for fear, and his princes shall be afraid of the ensign, saith the LORD, whose fire is in Zion, and his furnace in Jerusalem.*

240. *Isaiah 33:6: And wisdom and knowledge shall be the stability of thy times, and strength of salvation: the fear of the LORD is his treasure.*

241. *Isaiah 35:4: Say to them that are of a fearful heart, Be strong, fear not: behold, your God will come with vengeance, even God with a recompence; he will come and save you.*

242. *Isaiah 41:10: Fear thou not; for I am with thee: be not dismayed; for I am thy God: I will strengthen thee; yea, I will help thee; yea, I will uphold thee with the right hand of my righteousness.*

243. *Isaiah 41:13: For I the LORD thy God will hold thy right hand, saying unto thee, Fear not; I will help thee.*

244. *Isaiah 41:14: Fear not, thou worm Jacob, and ye men of Israel; I will help thee, saith the LORD, and thy redeemer, the Holy One of Israel.*

245. *Isaiah 43:1: But now thus saith the LORD that created thee, O Jacob, and he that formed thee, O Israel, Fear not: for I have redeemed thee, I have called thee by thy name; thou art mine.*

246. *Isaiah 43:5: Fear not: for I am with thee: I will bring thy seed from the east, and gather thee from the west;*

247. *Isaiah 44:2: Thus saith the LORD that made thee, and formed thee from the womb, which will help thee; Fear not, O Jacob, my servant; and thou, Jesurun, whom I have chosen.*

248. *Isaiah 44:8: Fear ye not, neither be afraid: have not I told thee from that time, and have declared it? ye are even my witnesses. Is there a God beside me? yea, there is no God; I know not any.*

249. *Isaiah 44:11: Behold, all his fellows shall be ashamed: and the workmen, they are of men: let them all be gathered together, let them stand up; yet they shall fear, and they shall be ashamed together.*

250. *Isaiah 51:7: Hearken unto me, ye that know righteousness, the people in whose heart is my law; fear ye not the reproach of men, neither be ye afraid of their revilings.*

251. *Isaiah 54:4: Fear not; for thou shalt not be ashamed: neither be thou confounded; for thou shalt not be put to shame:*

for thou shalt forget the shame of thy youth, and shalt not remember the reproach of thy widowhood any more.

252. *Isaiah 54:14: In righteousness shalt thou be established: thou shalt be far from oppression; for thou shalt not fear: and from terror; for it shall not come near thee.*

253. *Isaiah 59:19: So shall they fear the name of the LORD from the west, and his glory from the rising of the sun. When the enemy shall come in like a flood, the Spirit of the LORD shall lift up a standard against him.*

254. *Isaiah 60:5: Then thou shalt see, and flow together, and thine heart shall fear, and be enlarged; because the abundance of the sea shall be converted unto thee, the forces of the Gentiles shall come unto thee.*

255. *Isaiah 63:17: O LORD, why hast thou made us to err from thy ways, and hardened our heart from thy fear? Return for thy servants' sake, the tribes of thine inheritance.*

256. *Jeremiah 2:19: Thine own wickedness shall correct thee, and thy backslidings shall reprove thee: know therefore and see that it is an evil thing and bitter, that thou hast forsaken the LORD thy God, and that my fear is not in thee, saith the Lord GOD of hosts.*

257. *Jeremiah 5:22: Fear ye not me? saith the LORD: will ye not tremble at my presence, which have placed the sand for the bound of the sea by a perpetual decree, that it cannot pass it: and though the waves thereof toss themselves, yet can they not prevail; though they roar, yet can they not pass over it?*

258. *Jeremiah 5:24: Neither say they in their heart, Let us now fear the LORD our God, that giveth rain, both the former and the latter, in his season: he reserveth unto us the appointed weeks of the harvest.*

259. *Jeremiah 6:25: Go not forth into the field, nor walk by the way; for the sword of the enemy and fear is on every side.*

260. *Jeremiah 10:7: Who would not fear thee, O King of nations? for to thee doth it appertain: forasmuch as among all the wise*

men of the nations, and in all their kingdoms, there is none like unto thee.

261. *Jeremiah 20:10: For I heard the defaming of many, fear on every side. Report, say they, and we will report it. All my familiars watched for my halting, saying, Peradventure he will be enticed, and we shall prevail against him, and we shall take our revenge on him.*

262. *Jeremiah 23:4: And I will set up shepherds over them which shall feed them: and they shall fear no more, nor be dismayed, neither shall they be lacking, saith the LORD.*

263. *Jeremiah 26:19: Did Hezekiah king of Judah and all Judah put him at all to death? did he not fear the LORD, and besought the LORD, and the LORD repented him of the evil which he had pronounced against them? Thus might we procure great evil against our souls.*

264. *Jeremiah 30:5: For thus saith the LORD; We have heard a voice of trembling, of fear, and not of peace.*

265. *Jeremiah 30:10: Therefore fear thou not, O my servant Jacob, saith the LORD; neither be dismayed, O Israel: for, lo, I will save thee from afar, and thy seed from the land of their captivity; and Jacob shall return, and shall be in rest, and be quiet, and none shall make him afraid.*

266. *Jeremiah 32:39: And I will give them one heart, and one way, that they may fear me for ever, for the good of them, and of their children after them:*

267. *Jeremiah 32:40: And I will make an everlasting covenant with them, that I will not turn away from them, to do them good; but I will put my fear in their hearts, that they shall not depart from me.*

268. *Jeremiah 33:9: And it shall be to me a name of joy, a praise and an honour before all the nations of the earth, which shall hear all the good that I do unto them: and they shall fear and tremble for all the goodness and for all the prosperity that I procure unto it.*

269. *Jeremiah 35:11: But it came to pass, when Nebuchadrezzar king of Babylon came up into the land, that we said, Come, and let us go to Jerusalem for fear of the army of the Chaldeans, and for fear of the army of the Syrians: so we dwell at Jerusalem.*

270. *Jeremiah 37:11: And it came to pass, that when the army of the Chaldeans was broken up from Jerusalem for fear of Pharaoh's army,*

271. *Jeremiah 40:9: And Gedaliah the son of Ahikam the son of Shaphan sware unto them and to their men, saying, Fear not to serve the Chaldeans: dwell in the land, and serve the king of Babylon, and it shall be well with you.*

272. *Jeremiah 41:9: Now the pit wherein Ishmael had cast all the dead bodies of the men, whom he had slain because of Gedaliah, was it which Asa the king had made for fear of Baasha king of Israel: and Ishmael the son of Nethaniah filled it with them that were slain.*

273. *Jeremiah 46:5: Wherefore have I seen them dismayed and turned away back? and their mighty ones are beaten down, and are fled apace, and look not back: for fear was round about, saith the LORD.*

274. *Jeremiah 46:27: But fear not thou, O my servant Jacob, and be not dismayed, O Israel: for, behold, I will save thee from afar off, and thy seed from the land of their captivity; and Jacob shall return, and be in rest and at ease, and none shall make him afraid.*

275. *Jeremiah 46:28: Fear thou not, O Jacob my servant, saith the LORD: for I am with thee; for I will make a full end of all the nations whither I have driven thee: but I will not make a full end of thee, but correct thee in measure; yet will I not leave thee wholly unpunished.*

276. *Jeremiah 48:43: Fear, and the pit, and the snare, shall be upon thee, O inhabitant of Moab, saith the LORD.*

277. *Jeremiah 48:44: He that fleeth from the fear shall fall into the pit; and he that getteth up out of the pit shall be taken in the snare: for I will bring upon it, even upon Moab, the year of their visitation, saith the LORD.*

278. *Jeremiah 49:5: Behold, I will bring a fear upon thee, saith the Lord GOD of hosts, from all those that be about thee; and ye shall be driven out every man right forth; and none shall gather up him that wandereth.*

279. *Jeremiah 49:24: Damascus is waxed feeble, and turneth herself to flee, and fear hath seized on her: anguish and sorrows have taken her, as a woman in travail.*

280. *Jeremiah 49:29: Their tents and their flocks shall they take away: they shall take to themselves their curtains, and all their vessels, and their camels; and they shall cry unto them, Fear is on every side.*

281. *Jeremiah 50:16: Cut off the sower from Babylon, and him that handleth the sickle in the time of harvest: for fear of the oppressing sword they shall turn every one to his people, and they shall flee every one to his own land.*

282. *Jeremiah 51:46: And lest your heart faint, and ye fear for the rumour that shall be heard in the land; a rumour shall both come one year, and after that in another year shall come a rumour, and violence in the land, ruler against ruler.*

283. *Lamentations 3:47: Fear and a snare is come upon us, desolation and destruction.*

284. *Lamentations 3:57: Thou drewest near in the day that I called upon thee: thou saidst, Fear not.*

285. *Ezekiel 3:9: As an adamant harder than flint have I made thy forehead: fear them not, neither be dismayed at their looks, though they be a rebellious house.*

286. *Ezekiel 30:13: Thus saith the Lord GOD; I will also destroy the idols, and I will cause their images to cease out of Noph; and there shall be no more a prince of the land of Egypt: and I will put a fear in the land of Egypt.*

287. *Daniel 1:10: And the prince of the eunuchs said unto Daniel,
      I fear my lord the king, who hath appointed your meat and
      your drink: for why should he see your faces worse liking than
      the children which are of your sort? then shall ye make me
      endanger my head to the king.*

288. *Daniel 6:26: I make a decree, That in every dominion of my
      kingdom men tremble and fear before the God of Daniel: for
      he is the living God, and stedfast for ever, and his kingdom
      that which shall not be destroyed, and his dominion shall be
      even unto the end.*

289. *Daniel 10:12: Then said he unto me, Fear not, Daniel: for
      from the first day that thou didst set thine heart to understand,
      and to chasten thyself before thy God, thy words were heard,
      and I am come for thy words.*

290. *Daniel 10:19: And said, O man greatly beloved, fear not:
      peace be unto thee, be strong, yea, be strong. And when he had
      spoken unto me, I was strengthened, and said, Let my lord
      speak; for thou hast strengthened me.*

291. *Hosea 3:5: Afterward shall the children of Israel return, and
      seek the LORD their God, and David their king; and shall
      fear the LORD and his goodness in the latter days.*

292. *Hosea 10:5: The inhabitants of Samaria shall fear because
      of the calves of Bethaven: for the people thereof shall mourn
      over it, and the priests thereof that rejoiced on it, for the glory
      thereof, because it is departed from it.*

293. *Joel 2:21: Fear not, O land; be glad and rejoice: for the LORD
      will do great things.*

294. *Amos 3:8: The lion hath roared, who will not fear? the Lord
      GOD hath spoken, who can but prophesy?*

295. *Jonah 1:9: And he said unto them, I am an Hebrew; and I
      fear the LORD, the God of heaven, which hath made the sea
      and the dry land.*

296. *Micah 7:17: They shall lick the dust like a serpent, they shall move out of their holes like worms of the earth: they shall be afraid of the LORD our God, and shall fear because of thee.*

297. *Zephaniah 3:7: I said, Surely thou wilt fear me, thou wilt receive instruction; so their dwelling should not be cut off, howsoever I punished them: but they rose early, and corrupted all their doings.*

298. *Zephaniah 3:16: In that day it shall be said to Jerusalem, Fear thou not: and to Zion, Let not thine hands be slack.*

299. *Haggai 1:12: Then Zerubbabel the son of Shealtiel, and Joshua the son of Josedech, the high priest, with all the remnant of the people, obeyed the voice of the LORD their God, and the words of Haggai the prophet, as the LORD their God had sent him, and the people did fear before the LORD.*

300. *Haggai 2:5: According to the word that I covenanted with you when ye came out of Egypt, so my spirit remaineth among you: fear ye not.*

301. *Zechariah 8:13: And it shall come to pass, that as ye were a curse among the heathen, O house of Judah, and house of Israel; so will I save you, and ye shall be a blessing: fear not, but let your hands be strong.*

302. *Zechariah 8:15: So again have I thought in these days to do well unto Jerusalem and to the house of Judah: fear ye not.*

303. *Zechariah 9:5: Ashkelon shall see it, and fear; Gaza also shall see it, and be very sorrowful, and Ekron; for her expectation shall be ashamed; and the king shall perish from Gaza, and Ashkelon shall not be inhabited.*

304. *Malachi 1:6: A son honoureth his father, and a servant his master: if then I be a father, where is mine honour? and if I be a master, where is my fear? saith the LORD of hosts unto you, O priests, that despise my name. And ye say, Wherein have we despised thy name?*

305. *Malachi 2:5: My covenant was with him of life and peace; and I gave them to him for the fear wherewith he feared me, and was afraid before my name.*

306. *Malachi 3:5: And I will come near to you to judgment; and I will be a swift witness against the sorcerers, and against the adulterers, and against false swearers, and against those that oppress the hireling in his wages, the widow, and the fatherless, and that turn aside the stranger from his right, and fear not me, saith the LORD of hosts.*

307. *Malachi 4:2: But unto you that fear my name shall the Sun of righteousness arise with healing in his wings; and ye shall go forth, and grow up as calves of the stall.*

New Testament Verses: Fear

308. *Matthew 1:20: But while he thought on these things, behold, the angel of the Lord appeared unto him in a dream, saying, Joseph, thou son of David, fear not to take unto thee Mary thy wife: for that which is conceived in her is of the Holy Ghost.*

309. *Matthew 10:26: Fear them not therefore: for there is nothing covered, that shall not be revealed; and hid, that shall not be known.*

310. *Matthew 10:28: And fear not them which kill the body, but are not able to kill the soul: but rather fear him which is able to destroy both soul and body in hell.*

311. *Matthew 10:31: Fear ye not therefore, ye are of more value than many sparrows.*

312. *Matthew 14:26: And when the disciples saw him walking on the sea, they were troubled, saying, It is a spirit; and they cried out for fear.*

313. *Matthew 21:26: But if we shall say, Of men; we fear the people; for all hold John as a prophet.*

314. *Matthew 28:4: And for fear of him the keepers did shake, and became as dead men.*

315. *Matthew 28:5: And the angel answered and said unto the women, Fear not ye: for I know that ye seek Jesus, which was crucified.*

316. *Matthew 28:8: And they departed quickly from the sepulchre with fear and great joy; and did run to bring his disciples word.*

317. *Luke 1:12: And when Zacharias saw him, he was troubled, and fear fell upon him.*

318. *Luke 1:13: But the angel said unto him, Fear not, Zacharias: for thy prayer is heard; and thy wife Elisabeth shall bear thee a son, and thou shalt call his name John.*

319. *Luke 1:30: And the angel said unto her, Fear not, Mary: for thou hast found favour with God.*

320. *Luke 1:50: And his mercy is on them that fear him from generation to generation.*

321. *Luke 1:65: And fear came on all that dwelt round about them: and all these sayings were noised abroad throughout all the hill country of Judaea.*

322. *Luke 1:74: That he would grant unto us, that we being delivered out of the hand of our enemies might serve him without fear,*

323. *Luke 2:10: And the angel said unto them, Fear not: for, behold, I bring you good tidings of great joy, which shall be to all people.*

324. *Luke 5:10: And so was also James, and John, the sons of Zebedee, which were partners with Simon. And Jesus said unto Simon, Fear not; from henceforth thou shalt catch men.*

325. *Luke 5:26: And they were all amazed, and they glorified God, and were filled with fear, saying, We have seen strange things to day.*

326. *Luke 7:16: And there came a fear on all: and they glorified God, saying, That a great prophet is risen up among us; and, That God hath visited his people.*

327. *Luke 8:37: Then the whole multitude of the country of the Gadarenes round about besought him to depart from them; for they were taken with great fear: and he went up into the ship, and returned back again.*

328. *Luke 8:50: But when Jesus heard it, he answered him, saying, Fear not: believe only, and she shall be made whole.*

329. *Luke 12:5: But I will forewarn you whom ye shall fear: Fear him, which after he hath killed hath power to cast into hell; yea, I say unto you, Fear him.*

330. *Luke 12:7: But even the very hairs of your head are all numbered. Fear not therefore: ye are of more value than many sparrows.*

331. *Luke 12:32: Fear not, little flock; for it is your Father's good pleasure to give you the kingdom.*

332. *Luke 18:4: And he would not for a while: but afterward he said within himself, Though I fear not God, nor regard man;*

333. *Luke 21:26: Men's hearts failing them for fear, and for looking after those things which are coming on the earth: for the powers of heaven shall be shaken.*

334. *Luke 23:40: But the other answering rebuked him, saying, Dost not thou fear God, seeing thou art in the same condemnation?*

335. *John 7:13: Howbeit no man spake openly of him for fear of the Jews.*

336. *John 12:15: Fear not, daughter of Sion: behold, thy King cometh, sitting on an ass's colt.*

337. *John 19:38: And after this Joseph of Arimathaea, being a disciple of Jesus, but secretly for fear of the Jews, besought Pilate that he might take away the body of Jesus: and Pilate gave him leave. He came therefore, and took the body of Jesus.*

338. *John 20:19: Then the same day at evening, being the first day of the week, when the doors were shut where the disciples were assembled for fear of the Jews, came Jesus and stood in the midst, and saith unto them, Peace be unto you.*

339. *Acts 2:43: And fear came upon every soul: and many wonders and signs were done by the apostles.*

340. *Acts 5:5: And Ananias hearing these words fell down, and gave up the ghost: and great fear came on all them that heard these things.*

341. *Acts 5:11: And great fear came upon all the church, and upon as many as heard these things.*

342. *Acts 9:31: Then had the churches rest throughout all Judaea and Galilee and Samaria, and were edified; and walking in the fear of the Lord, and in the comfort of the Holy Ghost, were multiplied.*

343. *Acts 13:16: Then Paul stood up, and beckoning with his hand said, Men of Israel, and ye that fear God, give audience.*

344. *Acts 19:17: And this was known to all the Jews and Greeks also dwelling at Ephesus; and fear fell on them all, and the name of the Lord Jesus was magnified.*

345. *Acts 27:24: Saying, Fear not, Paul; thou must be brought before Caesar: and, lo, God hath given thee all them that sail with thee.*

346. *Romans 3:18: There is no fear of God before their eyes.*

347. *Romans 8:15: For ye have not received the spirit of bondage again to fear; but ye have received the Spirit of adoption, whereby we cry, Abba, Father.*

348. *Romans 11:20: Well; because of unbelief they were broken off, and thou standest by faith. Be not highminded, but fear:*

349. *Romans 13:7: Render therefore to all their dues: tribute to whom tribute is due; custom to whom custom; fear to whom fear; honour to whom honour.*

350. *I Corinthians 2:3: And I was with you in weakness, and in fear, and in much trembling.*

351. *I Corinthians 16:10: Now if Timotheus come, see that he may be with you without fear: for he worketh the work of the Lord, as I also do.*

352. *II Corinthians 7:1: Having therefore these promises, dearly beloved, let us cleanse ourselves from all filthiness of the flesh and spirit, perfecting holiness in the fear of God.*

353. *II Corinthians 7:11: For behold this selfsame thing, that ye sorrowed after a godly sort, what carefulness it wrought in you, yea, what clearing of yourselves, yea, what indignation, yea, what fear, yea, what vehement desire, yea, what zeal, yea, what revenge! In all things ye have approved yourselves to be clear in this matter.*

354. *II Corinthians 7:15: And his inward affection is more abundant toward you, whilst he remembereth the obedience of you all, how with fear and trembling ye received him.*

355. *II Corinthians 11:3: But I fear, lest by any means, as the serpent beguiled Eve through his subtilty, so your minds should be corrupted from the simplicity that is in Christ.*

356. *II Corinthians 12:20: For I fear, lest, when I come, I shall not find you such as I would, and that I shall be found unto you such as ye would not: lest there be debates, envyings, wraths, strifes, backbitings, whisperings, swellings, tumults:*

357. *Ephesians 5:21: Submitting yourselves one to another in the fear of God.*

358. *Ephesians 6:5: Servants, be obedient to them that are your masters according to the flesh, with fear and trembling, in singleness of your heart, as unto Christ;*

359. *Philippians 1:14: And many of the brethren in the Lord, waxing confident by my bonds, are much more bold to speak the word without fear.*

360. *Philippians 2:12: Wherefore, my beloved, as ye have always obeyed, not as in my presence only, but now much more in my absence, work out your own salvation with fear and trembling.*

Suly Rieman

361. *I Timothy 5:20: Them that sin rebuke before all, that others also may fear.*

362. *II Timothy 1:7: For God hath not given us the spirit of fear; but of power, and of love, and of a sound mind.*

363. *Hebrews 2:15: And deliver them who through fear of death were all their lifetime subject to bondage.*

364. *Hebrews 4:1: Let us therefore fear, lest, a promise being left us of entering into his rest, any of you should seem to come short of it.*

365. *Hebrews 11:7: By faith Noah, being warned of God of things not seen as yet, moved with fear, prepared an ark to the saving of his house; by the which he condemned the world, and became heir of the righteousness which is by faith.*

366. *Hebrews 12:21: And so terrible was the sight, that Moses said, I exceedingly fear and quake:*

367. *Hebrews 12:28: Wherefore we receiving a kingdom which cannot be moved, let us have grace, whereby we may serve God acceptably with reverence and godly fear:*

368. *Hebrews 13:6: So that we may boldly say, The Lord is my helper, and I will not fear what man shall do unto me.*

369. *I Peter 1:17: And if ye call on the Father, who without respect of persons judgeth according to every man's work, pass the time of your sojourning here in fear:*

370. *I Peter 2:17: Honour all men. Love the brotherhood. Fear God. Honour the king.*

371. *I Peter 2:18: Servants, be subject to your masters with all fear; not only to the good and gentle, but also to the froward.*

372. *I Peter 3:2: While they behold your chaste conversation coupled with fear.*

373. *I Peter 3:15: But sanctify the Lord God in your hearts: and be ready always to give an answer to every man that asketh you a reason of the hope that is in you with meekness and fear:*

374. *I John 4:18: There is no fear in love; but perfect love casteth out fear: because fear hath torment. He that feareth is not made perfect in love.*

375. *Jude 12: These are spots in your feasts of charity, when they feast with you, feeding themselves without fear: clouds they are without water, carried about of winds; trees whose fruit withereth, without fruit, twice dead, plucked up by the roots;*

376. *Jude 23: And others save with fear, pulling them out of the fire; hating even the garment spotted by the flesh.*

377. *Revelation 1:17: And when I saw him, I fell at his feet as dead. And he laid his right hand upon me, saying unto me, Fear not; I am the first and the last:*

378. *Revelation 2:10: Fear none of those things which thou shalt suffer: behold, the devil shall cast some of you into prison, that ye may be tried; and ye shall have tribulation ten days: be thou faithful unto death, and I will give thee a crown of life.*

379. *Revelation 11:11: And after three days and an half the Spirit of life from God entered into them, and they stood upon their feet; and great fear fell upon them which saw them.*

380. *Revelation 11:18: And the nations were angry, and thy wrath is come, and the time of the dead, that they should be judged, and that thou shouldest give reward unto thy servants the prophets, and to the saints, and them that fear thy name, small and great; and shouldest destroy them which destroy the earth.*

381. *Revelation 14:7: ...saying with a loud voice, Fear God, and give glory to him; for the hour of his judgment is come: and worship him that made heaven, and earth, and the sea, and the fountains of waters.*

382. *Revelation 15:4: Who shall not fear thee, O Lord, and glorify thy name? for thou only art holy: for all nations shall come and worship before thee; for thy judgments are made manifest.*

383. *Revelation 18:10: ...standing afar off for the fear of her torment, saying, Alas, alas, that great city Babylon, that mighty city! for in one hour is thy judgment come.*

384. *Revelation 18:15: The merchants of these things, which were made rich by her, shall stand afar off for the fear of her torment, weeping and wailing,*

385. *Revelation 19:5: And a voice came out of the throne, saying, Praise our God, all ye his servants, and ye that fear him, both small and great.*

EIGHT

The Fear of The Lord

Are you familiar with the word, sacred? What image comes to mind when you hear that word? Most likely the image of someone or something of value, worthy, set apart, holy, or sacrosanct. Well, although we travelled the journey of fear and how to overcome it, let me tell you about one scripture verse in Proverbs, which is very encouraging: *The fear of the Lord is the beginning of wisdom.* What? Fear God? Yes, however, the Lord is not asking that we cowardly fear Him or approach Him, He does not want that from us. No need for sweaty palms, rapid heart rate, high blood pressure, or heavy breathing. That is not what He wants from us or expects from us. He wants us to freely seek Him, freely approach Him and honor Him, respect Him, and be in awe of Him: give Him all the respect He is due.

The Lord is the King of Heaven: The Father, Son, and Holy Spirit. God is Love. He is the Prince of Peace, He is the Creator, Redeemer, Savior, Sovereign, Majesty, Miracle Maker, Promise Keeper, He is the Light, He is Perfect; He is Holy. He is the Ancient of Days. He is the Lamb of God. The Lord is the Lion of Judah, He is the Chain Breaker. God is the Judge, He is Compassionate, Loving, Kind; He is Merciful. He is the Word. The Lord is Omnipotent, Omniscient, He is for all eternity. He is Immutable: He is the same yesterday, today and tomorrow. I am in awe of God, and God deserves my honor, my respect, my complete reverence, my fear, because of who He is and His position, character, and attributes. John 4:24 tells us: *God is a Spirit: and they that worship him must worship him in spirit and in truth.* The Lord is worthy of my honor and my praise; He is Holy. I do not come before Him trembling; I come before Him in complete wonder, respect, love, gratitude, and adoration. I am not a puppet, I am not brainwashed, I do not belong to a cult. I am a sinner saved by His grace, forgiven, and an adopted daughter of the King. He is my Living Hope.

The rest of the verse in Proverbs chapter one reads: *But fools despise wisdom and instruction.* I know one thing, I do not want to be a fool when it comes to the Lord. I want to accept Him at His Word and learn from Him. I want to live a life which honors Him. I want to be humble and learn as much as I possibly can and share it with others. I need to be open minded to His instruction, and give Him all the respect which is due. When the Lord called Moses to the overwhelming task of freeing the Hebrew slaves, Moses asked what His name was, and the Lord's response was, *I am that I am.* God let Moses know He was everything which Moses needed to fulfil his task. God continues to be the Great I Am, all we have to do is trust Him. Will you trust Him too?

Names

Throughout scripture we read about how the Lord is described and the names used to bring clarity to His attributes. With each name we see a glimpse of who He is. I highly recommend that you use this list to find the scripture about the attributes of God and learn much about Him. Some of these phrases may be unfamiliar to you and I hope that you take a look at scripture and become familiar with the God who loves you more than you can ever possibly imagine.

The names of God make for an insightful Bible study and learn how He revealed Himself to the human race. In the book of Luke we find the question Jesus asked His disciples when he asked them, *Whom say ye that I am?* Actually, He asks this same question of you today.

1. Abba Father
2. Adonai
3. Alpha and Omega
4. Ancient of Days
5. Branch
6. Bread of Life
7. Creator
8. El Elyon
9. El Roi
10. Elohim
11. El-Shaddai
12. Everlasting Father
13. Friend of Sinners
14. God of your fathers
15. Good Shephard
16. Great Physician
17. Holy Spirit
18. I Am Who I Am
19. Immanuel
20. Jehovah Jireh
21. Jehovah Nissi
22. Jehovah Raah
23. Jehovah Rapha
24. Jehovah Shalom
25. Jehovah Shammah
26. Jehovah Tsidkenu
27. Jesus Christ
28. King of Kings
29. Lion of Judah
30. Living Hope

31. Living Water
32. Love
33. Messiah
34. Mighty God
35. Prince of Peace
36. Redeemer
37. Ruler of Israel
38. Savior
39. Son of God
40. Son of Man
41. Sovereign
42. The Light of the world
43. The Lord
44. The Vine
45. The Way, the Truth and the Life
46. Wonderful Counselor

Special Meaning

There are four names or attributes of God which make a meaningful impact on my life. Each name reveals a part of God' loving nature and encourages me with the personal relationship I have with my Lord. The first is Jireh, and the second is Chain Breaker, the third is Prince of Peace, and the fourth is Promise Keeper.

Jireh means God will Provide. Jireh reflects that God is everything, has everything and supplies exactly what I need in life when I need it. He is never early, He is never late; He is always on time. Sometimes, well, many times, this calls for patience on my part because God's timing is not my timing. I must trust that He will respond to my prayers, supply my needs, and wait on healing for others, in His time.

In scripture we have the story of Abraham and his son Isaac, and how they journeyed together to Mount Moriah to praise God with their sacrifice of a lamb. They travelled with their supplies and when they reached their destination, God provided the lamb. Jireh provided, and He was right on time. Bottom line, Jireh is enough for me every day. I do not have to be in control, I do not have to live in fear; He is enough so therefore I am enough. I trust Him and because of Him I can be victorious.

The song, *Jireh* by Elevation Worship and Maverick City Music is a song which drives home the point that He, the Lord provides and He is enough and therefore I am enough. I like this song and it is a wonderful reminder that the Lord is enough, and I am able to trust Him and be content, no matter what I experience. I am so grateful that I am already loved, I am already chosen, and all I must do is trust Him. *Jireh, You are Enough, I will be Content In every Circumstance, Jireh, You are Enough, Forever Enough, always Enough:* (rb.gy/panwm2).

Jireh is enough, so I am enough...

- When we struggle with fear of inadequacy...He is enough.
- When the medical test results do not look promising...He is enough.
- When the medication stops working...He is enough.
- When the doctor says there is nothing more that we can do...He is enough.
- When the fire or tornado or hurricane destroys everything... He is enough.
- When we fear we are not a good parent...He is enough.
- When the spouse walks out the door and abandons the family...He is enough.
- When friends betray us...He is enough.
- When the pet died...He is enough.
- When we think we are not good enough...He is enough.
- When the struggles come because of a job, or finding a job, or losing a job...He is enough.

- When there is too much month left and not enough money...He is enough.
- When the grave takes the person most loved...He is enough.
- When the accident happens...He is enough.
- When the storms of life hit hard...He is enough.
- When fear strikes the heart...He is enough.

We never need to try to be enough without the Lord because we will be unsuccessful. Anytime we try to completely rely on ourselves, we fail miserably. If we had the power to save ourselves, then Jesus's love and sacrifice is pointless. If we had the power to remove the fear and anxiety in our lives, then why do we continue to return to our human cycle of emotions? Without the Lord, we do not have the power or strength for life's battles. When we rely completely on the Lord in the midst of life's struggles, He is enough and therefore because of His strength, His love, we are enough.

You may be thinking, but you do not know my struggles, you don't know what I do or have done. You are absolutely correct, I do not know; however, God does and He understands and forgives. Take every struggle to Him, ask Him to help you fight the battle. Struggles come in all shapes and sizes and we assume or think we can control the things in our lives which control us; however, without God's help, we cannot. The Lord knows our struggles and He can help us since He is the chain breaker. The Lord is the chain breaker and He is more than enough to help us overcome anything in this life.

The Lord is able, and He has the power to break every sinful chain which stands in the way of giving everything in your life to Him.

- He can break the chain of your drug addiction.
- He can break the chain of your alcohol addiction.
- He can break the chain of your tobacco addiction.
- He can break the chain of your pornography addiction.

- He can break the chain of your gambling addiction.
- He can break the chain of your bullying addiction.
- He can break the chain of your stealing addiction.
- He can break the chain of your lying addiction.
- He can break the chain of your critical, judgmental thinking addiction.
- He can break the chain of your crime addiction.
- He can break the chain of your food addiction.
- He can break the chain of your sex addiction.
- He can break the chain of your internet addiction.
- He can break the chain of your shopping or spending addiction.
- He can break the chain of your lack of self-control.

The Lord can, and will break every chain which controls you, and so together we say, He will! Give your addiction to Him, ask Him to break the chains and release you into new found freedom. God waits for you to call out to Him. Like the Psalmist, ask God to create a new, clean heart in you. *Create in me a clean heart, O God; And renew a right spirit within me.* Psalm 51: 10.

Come to the altar and give every struggle to the Lord. Fight the battle on your knees, and let God be God and allow Him to work in your life. Where is the altar of God you ask? The altar of God is at your kitchen table where you can bow down to Him. The altar is in your living room or at the side of your bed where you can kneel and pray. You can pray at the park, on the train, on a bus, in a cab, in a prison, at a church, the beach, the mountain, anywhere. See, the altar of God is where your heart and devotion for God is, and the posture of worship that you have for Him. You can pray aloud or pray silently, you can pray alone or with a friend. If you are alone, call someone to pray along with you and for you.

Elevation Worship has a song, *O Come to the Father*, which I hope encourages you to come to the altar where God, the Father waits for you with open arms: (rb.gy/lcmef7). God waits on you to call out to Him, come to Him as you are, with all the hurts and imperfections of life. The Lord is waiting for you with a heart filled with pure love; He loves you. Take every care, every hurt, give Him your broken heart...He is waiting for you, call out to Him right now.

Are you hurting and broken within?
Overwhelmed by the weight of your sin?
Jesus is calling,
Have you come to the end of yourself?
Do you thirst for a drink from the well?
Jesus is calling, O come to the altar,
The Father's arms are open wide.

The name, Prince of Peace is very comforting to me for this life and the next. This name denotes that God is the ultimate ruler of peace. So here on earth what does peace look like for a believer, a follower of Christ? It means that we can be calm, that we can be at rest, and we can completely rely on Him and His power in the good times, the challenging times in the midst and middle of the storms. Like most people, I appreciate peace in my life. I enjoy living a peaceful life, in harmony with others and although trials abound, I can continue to have peace and joy and depend on the Lord and His grace to help me withstand the storms of life. I know that I am able to delight in the Lord and trust Him as He is the source of my joy, and not be overly concerned with happiness. Not that I do not enjoy and appreciate happiness; however, the source of happiness depends on a happening, a happenstance, and happiness is not long term. Joy is long term and does not depend on an event or situation or a happening. Joy depends on one person, and that person is the Lord, the Prince of Peace.

You may wonder, is there anything God cannot do? Yes, there is. God cannot lie. God cannot abandon us. He is the Promise Keeper. The Bible teaches that God is love and He Word is truth and therefore, we can trust Him. He never waves the carrot in front of us only to take it away. He never tells us one thing and then baits and switches on what He said or promised. He does not lie, nor will He ever abandon us: it is not part of His nature and it is not part of His attributes since He is righteous and holy.

The Bible is filled with God's promises which have been fulfilled and some yet to be fulfilled. His promises are irrevocable. That subject makes for another great Bible study topic. There are many promises found in the Old Testament which were fulfilled in the New Testament, and there are promises in the New Testament which will be fulfilled one day. Since the promises He made which have been fulfilled leads us to trust Him for the promises which will be fulfilled in His time, by His clock, not ours.

I Know Who I Am!

Knowing God and who He is and knowing His attributes helps me know who I am in Him. Because of Jesus' life, death, and resurrection, I am secure in Him. I have a name, a first name and a last name; however, now I have a new name. Because of Jesus, I too am called by my attributes in Him. I am very grateful to the Lord that I am not defined by the horrible names which I have been called by others in life, such as worthless, ugly, unlovable to name a few. I am not defined by the terrible things I have done, or the mistakes I make in life. I am not defined by my unwise choices in life. I am defined by God, who made me, and I am defined by the new names He gives to me.

In Christ, I am...

- ✓ Accepted
- ✓ Adopted
- ✓ Baptized
- ✓ Blessed
- ✓ Born of The Spirit

- ✓ Child of God
- ✓ Chosen
- ✓ Complete
- ✓ Daughter of the Most-High King

- ✓ Forgiven
- ✓ Heir
- ✓ Loved
- ✓ New Creation
- ✓ Reconciled
- ✓ Redeemed

- ✓ Sanctified
- ✓ Saved by grace
- ✓ Sealed
- ✓ Secure
- ✓ Wonderfully Made

What is your name? How do you believe the Lord sees you in His righteousness? I recommend that you make a list of all the horrible names which you have been called by others or you have called yourself. Pray, give each of those horrible names to the Lord and ask Him for His grace to replace them with His precious, new names for you. Take the list of old names and safely burn it; those are no longer your names! Ask Him to never allow you to see yourself by the old names because you are not defined by those old names. You are defined by the new names He gives you. Then take a moment and create the list of the new names which the Lord has given you as His child. Feel free to use my list as a guide or template and add to it as you see fit. Then seek out the Bible and find verses which support your new name in Christ. May those verses give you confidence, joy, strength and courage in the Lord. Place the list of your new names in a place where you will see it daily. Feel free to use the list of those new names as part of your daily affirmations.

There is one more name I want on my list which I pray I hear as I pass from this life to the next: faithful servant. I long to hear those words from the Lord as I enter His throne room in Heaven and He says, *Well done, my good and faithful servant.* May I run the race of life and complete my course ever faithful to the Lord. I pray that you are there with me too and that you live a faithful life and hear those same words from Him.

In Christ I am...

- ✓ Accepted
- ✓ Adopted
- ✓ Baptized
- ✓ Blessed
- ✓ Born of The Spirit
- ✓ Child of God
- ✓ Chosen
- ✓ Complete
- ✓ Daughter of the Most-High King
- ✓ Forgiven
- ✓ Heir
- ✓ Loved
- ✓ New Creation
- ✓ Reconciled
- ✓ Redeemed
- ✓ Sanctified
- ✓ Saved by grace
- ✓ Sealed
- ✓ Secure
- ✓ Wonderfully Made

NINE

Blessings

If you were to ask me to describe my life, one word comes to mind: blessed. I am very blessed by the Lord, indeed. Even when times seemed so hopeless, the Lord is always with me in the midst of the hopelessness and He restores my mind, my heart, my spirit, and my life. At one point, I worked three jobs in order to care for my children, and keep our household running, and one happy day, I was able to leave two of the jobs and focus on one. I was tired, my face showed signs of stress and age, and I was in need of rest and lots self-care. I prayed and I asked the Lord to restore to me what the locust took. This is from the book of Joel, in the Old Testament. In Joel 2: 25 we read: *And I will restore to you the years that the locust hath eaten…* I am blessed because the Lord heard and answered my prayer. I felt better, I was able to rest, eat on schedule and do the things I enjoyed, and most importantly, I was able to spend some quality time with my kids again. We rented a tiny house at the time, and the following year, we were able to move into our own home with a pool. We lived in a peaceful home, we enjoyed our house and the backyard, and our dogs enjoyed the pool too! It was nice to have a backyard again and have flowers and a small vegetable garden. Those are fond memories of the years we spent there.

Since then my life has changed again, and I am very blessed. Trust me when I say, I do not boast or brag about this for I cannot and do not take any of the credit; the blessings I have in life are wonderful gifts from my Lord. My children are now adults, and it is good to see the Lord work in their lives with challenges and blessings. If you have children, you know that as parents we want what is best for them and somedays, we can still worry about them; however, I know that I am able to trust the Lord with their lives since they were a gift from Him. From birth, I prayed for their salvation, their future spouses, and the plan He has for their lives. When my kids were young, I taught them God's Word, I taught them to pray and I had the privilege to lead them to the Lord. I know that He will do great things in their lives as long as they surrender to His perfect will.

I am blessed because I am able to spend time with them, and they seek my advice, which is such a blessing in life. Praise God, at this time, my needs are basic; I downsized and live in a little cottage with my girls, three dogs and one cat! I get to spend time with family and friends, I do the things I enjoy. Some days, I spend two to four hours outdoors, I work in the yard or the garden, and some days, I do not have to do much; it's wonderful. My life is far from perfect and I continue to face trials, actually the hardships will cease the day I take my last breath. I face challenges the same way you do. I struggle with the loss of three of my dear friends, I battled illness last year. I suffered smoke inhalation, and it took a physical toll on my strength. It took time to fully regain my voice, and I lost my singing voice for many months. This was challenging since I love to sing; at church I sang in the choir, on praise teams, and I sang solos. Some days, I was not able to sing for very long, and many days in church, I enjoyed listening to others sing. After several months, I regained my singing voice and I sing praise songs almost every day. Daily I suffer from chronic pain from the wear and tear of life on my body; however, I truly try not to complain about it. Sadly, one of my dogs was diagnosed with heart disease and was given a six months to one year to live; there are days I cry as I watch her struggle to breathe. I pray that with help of the medication, she can enjoy her last days with us. This is my reality, these are not complaints; I also face the same challenges you do with inflation, climate inconsistencies, and political unrest. In spite of trials, every day is a gift and blessing from the Lord and I continue to trust Him with every detail of my life. I am grateful for His goodness.

In this life we have trials, we have many problems; however, we do not have to despair by the pressures of our problems, we can depend on the Lord. Romans chapter five is a good reminder of the purpose of trials:...*but we glory in tribulations also: knowing that tribulation worketh patience; and patience, experience; and experience, hope: and hope maketh not ashamed; because the love of God is shed abroad in our hearts by the Holy Ghost which is given unto us.*

The second book of Corinthians gives me courage and is such a great reminder that through the trials and weaknesses, the Lord is always with me and it is His strength on which I depend.

And he said unto me, My grace is sufficient for thee; for my strength is made perfect in weakness. Most gladly therefore will I rather glory in my infirmities, that the power of Christ may rest upon me. Therefore I take pleasure in infirmities, in reproaches, in necessities, in persecutions, in distresses for Christ's sake: for when I am weak, then am I strong.

In the mornings I like to sing the *Doxology*. This hymn was written in 1709 by Thomas Ken, a bishop and song writer: (rb. gy/6md1nh). I raise a song of gratitude to the Lord, the Father, Son, and Holy Spirit. This songs helps me to have a correct, respectful posture of praise. It reminds me that I have nothing to do with the blessings which the Lord so freely gives to me because He loves me. I usually sing this song *a cappella* or without instruments.

If you are familiar with this hymn, sing along and if it is new to you, may it bless your heart as you sing praise to our God. *Anthem Lights* and *Selah* do a wonderful job as they sing the *Doxology*: (rb. gy/sxndfg).

Doxology
Praise God, from whom all blessings flow;
Praise him, all creatures here below;
Praise him above, ye heavenly host;
Praise Father, Son, and Holy Ghost. Amen.

I like the rhythm of *Blessings Flow,* because it makes me think of the footsteps I take in my journey of life and as I walk, as I run, the Lord blesses me. The blessings which the Lord gives are given so freely given, and each blessing is so personal. The Lord blesses us individually because He knows us and knows exactly what each of us needs.

May all the blessings flow, That come from Heav'n to here below, Now and forever, Falling from Your throne, To us Your own, A healing river flows, Now and forever: (rb.gy/tu5mqc).

When it comes to gift giving, I like to see people's reactions to the personalized gifts I purchase or make for them. Not that I have their names engraved on the gifts, I tend to give gifts people enjoy. I actively listen when people tell me about things they like, would like to have or never think of getting for themselves, and then I make a note for birthday and Christmas gifts. When it comes to gift getting, I will say, I am not so good with that because I rather give gifts than receive them; however, not when it comes to the Lord. When I pray specifically for something I need or would like to have and the Lord makes a way to provide it to me, I am thrilled! I freely accept the amazing blessings which the Lord so graciously gives to me and those I love. I am blessed by the Lord, and in turn, I want to be a blessing to others.

My prayer for this book is that the minds and hearts of many people will be touched and strengthen. I pray that you make a decision to become a follower of Jesus Christ and dedicate your life to the Lord. I pray that you find freedom from the bondage from fear, worry, anxiety, and depression. I pray that you reach out to a professional therapist, pastor, or counselor and find help for your mental health issues. I pray you find the help you need with your substance abuse issues. I pray that you decide to live, and not believe the lies of the enemy. I pray that lives and relationships are restored by the power of the Lord. I pray that you are empowered to live a life in the resurrected power of Jesus, I say Amen! Those are the blessings I seek, those are the blessings I desire from this book, and I wait on the Lord to answer those prayers.

I want to share a few last Bible verses with you and ask the Lord to bless you as you seek to live for Him. May you live in the power of Jesus and always remember that He is there for you in everything in this life.

Joshua 3:5: *And Joshua said unto the people, Sanctify yourselves: for to morrow the LORD will do wonders among you.*

Psalm 129:8: *We bless you in the name of the LORD.*

Lamentations 3:22-24: *It is of the LORD's mercies that we are not consumed, Because his compassions fail not. They are new every morning: Great is thy faithfulness. The LORD is my portion, saith my soul; Therefore will I hope in him.*

Jude 1:24: *Now unto him that is able to keep you from falling, and to present you faultless before the presence of his glory with exceeding joy.*

John 13:34: *A new commandment I give unto you, That ye love one another; as I have loved you, that ye also love one another.*

John 14:27: *Peace I leave with you, my peace I give unto you: not as the world giveth, give I unto you. Let not your heart be troubled, neither let it be afraid.*

I Thessalonians 5:18: *In every thing give thanks: for this is the will of God in Christ Jesus concerning you.*

I Thessalonians 5:23: *And the very God of peace sanctify you wholly; and I pray God your whole spirit and soul and body be preserved blameless unto the coming of our Lord Jesus Christ.*

TEN

My Story

When we started this journey, I mentioned that this story is not my story. You see, my story is not complete unless the Lord is at the forefront of my story, my life. He provides the gift of every breath I take each day, and every skill, every success and every blessing I have in my life. Without the Lord, my life would be empty, it would not make sense; I would aimlessly walk through life. I am so grateful to the Lord that He provides His Spirit and His purpose for my life. I do not have to fear or worry about success, since I do not need to compare my success to the success of others. I do not want to live my life for the applause of others. I want to live my life for the audience of one, the Lord Jesus Christ. I want to please and honor the Lord with everything in my life. Even in this, I need His help since I cannot do this without Him.

I really try to not compare myself to others since I know that path that God has for my life is not the path for others. Sometimes people ask me if my books are successful and I say, *yes*. Yes, because I do not measure the success of my books by the number of books which are sold, I measure success by the hearts and lives which are touched by my books. I firmly believe that if one person comes to the saving knowledge of the Lord Jesus Christ, then the books are successful. My goal is to reach as many people with the Good News of salvation through Jesus Christ. I want let everyone know that

Jesus is able to fix our brokenness. He can fix the messes in our lives, and He can mend our hearts so that we can go forth into the world and proclaim His name. My story is His story because without Him, my life would be empty, and my heart would be satisfied with temporary things which the world has to offer…which will fade away in time. The Lord offers so much more. With the Lord, I have a life secure in Him, and my salvation is eternal and His love and saving grace will never fade, never.

I will tell you, there were times that I wondered if I could ever complete this book. I faced some obstacles, and like other writers, I faced some self-doubt. There were some delays due to illness, the loss of a friend who decided to take her life; I was rear-ended as I exited the highway near my home, I spent many hours in physical therapy, and there were delays in the publication process. Of course, I wondered if anyone would be interested in reading what I wrote or if anyone else was excited about all the scripture verses on afraid and fear. I also wondered if sharing my story would matter or make an impact on anyone. I prayed often for this project and I had to remember that I am passionate about sharing the love of God with others and that helped me get back on track. I found a study plan for writers on *YouVersion: 5 Prayers for Christian Writers* which I had read about one year ago, and I decided to read it again. This was exactly what I needed to encourage me to keep going and trust that the Lord has a wonderful plan.

My prayer is that the Lord will be the center of your story. Allow Him to use you your life, with all the bumps and bruises of your story. Be willing to tell others about the wondrous things the Lord has done for you. He placed people in your life for you to speak with and to share the Good News of Jesus. He does not need you to be perfect, He needs you to be willing to share your story and His Word to encourage others the same way He comforted and encouraged you.

Blessed be God, even the Father of our Lord Jesus Christ, the Father of mercies, and the God of all comfort; who comforteth us in all our tribulation, that we may be able to comfort them which are in any trouble, by the comfort wherewith we ourselves are comforted of God. II Corinthians 1: 3, 4

Thank you travelling this fact-finding journey with me; I enjoyed the information I read, the things I learned. I am happy to share all the information and scripture with you, and trust that you will take time to learn more about the Bible. May the power of the Lord open your eyes to see His loving heart, and may His love touch your heart and life with His grace, mercy, and peace. I share these words with you as a reminder to allow the Lord to be part of your life, your story and give Him the praise which is due Him:

If I should speak then let it be, Of the grace that is greater than all my sin, Oh to tell you my story is to tell of Him: (rb.gy/iwybwc).

God Bless You. Peace to you.

The LORD bless thee, and keep thee:

*The LORD make his face shine upon
thee, and be gracious unto thee:*

*The LORD lift up his countenance upon
thee, and give thee peace.*

Numbers 6:24-26

Have not I commanded thee?
Be strong and of a good courage;
be not afraid, neither be thou dismayed:
for the Lord thy God is with thee
whithersoever thou goest.
Joshua 1:9

ACKNOWLEDGMENTS

A sincere Thank You to everyone who helped me with this project. I appreciate your support and kindness.

My son, Jonathan, thank you for your help with the voluminous data entry of scripture verses on fear, your efforts were such a time saver. Love you!

My son, Jared, thank you for your help with your editorial comments, and for being a grammar monitor. Love you!

Joel Thurston and Wade Myers, thank you for preaching the Word of God and your willingness to share your sermon notes so that I could share them with others.

Patrick McCalla, thank you for taking time from your busy life to write the Foreword. I am very grateful for our continued friendship.

YouVersion, www.bible.com for having the King James Version of the Bible available in digital form and available to share without written permission.

Thank you to everyone who prayed! I appreciate that you prayed for me, and for the powerful impact that this book makes on the lives of many people who find salvation in Jesus Christ.

ABOUT THE AUTHOR

Suly Rieman is a follower of Jesus Christ and a mom of two adult children. She is a career and life coach, a professional resume writer, a recruiter, an author and a public speaker. Suly Rieman mentors and coaches individuals to help them develop in their personal and professional lives. She provides counseling to grieving parents. She likes to read and learn. She has an associate degree in Business Administration, a bachelor degree in Applied Behavioral Sciences, and a master degree in Training and Development. She enjoys hiking and photography, and lives in a little cottage with her three dogs and one cat.

RESOURCES

365 Fear Nots: www.365fearnots.com

Adrian Rogers: rb.gy/x7k9db: https://www.christianquotes.info/images/5-reasons-wear-bible/

Adult & Teen Challenge: teenchallengeusa.org/

Alcoholics Anonymous: www.aa.org/

Al-Alon and Alateen: al-anon.org/

All Recipes: www.allrecipes.com/

All Sons & Daughters: *Great Are You Lord*: rb.gy/njv7cg: www.youtube.com/watch?v=uHz0w-HG4iU

American Psychiatric Association: Donald Black, M.D., *Anxiety Disorders*: rb.gy/if9nka: https://www.psychiatry.org/patients-families/anxiety-disorders

American Psychological Association: www.apa.org/

Anthem Lights, Selah: *Doxology:* rb.gy/sxndfg: www.youtube.com/watch?v=tQUTvMtUhw4

Anxiety & Depression Association of America: adaa.org/

Anxiety & Depression Association of America: *What Are Anxiety and Depression?* rb.gy/osvrob: https://adaa.org/understanding-anxiety

Barbour Publishing: *How To Pray; The Best of John Wesley on prayer*; 2007.

Barnes & Noble: www.barnesandnoble.com/

Be Brain Fit; Better Mind, Better Life: Deane Alban: *11 Benefits of Tapping for Anxiety Relief*: rb.gy/dcgj3l: bebrainfit.com/tapping-anxiety-benefits/

Becky Eldredge Ignatian Ministries: Charlotte Phillips: *Praying When It's Hard: Praying to Forgive Myself*: rb.gy/clv0d0: beckyeldredge.com/praying-when-its-hard-praying-when-trying-to-forgive-myself/

Bible Bookstore: biblestore.com/

Bibles: bibles.com/

Bibles At Cost: www.biblesatcost.com/

Big Daddy Weave: *My Story*: rb.gy/iwybwc: www.azlyrics.com/lyrics/bigdaddy weave/mystory.html

Brainy Quotes: rb.gy/fk1saa: Charles Swindoll: www.brainyquote.com/quotes/charles_r_swindoll_388332

Brainy Quotes: Ralph Abernathy: rb.gy/ogwfw5: www.brainyquote.com/quotes/ralph_abernathy_143902

Casting Crowns: *Oh My Soul*: rb.gy/x9ui6n: www.youtube.com/watch?v=Tn5aq54yu8A

Casting Crowns: *Praise You In This Storm*: rb.gy/ospfkf: www.youtube.com/watch?v=0YUGwUgBvTU

Celebrate Recovery: www.celebraterecovery.com/

Celebrate Recovery: Reinhold Niebuhr: *Prayer of Serenity*: rb.gy/lflgfu: www.celebraterecovery.com/resources/serenity-prayer

Chip Ingram: *Living on the Edge*: livingontheedge.org/

Chris Tomlin: *Good, Good Father*: rb.gy/ypyvz3: www.youtube.com/watch?v=iBmwwwiHrOk

Chris Tomlin: *Our God*: rb.gy/zjwcby: www.youtube.com/watch?v=O5d_gm9zrnY

Chris Tomlin: *Whom Shall I Fear*: rb.gy/rxm2tr: www.youtube.com/watch?v=q OkImV2cJDg

Christian Book Distributors: www.christianbook.com/

Christian History Institute: *Where Did We Get The Doxology?* rb.gy/6md 1nh: christianhistoryinstitute.org/magazine/article/where-did-we-get-the-doxology

Christian Today: JB Cachila: *One Big Reason Why We Should Not Trust in Our Feelings:* rb.gy/7isxnx: www.christiantoday.com/article/one-bi g-reason-why-we-should-not-trust-in-our-feelings/103841.htm

Christianity: Danielle Bernock: *What Are the Names of God Found in the Bible?* www.christianity.com/wiki/god/what-are-all-the-names-of-god.html

Christianity: *George Mueller, Orphanages Built by Prayer*: rb.gy/npwefg: www.christianity.com/church/church-history/church-history-for-kids/georg e-mueller-orphanages-built-by-prayer-11634869.html

Christianity Today: www.christiantoday.com/article/if-necessary-use-word s-what-did-francis-of-assisi-really-say/112365.htm

Chopra: Emily Holland: *The Side Effects of Worrying – What to do instead:* rb.gy/l5nuet: chopra.com/articles/the-side-effects-of-worrying-an d-what-to-do-instead

Cleveland Clinic: *Cortisol*: rb.gy/ljgwrt: my.clevelandclinic.org/health/articles/22187-cortisol

Cory Ashbury: *Reckless Love*: rb.gy/4teujc: www.youtube.com/watch?v=Sc6SSHuZvQE

Crisis Hotline: rb.gy/q7ehfr: www.crisistextline.org/topics/anxiety/#pass-741741-on-to-a-friend-10

Danny Gokey: *Tell Your Heart To Beat Again*: rb.gy/fsg29r: www.youtube.com/watch?v=F77v41jbOYs&list=RDF77v41jbOYs&start_radio=1

David Hoy & Associates: *5 Long-Term Benefits of Therapy*: rb.gy/qu6bch: https://davidhoy.com/5-long-term-benefits-of-therapy/

David Jeremiah, *Overcomer*: 2019; W Publishing, an imprint of Thomas Nelson.

David Jeremiah: *Turning Point*: www.davidjeremiah.org/

Day Designer: *Why It's Important to Spend More Time with Friends and Family*: rb.gy/oyc8pj: daydesigner.com/a/blog/why-its-important-to-spend-more-time-with-friends-and-family/

Dictionary: www.dictionary.com/

Discount Bible Book and Music Store: www.discountbibleonline.com/

Downy: Voices News: *5 Secular, non-biblical authors who verify Jesus' life and ministry:* rb.gy/anpy10: dowym.com/voices/5-secular-non-biblical-authors-who-verify-jesus-life-and-ministry/

Elevation Worship: *O Come to the Father*: rb.gy/lcmef7: genius.com/Elevation-worship-o-come-to-the-altar-lyrics

Elevation Worship & Maverick City: *Jireh:* rb.gy/panwm2: www.youtube.com/watch?v=w_gCSJI6DKM

Everyday Health: Maura Hohman: *Why Acupuncture Works for Anxiety Relief*: rb.gy/a3kuj7: https://www.everydayhealth.com/news/why-acupuncture-works-anxiety-relief/

Facebook: www.facebook.com

Faith Bible Church: www.fbcaz.org/

Flavius Josephus, *The Works of Josephus, Complete and Unabridged*; 1987; Translated by William Whiston, Hendrickson Publishers.

Free URL Shortener: free-url-shortener.rb.gy/

Good Reads: www.goodreads.com/quotes/486985-your-actions-speak-so-loudly-i-can-not-hear-what

Good Reads: Billy Graham: rb.gy/hqdlsv: www.goodreads.com/quotes/199683-the-will-of-god-will-not-take-us-where-the

Good Reads: John Wesley: rb.gy/lywtk3: www.goodreads.com/author/quotes/151350.John_Wesley/

Good Reads: Ralph Waldo Emerson: www.goodreads.com/quotes/486985-your-actions-speak-so-loudly-i-can-not-hear-what

GoodRx: Kara-Marie Hall, BSN, RN, CCRN: *A Guide to PTSD Triggers (and How to Cope)*: rb.gy/9my1eg: www.goodrx.com/conditions/ptsd/common-triggers

Grief Share: www.griefshare.org/

Harvard Medical School Publishing: Uma Naidoo, MD: *Nutritional strategies to ease anxiety*: rb.gy/1rsjzq: www.health.harvard.edu/blog/nutritional-strategies-to-ease-anxiety-201604139441

Health Resources & Services Administration: rb.gy/xukx69: www.hrsa.gov/behavioral-health/ptsd-national-center-ptsd

Help Guide: Lawrence Robinson, Melinda Smith, M.A., Jeanne Segal, Ph.D.: *Laughter is the Best Medicine*: rb.gy/uxqwx4: www.helpguide.org/articles/mental-health/laughter-is-the-best-medicine.htm

Henry Cloud, *Changes That Heal*: 1992; Zondervan.

Henry Cloud, John Townsend, *Boundaries; When to Say Yes, How to Say No to Take Control of Your Life:* 1992; Zondervan.

Huffpost: Jonathan Alpert: *What Fear Does to Your Body and How to Handle It*: rb.gy/d9sde9: www.huffpost.com/entry/what-fear-does-to-your-bo_b_7007940

Intermountain Healthcare: Kasee Bailey: *5 Powerful Health Benefits of Journaling*: rb.gy/ak57jz: intermountainhealthcare.org/blogs/topics/live-well/2018/07/5-powerful-health-benefits-of-journaling/

Insight for Living: insight.org/

J.D. Greear: jdgreear.com/

J.D. Greear: *Just Ask*: www.thegoodbook.com/just-ask

Jasmine Murray: *Fearless*: rb.gy/mdf0bz: www.youtube.com/watch?v=Yqtf71mILwY

Jason Gray: *Sparrows:* rb.gy/qsj4hx: www.youtube.com/watch?v=wRJZQFRyZ6s

Jonathan David and Melissa Helser: *No Longer Slaves:* rb.gy/lslqbf: www.youtube.com/watch?v=f8TkUMJtK5k

Jonathan, Melissa Helser: *Raise a Hallelujah*: www.youtube.com/watch?v=G2XtRuPfaAU

Journey Church: www.journeychurchaz.org/

Kaiser Permanente: *Why everyone should keep a journal – 7 surprising benefits*: rb.gy/5evyza: healthy.kaiserpermanente.org/health-wellness/health article.7-benefits-of-keeping-a-journal

Kendrick Brothers: kendrickbrothers.com/

King James Bible: www.kingjamesbibleonline.org/King-James-Version/

Lifeway: www.lifeway.com/

LinkedIn: www.linkedin.com/

Louie Giglio: *Don't Give The Enemy A Seat At Your Table, It's Time To Win The Battle Of Your Mind*; 2021; Passion Publishing.

Matt Maher: *Lord I Need You*: rb.gy/jy8kxk: www.youtube.com/watch?v=Luvf MDhTyMA

Matt Maher: *Run to the Father*: rb.gy/fx9dmg: www.youtube.com/watch?v=Rf vvEKMPGhA

Matt Maher: *Your Love Defends Me*: rb.gy/apklls: www.youtube.com/ watch?v=lW-pO78pcog

Mayo Clinic: *Stress relief from laughter? It's no joke*: rb.gy/ciicna: www.mayoclinic. org/healthy-lifestyle/stress-management/in-depth/stress-relief/art-20044456

Medical News Today: Jessica Caporuscio, Pharm. D., *What's the link between anxiety and shortness of breath?* www.medicalnewstoday.com/articles/32 6391#summary

Mercy Me: *I Can Only Imagine*: rb.gy/k4q2om: www.youtube.com/watch?v= DU0MwNpRq6M

Mindful, Healthy Mind, Healthy Life: *How to Mediate*: rb.gy/brkkio: www. mindful.org/how-to-meditate/

Mindful Moves: *15 Minute Yoga Flow for Anxiety*: www.healthline.com/health/anxiety/effects-on-body#Mindful-Moves:-15-Minute-Yoga-Flow-for-Anxiety

National Alliance on Mental Illness: rb.gy/9rlxp2: www.nami.org/About-Mental-Illness/Mental-Health-Conditions/Posttraumatic-Stress-Disorder

National Domestic Violence Hotline: www.thehotline.org/

National Institute of Mental Health: rb.gy/bzhz4b: www.nimh.nih.gov/health/topics/post-traumatic-stress-disorder-ptsd

National Suicide Prevention Lifeline: rb.gy/2tgsji: 988lifeline.org/talk-to-someone-now/

New Life Community Church: www.newlifeonline.com/

Nick Ortner: *The Tapping Solution*: www.thetappingsolution.com/

Passion City Church: passioncitychurch.com/

Passion Moment: passionconferences.com/

Pastor Chuck Swindoll: www.insight.org/

Polar: Bronwyn Griffiths: *How Exercise Affects The Brain, Does Your Workout Make You Smarter?* rb.gy/yzuxxv: www.polar.com/blog/how-exercise-affects-the-brain/

Positive Psychology: Courtney Ackerman MA: *28 Benefits of Gratitude & Most Significant Research Findings*: rb.gy/tuiuye: positivepsychology.com/benefits-gratitude-research-questions/

Positive Psychology: *What Are The Benefits of Music Therapy?* rb.gy/u9kjwh: positivepsychology.com/music-therapy-benefits/#benefits

Prevention: Hannah Chenoweth: *Binaural Beats Are Being Used as Sound Wave Therapy for Anxiety, but Does It Really Help?* rb.gy/uc6psz: www.prevention. com/health/mental-health/a35782370/binaural-beats-for-anxiety/

Psychology Today: James Lake, MD: *Massage Therapy for Anxiety and Stress:* rb.gy/kh7mwy: www.psychologytoday.com/us/blog/integrative-mental-health-care/201810/massage-therapy-anxiety-and-stress

Psychology Today: *Trauma*: rb.gy/dhyli7: www.psychologytoday.com/us/basics/trauma

Purim: www.britannica.com/topic/Purim

Recovery International: recoveryinternational.org/

Rend Collective: *Boldly I Approach*: rb.gy/egtk0d: www.youtube.com/watch?v=4QDnVD7gu5Y

Rend Collective: *Every Giant Will Fall*: rb.gy/3m73yo: www.youtube.com/watch?v=qW63lCBOaVo

Right Now Media: www.rightnowmedia.org/

Ryan Stevenson: *Eye of the Storm*: rb.gy/cmqgze: www.youtube.com/watch?v=-sx8wTnnfSc

Ryan Stevenson: *No Matter What*: rb.gy/hyoh7l: www.youtube.com/watch?v=CPeY_RK7akk

Scientific America: Annette Kämmerer: *The Scientific Underpinnings and Impacts of Shame*; *People who feel shame readily are at risk for depression and anxiety disorders*: rb.gy/nhyjcs: scientificamerican.com/article/the-scientific-underpinnings-and-impacts-of-shame/

Shadow Mountain Community Church: shadowmountain.org/

Sheila Walsh: *Blessings Flow*: rb.gy/tu5mqc: www.youtube.com/watch?v=XFsEyO_gSJo

Sheila Walsh: *Blessings Flow* lyrics: genius.com/Sheila-walsh-blessings-flow-lyrics

Shop The Word: www.shoptheword.com/

Smithsonian Magazine: Aarash Javanbakht, Linda Saab: *What Happens in the Brain When We Feel Fear*: rb.gy/nh3wuj: www.smithsonianmag.com/science-nature/what-happens-brain-feel-fear-180966992/

Smithsonian Magazine: Shannon Palus: *Light Therapy May Work on Chronic Mood Disorders, Too:* rb.gy/ehayly: www.smithsonianmag.com/smart-news/light-therapy-may-work-more-season-affective-disorder-180953431/

Stonebriar Community Church: www.stonebriar.org/

Stuart Smalley: rb.gy/sxe7zt: en.wikipedia.org/wiki/Stuart_Smalley

Substance Abuse and Mental Health Services Administration: www.samhsa.gov/

Suly Rieman: *Go Forth and Get A Job!* www.westbowpress.com/en/bookstore/bookdetails/703643-go-forth-and-get-a-job

Suly Rieman: *Surviving Grief:* www.westbowpress.com/en/bookstore/bookdetails/341915-surviving-grief

Summa Health: *7 Health Benefits to Getting a Good Night's Rest*: rb.gy/cldm36: www.summahealth.org/flourish/entries/2020/02/7-health-benefits-to-getting-a-good-nights-rest.

Tasha Cobbs: *Break Every Chain*: rb.gy/cneavm: www.youtube.com/watch?v=-pD2zIuiC2g

Tauren Wells: *Hills and Valleys*: rb.gy/alacxg: www.youtube.com/watch?v=8iDuZv_5MQk

Tenth Avenue North: *Afraid*: rb.gy/g2ik7b: www.youtube.com/watch?v=WohcTuNRBFE

Tenth Avenue North: *Control*: rb.gy/ateqbg: www.youtube.com/watch?v=kFfztu8-bBQ

The Afters: *I Will Fear No More*: rb.gy/1zf3ng: www.youtube.com/watch?v=wMm mbJlWhtk

The Compassionate Friends: www.compassionatefriends.org/

The Grable Group: Tim Grable: *27 Top Christian Comedians You Need to Know (Updated for 2020)*: www.thegrablegroup.com/entertainment/comedy/christia n-comedians-you-need-to-know/

The Hope Line: Dawson McAllister: *6 Myths About Forgiveness*: rb.gy/ mdoqqq: www.thehopeline.com/what-forgiveness-is-not-part-2/

The New Strong's Concise Concordance & Vine's Concise Dictionary of the Bible, 1997, 1999, Thomas Nelson, Inc.

The School of Life: www.theschooloflife.com/

The School of Life: *Why You Shouldn't Trust Your Feelings*: rb.gy/1npfkt: www. youtube.com/watch?v=nZYzzn6W2qc

The Summit Church: summitchurch.com/

Third Hour: Melissa Muse: *14 Clean Stand-Up Comedians That Will Have You Rolling With Laughter*: thirdhour.org/blog/buzz/entertainment/clean-stand-up-comedians/

US Department of Veterans Affairs: rb.gy/7mxano: www.ptsd.va.gov/

University of Minnesota; Earl E. Bakken Center for Spirituality & Healing: Louise Delagran, MA, MEd: *Impact of Fear and Anxiety*: rb.gy/7qagwu: www.taking charge.csh.umn.edu/impact-fear-and-anxiety

University of Rochester Medical Center: *5-4-3-2-1 Coping Technique for Anxiety*: rb.gy/pxiarf: www.urmc.rochester.edu/behavioral-health-partners/bhp-blog/april-2018/5-4-3-2-1-coping-technique-for-anxiety.aspx

University of Tehran, Institute of Biochemistry and Biophysics: *One of the Most Mysterious Solfeggio Frequencies 528Hz:* rb.gy/u1hohv: meditativemind. org/528hz-miraculous-healing-frequency/

Very well mind: Kendra Cherry: *List of Phobias*: *Common* Phobias *From A Through Z:* rb.gy/atgzfn: www.verywellmind.com/list-of-phobias-2795453

YouTube: www.youtube.com/

YouVersion: www.bible.com/

WhatsApp: www.whatsapp.com/

Wikihow: Trudi Griffin, LPC, MS: *How to Overcome Your Fears Through Visualization:* rb.gy/mqsx5u: www.wikihow.com/Overcome-Your-Fears-Through-Visualization.

Woman's Day: Olivia Muenter: *18 Calming Prayers for Anxiety That Offer Instant Stress Relief, These soothing words will bring comfort and inner peace to your heart*: rb.gy/taqgok: www.womansday.com/life/inspirational-stories/g29613781/prayers-for-anxiety/

Zach Williams: *Chain Breaker*: rb.gy/40blub: www.youtube.com/watch?v=JGY jKR69M6U

Zach Williams: *Fear is a Liar*: rb.gy/yyckpt: www.youtube.com/watch?v=sQTn REEtuNk

Printed in the United States
by Baker & Taylor Publisher Services